'The Condition of Menevia' Studies in the History of St Davids Cathedral

Special Issue of
The Journal of Religious History, Literature and Culture
2023

Edited by
JONATHAN M. WOODING and J. WYN EVANS

Volume 9 November 2023 Number 2
UNIVERSITY OF WALES PRESS
https://doi.org/10.16922/jrhlc.9.2

Editors
Professor William Gibson, Oxford Brookes University
Professor John Morgan-Guy, University of Wales Trinity Saint David
Dr Daniel Reed, Oxford Brookes University

Assistant Editor
Dr Thomas W. Smith, Rugby School

Reviews Editor
Dr Nicky Tsougarakis, University of Crete

Editorial Advisory Board
Professor David Bebbington, Stirling University
Professor Stewart J. Brown, University of Edinburgh
Dr James J. Caudle, Yale University
Dr Robert G. Ingram, Ohio University, USA
Professor Geraint Jenkins, Aberystwyth University
Dr David Ceri Jones, Aberystwyth University
Dr Paul Kerry, Brigham Young University, USA
Professor Frances Knight, University of Nottingham
Dr Robert Pope, Westminster College, Cambridge
Professor Huw Pryce, Bangor University
Professor Kenneth E. Roxburgh, Samford University, USA
Dr Eryn M. White, Aberystwyth University
Rt Revd and Rt Hon. Lord Williams of Oystermouth
Professor Jonathan Wooding, University of Sydney, Australia

Editorial Contacts
wgibson@brookes.ac.uk
j.morgan-guy@tsd.uwtsd.ac.uk
thomas.smith.2009@live.rhul.ac.uk
Tsougarakis@uoc.gr
d.reed@brookes.ac.uk

CONTENTS

The Contributors	v
Editors' Introduction	vii
List of Illustrations	ix

1   St Davids Before the Cathedral
    Jonathan M. Wooding   1

2   St Davids Cathedral: the 1182 Church
    Malcolm Thurlby   19

3   Building and Ornamental Stones of St Davids Cathedral
    Dyfed Elis-Gruffydd   45

4   Dundry Stone and other Limestones in the Fabric, Fittings,   61
    and Monuments of St Davids Cathedral
    Tim Palmer

5   The Shrine of St David
    John Crook   71

6   From Nash to Scott: The Maintenance of the Fabric and   95
    Worship of St Davids Cathedral 1793–1862
    Nigel Yates[†]

7   Llewelyn Lewellin and the Condition of St Davids   111
    J. Wyn Evans

8   Gilbert Scott and the Restoration of St Davids Cathedral   131
    Julian Orbach

9   'The Glow and The Glory': Contextualizing and Interpreting   147
    the Stained Glass of St Davids Cathedral
    John Morgan-Guy

Index   173

THE CONTRIBUTORS

John Crook is an independent architectural historian and archaeologist. Previously archaeological consultant to Winchester Cathedral, he continues in this role at St George's Windsor and elsewhere. He has a long-standing scholarly interest in the medieval cult of saints: published notably in two major books: *The Architectural Setting of the Cult of Saints in the Early Christian West* (2000) and *English Medieval Shrines* (2011). His latest book, on the domestic architecture of St George's Windsor, was published in February 2023.

Dyfed Elis-Gruffydd (1943–2023) was an Earth Scientist. He lectured in Geology and Geography at the City of London Polytechnic and also at Trinity College, Carmarthen (now University of Wales, Trinity Saint David). He was Head of the Publications Department for the Pembrokeshire Coast National Park Authority, Editor and Publishing Director of Gomer Press. Amongst his many publications are: *Wales: 100 Remarkable Vistas* (2017) and *Rocks of Wales* (2019).

J. Wyn Evans was Bishop of St Davids from 2008–16. Before that, he was Dean of St Davids from 1994–2008; and prior to that from 1982–1994, on the academic staff of Trinity College Carmarthen as Chaplain, Dean of Chapel and Head of the Theology and Religious Studies Department. He has lectured and published widely on the mediaeval and modern history of the church in Wales.

John Morgan-Guy is Professor of Practice in Cultural History at University of Wales Trinity Saint David. He has published widely in medical, art and church history. His most recent work is *Treasures: The Special Collections of the University of Wales Trinity Saint David* (2022). He is a fellow of the Royal Historical Society and of the Society of Antiquaries.

Julian Orbach is an author and lecturer in the field of architectural history. Amongst many publications, he co-authored three of the Buildings of Wales volumes (Pevsner Architectural Guides): *Pembrokeshire* (2004), *Carmarthenshire and Ceredigion* (2006), and *Gwynedd* (2009). He was architectural adviser to the Victorian Society in 1975–7 and wrote the *Blue Guide to Victorian Buildings in Britain* (1987).

Tim Palmer is retired from the Institute of Geography and Earth Sciences, Aberystwyth University. He is a geologist, sedimentologist, petrographer and palaeontologist with a special interest in limestones. He was executive officer of the Palaeontological Association from 2000–16.

Malcolm Thurlby is Professor of Art and Architectural History at York University in Toronto, Canada. He is the author of numerous studies of Romanesque architecture in Britain, including *Romanesque Art and Architecture in Wales* (2006).

Jonathan M. Wooding is a church historian specialising in the early Christianity of Celtic Britain and Ireland. He was Sir Warwick Fairfax Professor of Celtic Studies at the University of Sydney, Australia, from 2013–21. Prior to that he was Reader in Religious History at University of Wales, Trinity Saint David.

Nigel Yates (1944–2009) was Professor of Ecclesiastical History at the University of Wales, Lampeter (now University of Wales, Trinity Saint David) from 2005–9. Previously he had been head of the Kent Archives Service. His many publications included *Buildings, Faith, and Worship: The Liturgical Arrangement of Anglican Churches, 1600–1900* (2000) and *Anglican Ritualism in Victorian Britain, 1830–1910* (1999).

EDITORS' INTRODUCTION

The cathedral church of St Davids has stood for over eight centuries. It has survived periods of decay and neglect, as well as determined efforts by Reformation bishops to remove their throne to more centrally-located Carmarthen. By the time it was half-a-century old the cathedral had undergone major collapses which have left myriad traces on its walls. The ambitious restorations that saved it from further collapse in the nineteenth century left further complex traces. These should be regarded as scars of honour on a building that has evinced remarkable qualities of endurance and survival. In this volume they also are used as clues to reconstruct the history of this remarkable and beautiful building.

The editors had the pleasure, in 2007, of producing a volume of studies, by a range of distinguished specialists, on the history of the cult and church of St David. In 2023 we again have the pleasure of producing a collection on the architecture of the cathedral, which centres on the period of its first construction, in the twelfth/thirteenth century, and on the main period of its restoration, in the nineteenth. The twin focuses of this volume are areas in which there has been important new research, as well as significant revision of older historiographies. Attention is also paid to the personalities who were responsible both for construction, neglect, and restoration of this remarkable and evocative building.

In working on this volume we have amassed many debts for advice and assistance. The editors would especially like to thank the following for assistance on particular matters: Dr Stuart Harrison, Dr Karen Jankulak, Professor Densil Morgan, The Revd Dr Sarah Rowland Jones (Dean of St Davids Cathedral) and her staff, Professor Frances Knight, and Dr Paula Yates, together with the Staffs of the Manuscript Department of the National Library of Wales, the Roderic Bowen Library of the University of Wales Trinity Saint David, Pembrokeshire Archives and the Royal Commission on the Ancient and Historical Monuments of Wales (RCAHMW). Special thanks are also due to the editors of this journal, for the invitation to publish this collection and for their forbearance with delays in its production.

J. WYN EVANS and
JONATHAN M. WOODING

LIST OF ILLUSTRATIONS

Plan of St Davids Cathedral, from *The Builder*, December 1892   xii
(image courtesy of RCAHMW)

Chapter 2

1   St Davids Cathedral, presbytery and crossing to west   21
2   Detail of west bay of south arcade of nave, showing   22
    awkward junction
3   Nave, interior to east showing triforium and clerestorey   22
4   St Davids Cathedral, north nave doorway   23
5   Llanthony Priory, slype vault   26
6   St Davids Cathedral, presbytery north arcade, westernmost   27
    column
7   St Davids Cathedral, presbytery, interior to E   27
8   St Davids Cathedral, S presbytery aisle, interior to W   28
9   St Davids Cathedral, S presbytery aisle, western arch   29
10   St Davids Cathedral, presbytery north aisle, penultimate   29
    west bay

Chapter 3

1   Simplified geological map of the St Davids Peninsula   47
2   Exterior wall, South Nave Aisle (Photo: Dyfed Elis-Gruffydd)   49
3   Exterior wall, Lady Chapel (Photo: Dyfed Elis-Gruffydd)   50
4   Exterior south-facing wall, South Transept   52
    (Photo: Dyfed Elis-Gruffydd)
5   Building and ornamental stones of St Davids Cathedral,   57
    St Mary's College and Porth y Tŵr: age, nature, source and use

Chapter 4

1   Cut surfaces of Dundry Stone (left) and Bath Stone (right)   67
    as seen with a magnifying glass
2   Southern screen of the Bishop Vaughan Chapel, showing   67
    pieces of original Bath, Dundry, and Sutton stones, and
    replacement pieces of Bath Stone from the late nineteenth-
    century repairs

List of illustrations

3   Sutton Stone early-replaced mullions in the Bishop Vaughan   68
    south screen

Chapter 5

1   The shrine from the south-west after the conservation   72
    programme of 1911–12, showing its architectural context
    (Photo: John Crook)
2   The shrine from the south-west before conservation in   73
    1911–12 (Photo: John Crook)
3   Cross-section through the centre of the monument viewed   79
    from the west
4   Rectified photograph of the south side of the monument   80
    (Photo: John Crook)
5   Plan view of the *mensa* (Photo: John Crook)   81
6   Head stops of the triple arcade (not to same scale)   83
    (Photo: John Crook)
7   Rectified photograph of the north side of the monument   84
    (Photo: John Crook)
8   Plan of the monument (north at top) showing position   85
    of the niches
9   Whitchurch Canonicorum (Dorset). Shrine of St Wita in   89
    north transept (Photo: John Crook)
10 St Davids Cathedral. Shrine of St Caradoc   90
    (Photo: John Crook)

Chapter 8

1   St Mary Stafford, prior to Scott's restoration   133
2   St Mary Stafford in 1852, after Scott's restoration   134
3   Elevation of the south side of St Davids Cathedral   137
    by A. W. Pugin (copyright Pembrokeshire County Council,
    used with kind permission)
4   Presbytery, St Davids Cathedral, prior to Scott's restoration 139
5   Presbytery, St Davids Cathedral in the late nineteenth   139
    century
6   Cathedral from south-east, showing Scott's restoration   142
    of tower and east end
7   Photo of G. G. Scott, E. A Freeman and others at St Davids, 143
    1877 (image courtesy of RCAHMW)
8   Photo, *c.*1890, of roofless East End of St Davids Cathedral 144

List of illustrations

Chapter 9

1   East end of the presbytery, St Davids Cathedral, stained   149
glass by John Hardman & Co. 1870, glass mosaic by
Salviati & Co., 1871 (Photo: Martin Crampin)

2   Salviati & Co., The Brazen Serpent, 1871, designed by   154
John Hardman Powell, presbytery (Photo: Martin Crampin)

3   John Hardman & Co., The Nativity, 1870, designed by   157
John Hardman Powell, presbytery (Photo: Martin Crampin)

4   James Powell & Sons, St Nicholas, 1904, Chapel of   160
St Nicholas, east wall of the north aisle of the retrochoir
(Photo: Martin Crampin)

5   C.E. Kempe & Co., The Risen Christ with St David and   162
St George, and Archangels, 1923, west wall of the nave
(Photo: Martin Crampin)

6   William Morris & Co. (Westminster), The Israelites Crossing   165
the Red Sea and the Ark of the Church, 1956, designed by
Frederick Cole, baptistry window, west end of the south aisle
(Photo: Martin Crampin)

7   Carl Edwards, Thomas Becket Enthroned, 1958, east wall   167
of the Chapel of St Thomas Becket (Photo: Martin Crampin)

*Except where otherwise identified or credited, the illustrations are from
the authors' collections or are free of copyright.*

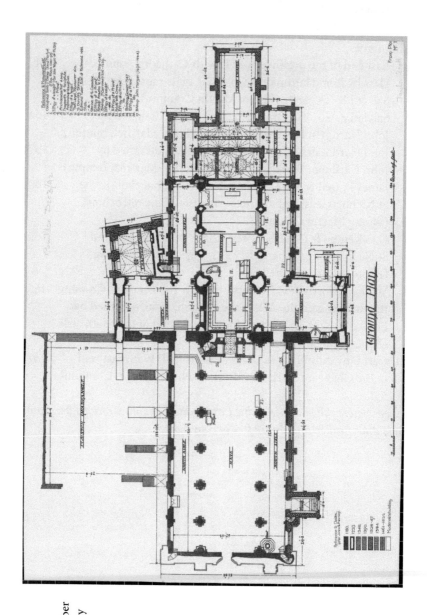

Plan of St Davids Cathedral, from *The Builder*, December 1892 (image courtesy of RCAHMW)

1.
ST DAVIDS BEFORE THE CATHEDRAL

Jonathan M. Wooding

The Welsh annals record under 1182 that: 'the church of Menevia is demolished and begun anew' (*Ecclesia meneuensis diruitur et de nouo inchoatur*). The earlier church was of no great antiquity, dedicated only in 1131; its replacement has stood already for more than eight centuries.[1] If this seems a very long span of time, we might remind ourselves that by 1182 the history of the church at Menevia reached back much further, arguably to the time of St David himself. The history of this earlier period will be the subject of this chapter; in particular it will be concerned with aspects of that history which potentially have influenced the form and the context of the cathedral.

A cathedral is simply the church where the bishop has their throne, so the title of my chapter is slightly mischievous. The 1131 *ecclesia* was also a cathedral, as indeed were an unknown number of its predecessors. Yet it is intended to draw attention to the challenge of envisaging an earlier St Davids of much less substantial architecture, for which task have only traces of evidence to work from. The 1182 cathedral is, as described by Malcolm Thurlby (*infra*), an ambitious exercise in an international style, on a scale unprecedented in Wales. Its footprint indeed is so large that it almost certainly lies on top of a great part of the remains of its predecessors. The documentary record can create something of the same impression. The period *c*.1080–1200 in south Wales – which I will term the 'long twelfth century', in preference to the 'Norman era' – has left a substantial corpus of writing concerned with the history of the cathedrals, their territories, and their patron saints. It is evident that this work incorporated and redacted sources from earlier centuries which are mostly now lost. The large scale of twelfth-century creation thus not only contrasts sharply with what survives from previous centuries, but sometimes appears to actively suppress it.[2] These fault-lines in our evidence, literary and material, coincide with a period of transition, which saw the arrival of Norman settlers and ecclesiastical re-organisation under the

https://doi.org/10.16922/jrhlc.9.2.1

influence of the Gregorian reform of the western church. Norman secular settlement was unambiguously colonial, albeit politically fragmented, but on the ecclesiastical side the new fashions in reform and church architecture had patronage from Welsh as well as Norman rulers, while bishops of Welsh, English, as well as Norman origin supported historic claims of the Welsh churches against the centrism of Canterbury. It can be easy in this environment to focus too much on change at the expense of continuity, which will be a key theme in what follows.[3]

Roger Stalley has observed that 'there is every likelihood that the 1131 structure affected the layout and design of the existing cathedral', as well as noting that 'several churches and chapels' are likely to have preceded it;[4] we will consider below some comparative evidence for what these buildings may have been like. Such continuity is to be expected on a long-established church site. An early medieval cathedral and cult-centre would have had multiple buildings; new structures needed to accommodate the existence of previous and continuing ones. Continuous performance of devotions on a church site also provides a less visible, but relentless discourse of continuity: a daily cycle of prayer, alongside separate devotions to multiple saints, day after day, year after year. Such liturgical performance over time marks out enduring zones of sacred space and relationships between them, which may be referenced in later buildings.

Sources and Approaches

Our main documentary sources for the pre-*c.*1100 period at St Davids are the Welsh annals, brief yearly chronicles that had been kept at St Davids since around 800, and the more discursive writings of two remarkable scholars: Rhygyfarch ap Sulien (d. 1099), the son of a bishop of Menevia, and Gerald of Wales (d. *c.*1223), who was controversially bishop-elect in 1198–1203. Rhygyfarch and Gerald were enmeshed in the affairs of the diocese at a time of heated debates over its territories and status, so it is right to see their work as projecting an image of early medieval St Davids within this context. This caveat, along with their distance in time from events, puts limits on accepting their accounts of the earlier period without corroborative evidence. We should not, however, be lured into viewing their writings only (or in Rhygyfarch's case, even mainly) as pursuing a political agenda. It is presently fashionable to interpret 'Celtic' hagiography in terms of political and 'notarial' content – what David Dumville has termed 'the Cork method' – and sometimes to see such texts as intended to actively support, or even to effect, substantial changes to the identity of churches.[5] Latin texts necessarily had a limited reception, so there is a danger of overstating their connection to real events – unless we see them as reflecting what was already widely thought.[6]

Our perceptions of the nature of change in the twelfth century can also be tacitly influenced by the legacy of another, older, model of Celtic historiography that can be termed the 'Celtic church'. This creates what we might consider an 'ethnic' distinction between the pre- and post-reform church. Substantially an outgrowth of Georgian church historiography, but adopted into influential studies of Celtic saints in the twentieth century, it ascribes to the Welsh church in the first millennium what Owen Chadwick termed an 'abnormal' ecclesiology, deriving from monastic settlements during a semi-mythical 'age of the saints' and persisting in isolation up to the Gregorian reform.[7] This somewhat synchronic and un-diverse – as well as, in origin at least, sectarian – model tends to obscure the extent of evolution in the organisation of the Welsh church up to and beyond 1100 and, in particular, that such development often seems to be in step with that in neighbouring churches.[8] It also inspires the conflation the spheres of influence of the saints in their own lifetimes with the geography of their cults.[9]

The Historical Identity of St David

David was clearly an historical person who lived in the mid- to late sixth century. His death is recorded by Irish annalists, possibly in a contemporary entry, at AD 589; the Welsh annals, for David's era only retrospective – though probably compiled *at* St Davids – place his death just after AD 600.[10]

Rhygyfarch portrays David as a monastic leader with a very austere regime of unceasing prayer, drinking only water, and eating only bread and herbs. The authenticity of this portrayal is supported by early sources, notwithstanding the strong possibility that this spirituality also had a particular appeal to Rhygyfarch's contemporaries.[11] The ninth-century Life of a Breton bishop, Paul Aurelian, ascribes to David the epithet *Aquaticus* ('Waterman'), because he fed on bread and water.[12]

3

John Morris and David Dumville further note the similarity, extending to some of the phraseology Rhygyfarch uses, of a broadside written by the sixth-century churchman Gildas.[13] These comparisons suggest that Rhygyfarch referred to a copy of the same, or a very similar, rule,[14] maybe found amongst the books at David's 'own city' (*ipsius ciuitatis*): 'eaten away along the edges and the spines by the constant devouring of grubs and the ravages of the passing years, and written in the handwriting of our forefathers'.[15]

We cannot claim as long and consistent a record for David's identity as a bishop. Rhygyfarch claims (ch. 46) that David was consecrated an archbishop in Jerusalem and that subsequently, at a synod in Llanddewi Brefi (Ceredigion): 'his monastery was dedicated as the metropolitan church of the whole country, so that whoever might govern it should be accounted archbishop' (ch. 53).[16] We can see anachronism here. In the context of the sixth century it is difficult to credit a British bishop being consecrated in Jerusalem. The metropolitan claim, which would have accorded St Davids authority equal to Canterbury, can be seen as pushback against the centrism of the Gregorian reform. Rhygyfarch did not, however, invent the claim of archiepiscopal status. Asser, writing in 893, describes his cousin Nobis at St Davids as 'archbishop' (*archiepiscopus*),[17] located at the *monasterium et parochia* 'of David' (*Degui*).[18] All these terms are potentially false friends. *Monasterium et parochia* in this period may describe a collegiate-type community and its remit, rather than the more familiar 'monastery and parish'; what *archiepiscopus* meant in early medieval Wales is also controversial.[19] We can at least say two things here pertinent to our subject. The first is that bishops of St Davids claimed the status of archbishop in the first millennium. The second is that whatever the actual privileges attached to this office, the metropolitan claim must represent a nuancing of the title for a different, reformed, context. These changing conceptions would have born upon the architecture on the site over time.

In the annals David's successors are only designated 'bishop' (*episcopus*), but, as we have already noted, these are not contemporary records before c.800. That David was certainly an ascetic monk does not preclude that he was also a bishop; abbots are candidates for the episcopate and early monks are described in Welsh and Irish hagiography as accepting pastoral roles after youthful experiences of ascetic monasticism.[20] We also, however, cannot rule the possibility that David was retroactively inserted into a later succession of bishops based at his monastery.

The Personality of Menevia

Rhygyfarch (ch. 8) says that David had his early education in a monastery at *Vetus Rubus* (see below), before establishing his own monastery at a *Vallis Rosina*, 'which the Welsh are in the habit of calling by the common name of Hoddnant' (*quam uulgari nomine Hodnant Brittones uocitant*). Later in the Life, we are told that the latter was near the River Alun (*flumen quod dicitur Alun*).[21] The river alongside the current cathedral is named the Alun/Alan and 'Merrivale', a name used locally for the valley, is a direct English translation of Welsh *Hoddnant*.[22]

Neither Rhygyfarch nor Asser use the name most commonly used for St Davids in the Welsh sources: *Mynyw* (Latin *Menevia*). The Irish annals refer to David as *Dauid Cille Muine* ('David of the Church of Mynyw') under 589, as does the Irish martyrology of Oengus (*Félire Oengusso*) written *c*.830.[23] Gerald of Wales (d. *c*.1223) claims that the name is derived from an Irish word *muni*, meaning 'thicket'.[24] We might see in Gerald's etymology a reference to the type of overgrown or waste spaces that are the natural habitat of eremites.[25] An inconspicuous, low-lying, site alongside a river is also characteristic of a number of Welsh churches which are reputed to have been founded first as monasteries: for example, Bangor Cathedral in Gwynedd, as well as Llancarfan and Llanilltud Fawr in the Vale of Glamorgan.

The setting of the cathedral in a remote, low-lying, narrow and damp valley bottom can thus be attributed to its primary origin in a community that retreated from the secular world and from the public gaze.[26] This has unhelpfully constrained later development. That the valley floor is not an ideal foundation for a massive stone cathedral is witnessed by the collapses of the partly-built cathedral in 1220 and 1248, as well as the outward rotation of the nave columns (see Thurlby, *infra*). The damp environment no doubt was also detrimental to an unknown number of earlier timber buildings.

The remoteness of the setting was not necessarily a continuous factor. To some extent at least, a major shrine, once established with whatever original cause, *makes* itself a central place. A. W. Wade-Evans observed that St Davids was not really isolated if viewed with respect to maritime connections in the Irish Sea.[27] Though he was thinking in the context of a dated 'saints and seaways' model, in which Wales derived its monasticism from seaborne missions, his point is still valid as there is evidence of strong links between St Davids and Ireland.[28] In the sixth and seventh centuries St Davids could have participated in international exchange networks of the Irish Sea in which we know some other large coastal sites shared.[29] By the tenth and eleventh centuries, however, political change in the Irish Sea saw coastal sites such as St Davids made vulnerable to repeated events of seaborne raiding and this is one definite context in which continuity of settlement is likely to have been broken, at least for short periods.[30]

In the twelfth century, Pope Calixtus II (see *infra*), could deem the journey to David fully half as difficult as one would make to Rome – but measured from the perspective of English pilgrims. The extreme western location did not appeal at all to Reformation bishops who, wholly despising its appeal to 'vacabounde pilgremes', withdrew to the more central town of Carmarthen, to the inevitable neglect of the fabric of the cathedral.[31]

In amongst such changing conceptions of role and orientation of sites, our sources evince a tension between the careers of real holy persons and the subsequent histories of the churches they founded, or were founded in their name. Rhygyfarch, as we have noted, describes David's place of education as *Vetus Rubus* (Latin: 'old briar'). Gerald identifies this with Henfynyw (Welsh: 'old Mynyw') on the Ceredigion coast, near modern Aberaeron. That Henfynyw was in a different kingdom (Ceredigion) to St Davids (Dyfed) in the sixth century does not militate against its identification as David's place of formation; it is a known pattern that early Irish and Welsh monks retreated across internal borders to set up monasteries of their own.[32] Archaeological finds at Henfynyw confirm it as an early medieval church. An inscribed stone preserved here dates to the seventh through ninth centuries; some more recent finds of stone sculpture from the vicinity are also of early medieval date.[33] There are some grounds then, to see Gerald's identification as plausible.

The church at Henfynyw is also dedicated to St David; such dedications and other commemorations to David in Ceredigion are more numerous than in Pembrokeshire, but we should see this as part of a separate process, in which churches with and without direct connections to the saint became part of his 'cult'. A logical context for the expansion of David's cult into Ceredigion would be the merger, *c*.900, of Ceredigion with Dyfed to become Deheubarth. Wyn Evans, who has considered in detail the relationship between these churches, has proposed that the community of St Davids may have withdrawn inland for a period in the face of the raids of the tenth and eleventh centuries, in a similar way to the movement of the community of St Cuthbert in Northumbria in the Viking era.[34] This seems a more probable scenario than Evan's other suggested model, which is that Henfynyw was the actual early seat of the bishops of Menevia, only moved to St Davids in Pembrokeshire perhaps as late as the eleventh century, with Bishop Sulien (1073–78/1079–6): 'commissioning his son Rhygyfarch to write a *Vita*, thereby justified and created a new scenario'.[35] This would, in effect, cast Rhygyfarch's Life into a role comparable to that the Book of Llandaf, a dossier annexing texts and cults of varying antiquity, and creating others, compiled under Bishop Urban in Glamorgan in the twelfth century to lend a spurious historical depth to what we suspect was a largely new episcopal seat at Llandaf.[36] What Patrick Sims-Williams has observed there, however, also applies here: 'Certainly it is difficult to imagine how Urban could have begun to attempt to foist Llandaf on his contemporaries if it had no history *at all* behind it'.[37] Evans himself describes this rather eye-watering shift of site to be a 'more unlikely' explanation, but John Reuben Davies has developed it further in two recent studies.[38]

As Gerald and Rhygyfarch are unambiguous as to *Vetus Rubus* and *Vallis Rosina* being separate places it is hard to see sufficient cause to suspect such a manipulation of history here. This desire to move early St Davids away from modern St Davids is not unprecedented. There have been suggestions of it being originally at shoreline site such as Whitesands, near St Davids, though in this case we should observe its links to the dated model of 'saints and seaways'.[39] We admittedly lack the sort of archaeological evidence from St Davids that would demonstrate continuity there from the time of St David. None of the datable inscriptions from the vicinity of the cathedral take us earlier than around the ninth century.[40] There is a monument to Sulien's contemporary, Bishop Abraham (d. 1080), at St Davids and a SATURNBIU commemorated on a monument from Ramsey Island, 5kms west of St Davids cathedral, is plausibly, but not conclusively, equated with Bishop Saturnbiu Hail (d. 831).[41]

Evans and Davies identify some potentially important ambiguities in the evidence. As noted above, neither Asser nor Rhygyfarch use the name Menevia/Mynyw – in the latter's case not even for the 'old' Mynyw in Ceredigion. Evans also highlights an interesting ambiguity in the Life of Gruffydd ap Cynan (*c.*1137–48), which, in describing a procession near St Davids in 1081, places the bishop (*Menevensis episcopus*) and all the clergy 'of Menevia' (*clerique omnes Menevnenses*) in the company of a choral community 'of St David' (*chorus universus Sancti Davidis*).[42] These could point to the existence of different framing institutions, if not necessarily separate places; perhaps the *parochia Degui* of the archbishop (as in Asser) was in some way distinct from Menevia? It also might reflect evolution in pastoral provision: to give one example, the supplementing or replacement of secular by religious canons under the influence of the monastic reform, such as we see, for example, at Winchester in the tenth century.[43]

Settlement at St Davids in the Sixth through Eleventh Centuries

In the light of the above there seems limited grounds to question the consistent association of David's own monastery with the cathedral site.

If we were to picture the cathedral close in the mid-twelfth century, we should envisage a range of buildings, probably of wood, clustered around a stone cathedral of Romanesque style, lime-plastered on its exterior, as also was originally the case with 1182 cathedral.[44]

The 1131 cathedral, built by Bishop Bernard (1115–48) was unquestionably on, and/or adjacent to, the site of the present cathedral. Gerald, who knew St Davids before and during the construction of the 1182 cathedral, describes how Henry II, returning from Ireland in 1171, crossed to it over a large marble slab, the *Llech Llafar*, that served as a bridge 'where the River Alun flows, which divides the cemetery from the northern side [of the church]'.[45] The 1182 annal implies that the new cathedral was close enough to the site of its predecessor that the 1131 structure required to be removed before work could commence on the new one.[46]

Pope Calixtus II's bull of 25 May 1123, described Bernard as 'bishop of the church of Andrew the Apostle and St David' and Giraldus describes Henry II's visit (*supra*) as to the 'cathedral of St Andrew and St David'. In his *De Invectionibus*, Gerald describes an event, probably around 1200, when the canons gathered 'in the old church of St Andrew (*in veteri ecclesia Sancti Andrae*)'and a vision of a flaming lion went around the outside [the old church] and the greater church three times (. . .*tam illam quam etiam majorem ecclesiam ter circuivit*).[47] The 'greater church' would be the new cathedral, still under construction, the 'old church' almost certainly a remnant of the 1131 cathedral, left standing while the new one was being built. This story reminds us the construction of the 1182 cathedral took place surrounded by the standing structures of a crowded cathedral close.

Edwin Lovegrove, in an architectural survey of 1922, proposed that the presbytery of the 1131 church was left standing while the new nave was built and that it was originally intended to be incorporated into the new building; in a second study in 1926 he attributed the fall of the tower in 1220 to the process of removing the 1131 fabric.[48] It may be of interest to note here Thurlby's recent survey of Llandaf Cathedral, where he argues that most of the main chamber of the presbytery – which is closely comparable in width (c.10m) to that of St Davids – was retained from Urban's cathedral of the 1120s in its rebuilding at the end of the twelfth century, fragments of older window arches helping to clearly identify fabric of the 1120s.[49] This comparison lends plausibility to Lovegrove's suggestion, though the seismic disruption of the fabric at St Davids during the construction of the presbytery renders any such argument difficult of proof.

Wyn Evans has offered another possibility for a fossilised element of Bernard's cathedral, proposing that the present chapel of St Thomas Becket, which opens off the east side of the north transept, may preserve part of the 1131 cathedral. The St Thomas chapel incorporates thirteenth-century decorative features, but these might not serve to date the whole fabric, which might incorporate older footings. The building extends east alongside the wall of the presbytery, but varying from its alignment by around 13 degrees. If this is the remains of the east end of Bernard's cathedral, it would have been narrower (c.8.5m) than, for example, Urban's contemporary church at Llandaf (c.10m); the remaining floor-plan of the whole building, of indeterminate length, would run under the north transept and north aisle of the nave – the type of relationship we see, for example, between the Old Minster and the later cathedral at Winchester.[50] At Winchester the point of intersection allowed the site of the shrine of St Swithun to stand in relationship to both the old and new buildings and influenced its placement in the new structure.[51] The difference in alignment at St Davids might also accord with the St Thomas chapel being the fossil of an external chapel standing on a different alignment to the main church, such as is seen at the large churches of Clynnog Fawr (Gywnedd) and Llanelian (Anglesey).[52]

9

Monasteria, Cathedrals, and Pilgrimage in First Millennium Britain

What type of church stood at St Davids before 1131 is unknown. We have an account of the one at Llandaf before Urban's cathedral: it is recorded that it measured only 'twenty-eight feet in length, fifteen in breadth, and twenty in height; there were two aisles, one on each side, of very small size and height; and a sanctuary of rounded structure, twelve feet in length and breadth': around 8.5m × 4.6m, not much larger in ground-plan than the *c.*1100 chapel at Whitesands (9.1m × 3.2m), near St Davids, though with aisles and an apse.[53]

A medieval church, however, subsists in a wider complex of structures. Sometimes these are parts of a larger church, but still different rooms. In an early medieval building these spaces might comprise freestanding structures, perhaps linked by walkways which perform the same functions as ambulatory in a great medieval cathedral. A very small church might be sufficient for a community of limited numbers, in a similar way to a college chapel in the modern period. A major shrine, visited by pilgrims, would require larger spaces. If, as has been argued in a range of recent studies, Llandaf was not the diocesan centre or a major shrine in early medieval Glamorgan it might not have required a large church. For St Davids, however, we might expect something larger.

Many studies of early medieval shrines begin with Cogitosus' famous description of the shrine at Kildare, in Ireland, in the seventh century. Though an Irish and not a British site, its basic premises for division of space are likely to have been shared through monastic networks around the Irish Sea:

> In its suburbs, which Saint Brigit had marked out by a definite boundary, no human foe or enemy attack is feared; on the contrary, together with all its outlying suburbs it is the safest city of refuge in the whole land of Ireland for fugitives . . . In one vast basilica, a large congregation of various rank status, rank, sex and local origin, with partitions placed between them, prays to the omnipotent master, differing in status, but one in spirit.[54]

It is now strongly debated by economic historians whether such sites had a genuinely 'urban' quality, but in theological terms they were understood as 'cities' on analogy with St Augustine's two cities, or Biblical models such as the Levitical cities of refuge.[55] Rhygyfarch describes St Davids as a *civitas*, but whether this reflected a general usage, or his simply his own desire to underscore its 'metropolitan' status is not able to be determined.

Offering sanctuary was certainly a primary function of large regional churches in Wales, within a zone of sanctuary (*noddfa*) marked out around it.[56] Hiberno-Latin Canon Law set out a taxonomy of zones of sanctity around a major church. Again, though these were composed in an Irish ecclesiastical context, they had a wider currency in monastic networks and Peter Hill and David Jenkins have applied them effectively to the evidence from a large multi-period excavation at Whithorn in 1984–92.[57]

Whithorn, in Galloway, was in a British (i.e. speaking a language derived, like Welsh, from proto-British), not Gaelic-speaking region during the first millennium. Its site has many points of comparability to St Davids, being a cathedral and *monasterium* at the shrine of an early saint (Ninian), located in the centre of a peninsula reaching into the Irish Sea. Like St Davids, it came under English influence in the later first millennium, but in this case being absorbed into the English kingdom of Northumbria, which led to a realignment of the site and some culturally English architectural influences after *c*.700, which we thus would not expect, or at least not on the same scale, at St Davids. The excavated remains are, however, a substantial glimpse of the diachronic evolution of a large early-medieval centre of the culturally 'British' church, with a continuous sequence of building and rebuilding of wooden structures from the sixth century into the second millennium.[58]

Of particular interest at Whithorn is an impressive sequence from the north of the excavated area, situated around 40m from the nave of the standing twelfth-century cathedral/priory, which we might presume to stand on the sacred core of the earlier site. The sector in question was at the edge of what the excavator defined as an 'inner precinct', marked by a vestigial, but discernible boundary in the sixth through seventh centuries, inside which was primarily a cemetery. In the putative outer precinct were what were likely to be workshop and settlement buildings, this sector reaching as far as 70m from the cathedral. As early as the sixth and seventh centuries, there was evidence of participation in exchange networks, including of goods imported directly to western Britain from North Africa and Gaul.[59] From the early 700s, the inner precinct, now enclosed by a stone boundary on a new alignment, supported a range of buildings, including, amongst a range of buildings, a bicameral wooden church of 17.9m × 4.5m which stood from *c*.730 into the mid-800s. This church would in chronological terms be from the 'Northumbrian' period, but the excavator did not find straightforward parallels for it in Northumbrian architecture.[60] It had replaced two earlier, separate clay-walled oratories that occupied approximately the same area. The new church was periodically rebuilt with addition of aisles, internal screens, and a new doorway across nearly a century, before being destroyed by fire in *c*.845. It was subsequently replaced by a smaller, stone, church, around 12m in length.[61] What was striking was the clear relationship of this sequence of buildings to the earlier cemetery and 'special graves' within it, a relationship maintained over some four centuries of redevelopment, including a shift of alignment around 700. As in Cogitosus' description of Kildare, we see here evidence for an architecture which provided for people venerating in separate spaces, with paths that channel visitors through routes appropriate to their status, or to the liturgical narrative they were re-enacting. We also see evidence for zoning of activities in what Cogitosus would term the 'suburbs'.

In 1979 Laurence Butler made a preliminary attempt to apply the Irish model of zones of sacred monastic space to St Davids, in the context of a wider debate about 'monastic cities'.[62] In this he identified the medieval cathedral close as a possible inner zone, with features such as the coastal chapel-sites and the linear earthwork Ffos y Mynach as markers of a possible outer zone on a 2–3km radius around the cathedral. Further cataloguing and dating of landscape features by Heather James and others offers the potential to pursue this model further, though this is beyond the scope of the present study.[63]

Conclusion

The aim of the foregoing has been, firstly, to sketch a model for the history of the development of St Davids as an ecclesiastical centre up to the twelfth century that is diachronic rather than synchronic. Setting aside older dichotomies such as 'Norman' vs 'native' or 'Roman' vs 'Celtic', there is a need to focus more on the strands of continuity of material and religious life, over a period of centuries, which may have fed into the conception and design of the medieval cathedral. The history of the Welsh church in the eleventh and twelfth centuries admittedly offers numerous challenges to tracing continuity. St Davids in the tenth century was subject to repeated destructive raids, which might have caused a break with the past. When a pilgrim priest came to St Davids towards the end of the century, he found the site temporarily abandoned and he struggled for seven days 'uprooting thorns and thistles' until he reached the founder's tomb.[64] But it *was* still there and able to be located, even if we are unsure what happened to his relics. Sources from the tenth century and earlier are mostly lost. Gerald of Wales was unsure whether it was the raids, or simple effluxion of time, that were responsible;[65] Rhygyfarch, however, had found old manuscripts surviving there in his own time.[66] And perhaps we should occasionally question the persistent association of the writing of Rhygyfarch's Life of St David with William I's visit to St Davids and the new order it presaged. Rhygyfarch was first of all a churchman and he wrote his Life of David within a very few years of the fifth centenary of his patron's death – a natural enough time to celebrate, as much as boost, the enduring influence of a popular saint.[67]

Notes

[1] *Annales Cambriae* s.a. 1131 and 1182, ed. J. Williams ab Ithel, Roll Series (London, 1860) pp. 39, 55, but note the new editions by Henry Gough-Cooper (*http://croniclau.bangor.ac.uk/editions.php.en*). Also see Also see comprehensive reassessment of the annals in B. Guy, G. Henley, O. Wyn Jones and R. Thomas (eds), *The Chronicles of Medieval Wales and the March* (Turnhout, 2020).

[2] *Viz.* Roger Brown, who perhaps rather harshly judges Rhygyfarch and Gerald to have 'bedevilled' the earlier history: 'The Age of Saints to the Victorian Church', in N. Doe (ed.), *A New History of the Church in Wales* (Cardiff, 2020), pp. 9–26: 9.

[3] See, in general, the remarks of Wendy Davies, 'Property Rights and Property Claims in Welsh *vitae* of the eleventh century', in *Hagiographie, cultures et sociétés IVe–XIIe siècles* (Paris, 1981), pp. 515–33.

[4] R. Stalley, 'The Architecture of St David's Cathedral: Chronology, Catastrophe and Design', *Antiquaries Journal*, 82 (2002), pp. 13–45: 18.

[5] D. Dumville, Review of K. McCone, *Pagan Past and Christian Present, Peritia*, 10 (1996), pp. 389–98: 395.

[6] See thoughtful comment by Rebecca Thomas, *History and Identity in Early Medieval Wales* (Woodbridge, 2022), p. 4.

[7] For example, Bishop Thomas Burgess, *Tracts on the Origin and Independence of the Ancient British Church* (London, 1815), e.g. pp. 98–106, 144–5, and Rice Rees, *An Essay on the Welsh Saints or the Primitive Christians, Usually Considered to have been the Founders of the Churches in Wales* (London and Llandovery, 1836), e.g. p. 70; for criticism, see: J. R. Davies, 'The Saints of South Wales and the Welsh Church', in A. Thacker and R. Sharpe (eds), *Local Saints and Local Churches in the Early Medieval West* (Oxford, 2002), pp. 361–95, pp. 361–5.

For the twentieth century: John Fisher, 'Welsh Church Dedications', *Transactions of the Honourable Society of Cymmrodorion* (1906–7), pp. 76–108; E. G. Bowen, *Saints, Seaways and Settlements in the Celtic Land* (Cardiff, 1969); critique by: R. Sharpe, 'Martyrs and Local Saints in Late Antique Britain', in Thacker and Sharpe (eds), *Local saints*, pp. 75–154: 94–102; O. Chadwick, 'The Evidence of Dedications in the Early History of the Welsh church', in N. K. Chadwick (ed.), *Studies in Early British History* (Cambridge, 1954), pp. 173–88.

[8] J. Blair, *The Church in Anglo-Saxon Society* (Oxford, 2005), pp. 345.

[9] K. Jankulak, 'Adjacent Saints' Dedications and early Celtic History', in S. Boardman, J. R. Davies and E. Williamson (eds), *Saints' Cults in the Celtic World* (Woodbridge, 2009) pp. 91–118; J. M. Wooding, 'The Figure of David', in J. W. Evans and J. M. Wooding (eds), *St David of Wales: Cult, Church and Nation* (Woodbridge, 2007), pp. 1–19: 7–10.

[10] T. Charles-Edwards, *The Chronicle of Ireland*, 2 vols (Liverpool, 2006), vol. i, pp. 7–9; *Annales Cambriae*, ed. Williams ab Ithel, p. 6.

[11] Hermits born in the eleventh century were promoted as saints by St Davids (Caradog Fynach) and Llandaf (Elgar) in the twelfth; also see Gray, in David Ceri Jones, Barry J. Lewis, Madeleine Gray and D. Densil Morgan, *A History of Christianity in Wales* (Cardiff, 2022), p. 100.

[12] C. Cuissard (ed.), 'Vie de saint Paul de Léon en Bretagne d'après un manuscrit de Fleury-sur-Loire conservé à la Bibliothèque publique d'Orléans', *Revue celtique*, 5 (1881–3), pp. 413–60: 421.

[13] J. Morris, 'The Dates of the Celtic Saints', *Journal of Theological Studies*, n.s. 17 (1966), pp. 342–91: 349, 384–5, D. N. Dumville, *St David of Wales* (Cambridge, 2001), pp. 12–22; Gildas, *Fragmenta*, ed. and trans. M. Winterbottom, *Gildas the Ruin of Britain and other Works* (Chichester, 1980), pp. 143–5, notes 154–5. On Gildas' *floruit*: Charles-Edwards, *The Chronicle of Ireland*, vol. i., p. 108, n. 4.

[14] A. W. Wade-Evans (trans.), *Life of St. David* (London, 1923), p. 62, offers other potential references to saints as '*Aquatici*' in early Wales.

[15] *Vita S. Dauid*, ch. 66, ed. and trans. R. Sharpe and J. R. Davies, in Evans and Wooding (eds), *St David of Wales*, pp. 152–3.

[16] Rhygyfarch, *Vita S. Dauid* ch. 53, ed. Sharpe and Davies, pp. 146–7.

[17] Asser, *Vita Ælfredi regis* ch. 79, ed W. H. Stevenson, *Asser's Life of King Alfred* (Oxford 1904), p. 65. In *Annales Cambriae*, s.a. 840, Nobis is *episcopus in Miniu*, ed. Williams ab Ithel, p. 11.

[18] Asser, *Vita Ælfredi regis* ch. 79, ed Stevenson, pp. 65–6.

[19] T. Charles-Edwards, *Wales and the Britons 350–1064* (Oxford, 2013), pp. 597–8; T. Charles-Edwards, 'The Seven Bishop-Houses of Dyfed', *Bulletin of the Board of Celtic Studies*, 24 (1970–2), pp. 247–62; Lewis, in *A History of Christianity*, pp. 75.

[20] J. M. Wooding, 'The Representation of Early British Monasticism and *Peregrinatio* in *Vita prima S. Samsonis*', in L. Olson (ed.), *St Samson of Dol and the Earliest History of Brittany, Cornwall and Wales* (Woodbridge, 2017), pp. 137–61: 149–53; also, *Vita S. Columbae*, I.20, ed. A. O. and M. O. Anderson (London, 1961), pp. 248–51.

[21] *Vita S. Dauid*, chs. 17 and 15 ed. and trans. Sharpe and Davies, pp. 120–23.

[22] B. G. Charles, *The Placenames of Pembrokeshire* (Aberystwyth, 1992), pp. 296–7.

[23] T. Charles-Edwards, *The Chronicle of Ireland*, vol 2, pp. 7–9 and W. Stokes (ed. and trans.), *Félire Oengusso, the Martyrology of Oengus the Culdee* (London, 1905), p. 80.

[24] Giraldus Cambrensis, *Vita S. Dauid*, ed. P. Russell, *https://saints.wales/theedition*.

[25] B. McGinn, 'Ocean and Desert as Symbols of Mystical Absorption in the Christian Tradition', *Journal of Religion*, 74 (1994), pp. 155–81.

St Davids Before the Cathedral

26   At least ostensibly, as one may credit a degree of exhibitionism to eremites: see M. Mott, *The Seven Mountains of Thomas Merton* (Boston, 1984), p. 297.

27   Wade-Evans, *Life of St. David*, p. 268; the Irish themselves claimed that their ritual of the Mass came via the British saints David, Gildas and Docco: W. W. Heist (ed.), *Vitae Sanctorum Hiberniae ex codice olim Salmanticensi* (Brussels, 1965), pp. 82.

28   See discussion in J. M. Wooding, 'Island and Coastal Churches in Medieval Wales and Ireland', in K. Jankulak and J. M. Wooding (eds), *Ireland and Wales in the Middle Ages* (Dublin, 2007), pp. 201–28: 214–18.

29   P. Hill, *Whithorn and St Ninian: the Excavation of a Monastic Town* (Stroud, 1997), pp. 297–332; but cf. E. Campbell, *Continental and Mediterranean Imports to Atlantic Britain and Ireland*, AD 400–800 (York, 2007).

30   It is common to refer to the Norse raids as 'Viking', but these raids were sometimes linked to Welsh politics: see B. Hudson, *Viking Pirates and Christian Princes: Dynasty, Religion, and Empire in the North Atlantic* (Oxford, 2005), pp. 60, 152, 168–70; *Annales Cambriae*, ed. Williams ab Ithel, pp. 20–9.

31   T. Wright (ed.), *Three Chapters of Letters Relating to the Dissolution of the Monasteries* (London, 1843), pp. 183–6: 185, 206–10.

32   T. Charles-Edwards, 'The Social Background to Irish *Peregrinatio*', *Celtica*, 11 (1976), 43–59; on the Welsh manifestation of *peregrinatio* see Wooding, 'The Representation', pp. 155–6.

33   N. Edwards et al. *A Corpus of Early Medieval Inscribed Stones and Sculpture in Wales: Volume II South-West Wales* (Cardiff, 2007), pp. 132–4 and Robert Gapper, *pers. comm.*

34   J. W. Evans, 'St David and St Davids: Some Observations on the Cult, Site and Buildings', in J. Cartwright (ed.), *Celtic Hagiography and Saints' Cults* (Cardiff, 2003), pp. 10–25: 15; J. W. Evans, 'Transition and Survival: St David and St Davids Cathedral', in Evans and Wooding (eds), *St David*, pp. 20–40: 39. Also I note the recent redating to ninth century of the IDNERT stone at Llanddewi Brefi, with its reference to the 'plunder of St David' (*predam sancti Dauid*) (Edwards, *Corpus*, pp. 150–3).

35   Evans, 'Transition and Survival', pp. 38–9.

36   See, *passim*, J. R. Davies, *The Book of Llandaf and the Norman Church in Wales* (Woodbridge, 2003); P. Sims-Williams, *The Book of Llandaf as a Historical Source* (Woodbridge, 2019).

37   Sims-Williams, *The Book of Llandaf*, pp. 7–8.

38   J. R. Davies, 'Cathedrals and the Cult of Saints in eleventh and twelfth century Wales', in P. Dalton, C. Insley, and L. J. Wilkinson (eds), *Cathedrals, Communities and Conflict in the Anglo-Norman World* (Woodbridge, 2011), pp. 99–115: 100–1; J. R. Davies, 'The Medieval Church', in G. H. Jenkins, R. Suggett and E. White (eds), *Cardiganshire County History Vol 2. Medieval and Early Modern Cardiganshire* (Cardiff, 2019), pp. 175–96: 178–80. He cites as support for Evans's model Richard Sharpe's theory concerning Rhygyfarch's treatment of *mynyw*, though I don't see it as clearly doing so: R. Sharpe, 'Which Text is Rhygyfarch's *Life* of St David?', in Evans and Wooding (eds), *St David*, pp. 90–106: 99.

39   M. L. Dawson, 'Notes on the Monastery of Rosnat or Ty Gwyn, Pembrokeshire', *Archaeologia Cambrensis* (1898), pp. 1–20; H. James, 'The Cult of St. David in the Middle Ages', in M. Carver (ed.), *In Search of Cult: Archaeological Investigations in Honour of Philip Rahtz* (Woodbridge, 1993), pp. 105–12: 106; Evans, 'St David and St Davids: Some Observations', p. 11. A similar claim once made for Whithorn is belied by more recent archaeological evidence: J. M. Wooding, 'St Ninian: Archaeology and the *Dossier* of a Saint's Cult', in J. Murray (ed.), *St Ninian and the Earliest Christianity in Scotland* (Oxford, 2009), pp. 9–18: 10.

40   Edwards, *Corpus*, pp. 427–56.

41   Edwards, *Corpus*, pp. 440–4 and 447–9.

[42] P. Russell (ed. and trans.), *Vita Griffini Filii Conani: the Medieval Latin Life of Gruffudd ap Cynan* (Cardiff, 2005), pp. 68–9; Evans, 'St David and St Davids: Some Observations', pp. 14–15. The *chorus universus*, is a '*clas*' in the Welsh translation of the Life.

[43] J. M. Wooding, 'Pilgrimage and Cathedrals in Early Medieval Britain', in D. Dyas and J. Jenkins (eds), *Pilgrimage and England's Cathedrals: Past, Present and Future* (London, 2020), pp. 29–48: 36; Blair, *The Church*, pp. 344–54.

[44] On possible symbolism of rendering, see: J. Howe, *Before the Gregorian Reform* (Ithaca NY, 2016), pp. 87–9.

[45] '*Labitur hic autem Aluni fluvius . . . coemiterium lateralitur a borea disterminans*', in J. F. Dimock (ed.), *Itinerarium Kambriae* Rolls Series 6 (London, 1868), p. 107. Another version in *Topographia Hibernica* ch. I.38, ed. J. F. Dimock, Rolls Series 5 (London, 1867), p. 287.

[46] B. Guy, G. Henley, O. Wyn Jones and R. Thomas (eds), *The Chronicles of Medieval Wales and the March*.

[47] Giraldus, *De invectionibus*, 6.10, ed. W. S. Davies, *Y Cymmrodor*, 30 (1920), p. 211. This vision pertains to his campaign after the death of Peter de Leia (1198), so to be probably assigned to near that date.

[48] E. W. Lovegrove, 'St. David's Cathedral', *Archaeologia Cambrensis* (1922), pp. 360–82: 368, 375–6; 'The Cathedral Church of St Davids', *Archaeological Journal*, 83 (1962), pp. 255–83: 261–2.

[49] M. Thurlby, 'The Romanesque Fabric of Llandaff Cathedral', *Archaeologia Cambrensis* (2021), pp. 159–91: 171–84.

[50] T. B. James, *Winchester* (London, 1997), pp. 44–66.

[51] Wooding, 'Pilgrimage and Cathedrals', p. 37.

[52] David Petts, *The Early Medieval Church in Wales* (Stroud, 2009), pp. 58–9; at Clynnog, unfortunately from pre-modern excavations, there seems to be evidence of earlier phases, on the same alignment, of the extant medieval structure: B. Stallybrass, 'Recent Discoveries at *Clynnog Fawr*', *Archaeologia Cambrensis* (1914), 271–96.

[53] J. Gwenogvryn Evans (ed.), *The Text of the Book of Llan Dâv* (Oxford, 1893), p. 86; On excavations at Whitesands: K. Murphy and K. A. Hemer, *Excavation of an Early Medieval Cemetery at St Patrick's Chapel, St Davids, Pembrokeshire*, DAT Report No. 2022–46 (Llandeilo, 2021), p. 47–51.

[54] S. Connolly and J.-M. Picard (trans.), 'Cogitosus: Life of Saint Brigid', *Journal of the Royal Society of Antiquaries of Ireland*, 117 (1987), pp. 5–27: 25–6.

[55] C. Etchingham, *The Irish 'Monastic Town': is this a Valid Concept?* Kathleen Hughes Memorial Lecture (Cambridge, 2010).

[56] H. Pryce, *Native Law and the Church in Medieval Wales* (Oxford, 1993), pp. 168–73; Lewis, in *A History of Christianity*, pp. 78–9.

[57] Hill, *Whithorn*, pp. 3–35; D. H. Jenkins, '*Holy, holier, holiest': the Sacred Topography of the Early Medieval Irish Church* (Turnhout, 2010), 31–2, 48–52, 88.

[58] My discussion is sourced both from Hill's report and my own experience as a member of the excavation team for periods in 1987–9 and 1991.

[59] Hill, *Whithorn*, pp. 35–7; Campbell, *Continental and Mediterranean Imports*, *passim* and pp. 117–18 for summary of Welsh connection.

[60] Hill, *Whithorn*, pp. 44–5, 138.

[61] Hill, *Whithorn*, esp. pp. 103–18, 140–60.

[62] L. A. S. Butler, 'The Monastic Town in Medieval Wales', *Bulletin of the Board of Celtic Studies*, 28 (1978–80), pp. 458–67: 462–6.

[63] James, 'The Cult of St David', and H. James, 'The Geography of the Cult of St David: a Study of Dedication Patterns in the Medieval Diocese', in Evans and Wooding (eds), *St David*, pp. 41–83: 47–56; B. Vyner, Ffos y Mynach, St Davids: an Exploration and a Biography of the Monk's Dyke, *Archaeologia Cambrensis* (2021), pp. 77–110.

[64] *Life* of St Caradog Fynach, ed. and trans, Francesco Marzella: 'Seintiau' (*https://saints.wales*), forthcoming. Also, Francesco Marzella, 'Gerald of Wales and the Life of St Caradog', in D. Parsons and P. Russell (eds), *Seintiau Cymru / Sancti Cambrenses: Studies in the Saints of Wales* (Aberystwyth, 2022), pp. 299–316. I would like to thank Dr Marzella for kindly sending me his edition in advance of publication.

[65] Giraldus Cambrensis, *Vita S. Dauid* ch. 43, ed. P. Russell, *https://saints.wales/theedition*

[66] See note 15.

[67] I would like to especially thank Karen Jankulak, as always, for her support as well as useful criticism a draft. Conversations with Wyn Evans over many years inform all my approaches to the cathedral – even if we sometimes disagree!

2.
ST DAVIDS CATHEDRAL: THE 1182 CHURCH

Malcolm Thurlby

Introduction

Nineteenth- and twentieth-century accounts of the late twelfth- and early thirteenth-century fabric of St Davids Cathedral have frequently questioned the classification of the building; is it Romanesque or Gothic?[1] Useful as these labels are in the general ordering of European art and architecture, they were not in use in the late twelfth century and will be avoided in the following discussion.[2] Instead, focus will be on the reconstruction of the church as designed in 1182. Associations will be sought with earlier and near-contemporary buildings with the view to understanding the place of St Davids Cathedral in late twelfth-century architecture, where the masons were trained, why the building was constructed and for whom.

Documentation

The documentation that relates to the present building provides an essential framework for our analysis of the building and yet, as is so often the case, it supplies so little of the detail we crave to know. The *Annales Cambriae* (*Annals of Wales*) record that in 1182 the church of St Davids was destroyed and work on the present cathedral church was commenced.[3] In 1188 Baldwin, archbishop of Canterbury, said Mass at the high altar during his tour of Wales.[4] This may be taken to mean either that part of the old cathedral was still in use or that the sanctuary of the new church was completed. In 1189, the papal legate, John of Anagni, granted Gerald of Wales and Bishop Peter de Leia release from their vows to join the crusade, on condition that they contributed to the

https://doi.org/10.16922/jrhlc.9.2.2

rebuilding (*reparationem*) of the church of St Davids.[5] This indicates that building was still ongoing. In 1197 Lord Rhys of Deheubarth was buried in the cathedral. In 1198 Bishop Peter de Leia died, and his obit records that he began (*incoepit*) the new work on the cathedral.[6] The implication is that it was not yet finished. In 1220 the new tower collapsed.[7] This has been taken universally to refer to the crossing tower. In 1248 an earthquake damaged 'a great part' of the church.[8] These events, along with the work of subsequent restorations, account for the complexity of what we see today.

The floor-plan of the 1182 church has come down to us in its entirety. There is an aisled presbytery of four bays, a crossing tower under which there is the liturgical choir. The aisleless transepts have three bays and communicate through doors with the aisles of the six-bay nave. The retrochoir and Lady Chapel are later additions that extend to the original floor-plan to the east.

The Archaeology of the Fabric: the Crossing

Given that the crossing tower is the only part of the building that can be specifically associated with the documentation, it provides a good starting point for our investigation. This allows us to identify features that are specific to the 1180s and the 1220s. Examination of the nave, presbytery and transepts will follow with the view to separating 1180s, 1220s and post-1248 work. We will then be in a position to reconstruct the appearance of the 1182 design of the cathedral.

The differences between the west and the other crossing arches illustrate changes between the 1180s and post-1220 work (Fig. 1). They are: from round-headed to pointed arches, from nibs to fillets on the shafts, from some capitals without necking to the consistent use of necking, and from deeply cut and projecting mouldings to shallow mouldings and simple chamfers. There is also a change from deep to shallow carving in the capitals which is especially noticeable in the foliated trumpet-scallop types in the north, south and east arches. There are analogous contrasts between the arcading towards the east above the west crossing arch and the arcades above the other three crossing arches.[9]

We now turn our attention to the nave in which we find close analogues for the 1180s work in the western crossing arch as well as other details that fit with a date in the 1180s.

St Davids Cathedral: The 1182 Church

Figure 1: St Davids Cathedral, presbytery and crossing to west

The Nave

The six-bay nave has wide, round-headed arches except in the narrow west bay where the arch is pointed. The relatively squat columns alternate round and octagonal and have attached shafts on the cardinal axes to create what is usually called a *pilier cantonné*. The detached shafts of the west responds are exceptional.[10] On the aisle side of the piers there are stepped triple shafts with capitals and abaci that project beyond the plane of the wall intended to support the ribs of an aisle vault. The main arcade arches have three orders, of which the inner one is plain with hollow chamfers. The second order towards the nave is adorned with rich chevron ornament, which changes in detail from bay to bay, and which is framed by a segmental roll moulding. The outer order towards the nave has two roll mouldings, the inner one of which is nibbed. In the western bay of the north arcade the chevron in the left arc of the arch does not match that on the right and there is an awkward junction between the two at the apex (Fig. 2). There is a set back at the triforium sill to facilitate the placement of vault shafts; a triplet above the columns and a single shaft above the middle of the main arcade arch (Fig. 3). The upper half of the nave elevation appears to link a triforium and clerestory under a single giant arch carved with chevron or meander ornament that

21

Figure 2 (*above*): Detail of west bay of south arcade of nave, showing awkward junction

Figure 3: Nave, interior to east showing triforium and clerestorey

changes from arch to arch. In fact, there is no division within the passage between triforium and clerestory. The triforium arches are sharply pointed and have two continuous orders, the inner with a quadrant roll, the outer with a roll moulding. Between the heads of the arches there is a pierced roundel with a variety of carved detail.

The west front is the product of Scott's restoration, and as a reflection of the actual 1180s design it must be used with caution and in conjunction with pre-restoration photographs and antiquarian drawings.[11] The south doorway dates from the fourteenth century but the three-order, round-headed north doorway is contemporary with the rest of the nave (Fig. 4). The inner order is continuous and has a quadrant roll moulding. Orders two and three both have poorly preserved chevron in the arch and are carried on capitals atop nibbed shafts and moulded bases. The chevron on order two has a lattice pattern while in order three it was a saw-tooth form with outer and central thin roll mouldings. The two left, and the outer right capitals have remnants of foliage decoration. The damaged inner right capital takes the form of a grotesque mask. The hood mould is carved with shuttlecocks and has a mask at the apex and damaged dragon's-head stops.

Figure 4: St Davids Cathedral, north nave doorway

There was a remodelling of the nave aisles in the time of Bishop Gower (1328–47) when the walls were heightened and larger windows inserted. However, the walls up to the string-course at windowsill level and the triple-shafted vault responds up to the level of the nave arcade capitals belong to the 1180s build. At the west end of the south aisle below the rose window there is part of the lower frame of its predecessor. The abandonment of the lower window and the subsequent rebuilding at a higher level may have been precipitated by damage caused in the 1248 earthquake.

The capitals of the main arcades boast a fine array of different designs from simple trumpet-scallops to richly foliated and even figured versions of the type, to a range of foliage forms that includes experimental varieties of stiff-leaf. Some of the capitals atop the attached shafts are without necking but on the core capital necking is used.[12]

The triple-shaft groups on the aisle side of the nave arcade piers, in which plain shafts flank a nibbed shaft, are a compact version of the responds of the soffits of the west crossing arch. The abaci of the main arcade capitals are the same as on the west crossing capitals. The capitals without necking in the nave arcades and atop the single high-vault shafts are used throughout the west crossing arch responds. Trumpet scallops with a clear separation between the individual elements, richly foliated scallops, and trefoil leaves with a gorged central lobe that grow from the bell of the capital, are also common to the nave and west crossing arch). Gaping chevron is common to the westernmost clerestory arch on the north side of the nave and the west face of the west crossing arch. Finally, the stepped roll moulding with a central nib on the west crossing arch appears in reduced form on the outer order of the nave arcades.

The alternation of triple shafts above the main arcade piers with single shafts above the centre of the bay indicates that a six-part vault over single bays was planned. The set-back above the main arcades to create a sill for the triforium and vaulting shafts confirms the intention to vault. Where such set-backs occur in English Romanesque architecture, as in the presbytery and transepts of Durham cathedral, the nave of Lindisfarne priory, the nave of St Peter's abbey (now cathedral), Gloucester, and the presbytery of Malmesbury abbey, high vaults were constructed.[13] Of these churches, the nave of Gloucester is the likely point of departure for the St Davids scheme. In some cases the wall arches or *formerets* that define the edge of the vault are chiselled back. This suggests that the masonry web of a high vault was mortared to the *formeret*. This evidence may be contrasted with the *formerets* in the nave at Llanthony priory which remain in near-perfect condition after the removal of the former wooden high vault.[14] Indeed, it will be noticed that the label stops of the arches are even preserved. On the other hand, the remains of vaults in the Great Church of Glastonbury abbey present a more involved picture. Above the *formeret* to the left the stones of the vault web – limestone below and tufa above – are intact.[15] The same is true for the limestone springer and the first two pieces of tufa above the right *formeret*, but above this the vault web has fallen away and thus the *formeret* stands alone.

Roger Stalley suggested that the nave high vault would have had a domical trajectory, and this can be visualized with reference to the west crossing arch or to the large, round-headed arch on the inside of the west wall that encloses the windows of the west front.[16] The capitals of these arches are at the same level as the capitals of the high vault, while the head of the arch disappears behind the present ceiling.

The only stone suitable for the webbing of the high vault is tufa. In spite of Stalley's reservation as to the daring of the masons about trying to build a high vault, even in lightweight tufa, there is such a good tradition of tufa vaults in the West Country that such a bold move should come as no great surprise.[17]

Reconstruction of a high stone vault in the nave of St Davids strongly suggests that aisle vaults were also built. This is confirmed by the offset on the east wall of the nave south aisle, by the triple shafts on the aisle side of the main arcade piers and the responds against the aisle walls. The space for the St Davids aisle-vault springers is unusually narrow, but a close parallel is in the near-contemporary slype vault at Llanthony priory where each rib is cut from a different stone all distinct from the wall arch as would have been the case at St Davids (Fig. 5).

The Presbytery

The elevation of the presbytery comprises two storeys, a pointed main arcade surmounted by pointed clerestory windows (Fig. 1). Work remains from all three building campaigns, 1182, post-1220 and post-1248. The archaeology is involved and has been analyzed in detail elsewhere.[18] In short, the high vault capital above the westernmost column of the main arcade on the north side is of the same type of decorated scallop as on the eastern side of the crossing. The distinct differences between this capital type and those used in the 1180s work makes it clear that the vault

Figure 5: Llanthony Priory, slype vault

capitals belong with the post-1220 rebuild. Above the high-vault capital are the remains of wall arches and space for the springing of the vault, on either side of which there is the clerestory string-course. Here the springers of the *formerets* have been chiselled back like those in the nave (Fig. 6). There is similar evidence for a high vault in the south-west and north-west angles of the presbytery. Above the westernmost column on the north side, a large trefoil niche interrupts the lines of the high vault (Fig. 6). Clearly the high vault and the niche are incongruous and this is explained by the removal of the high vault, presumably after the 1248 earthquake, and the subsequent introduction of the niche. In the east clerestory, which was accurately restored by Scott, the lateral windows are too tall to accommodate a high vault (Fig. 7). It follows that this range of windows must date after 1248.

The east responds of the main arcades are compound and have an inner order of stepped triple shafts – the middle one of which is nibbed – and hollows between the shafts as on the responds of the western crossing arch). The second order has a single nibbed shaft and a foliage capital, while the outer order is a nibbed roll set between hollow mouldings and continues directly to the abacus. On the aisle side of the main arcade columns there are triple-shaft groups that carry trumpet-scalloped capitals as if to support vault ribs (Fig. 8). Curiously, they are

St Davids Cathedral: The 1182 Church

Figure 6: St Davids Cathedral, presbytery north arcade, westernmost column

Figure 7: St Davids Cathedral, presbytery, interior to E

27

Figure 8: St Davids Cathedral, S presbytery aisle, interior to W

set three courses below the capital of the main arcade and, consequently, the present system could not have included aisle vaults. The bases of the west responds overlap those to the left and right from the 1180s and therefore the responds must be larger than in the 1180s work. The succulent waterleaf capitals of the west responds are paralleled in the post-1220 crossing capitals rather than in the 1180s work.

At the east end of the aisles there are round-headed wall arches (Fig. 9). In the south aisle this arch is carried on a trumpet-scallop capital to the north but is suspended to the south. The capital is set at a lower level than the capitals of the main arcade and yet is at the same height as the capitals atop the triple shafts at the back of the main arcade piers. The wall arches and the capitals at the back of the arcade piers are normally associated with the intention to vault the aisles. However, the placement of the capitals of the main arcade just three courses above the 'vault' shafts at the back of the piers has suggested to most commentators that the vaults were never built. Be that as it may, in the penultimate west bay of the north aisle there is further evidence of at least the intention to vault (Fig. 10). Here the scars of the junction of the putative vault are

Figure 9: St Davids Cathedral, S presbytery aisle, western arch

Figure 10: St Davids Cathedral, presbytery north aisle, penultimate west bay

preserved in the restored pointing above and to the outside of a former round-headed window. To the east the scar descends to the side of a triple-shaft vault respond at which point there is a significant change. Below the junction there is a hollow to either side of the respond but this feature is lacking above. The change marks the original setting of the vault capital, while the present position of the capital dates from Bishop Gower's heightening of the aisle wall.

The seemingly insoluble problem of the aisle vault can be resolved if we accept that the aisle vault capitals belong to the 1180s while the main arcade capitals are from post-1220 rebuilding. The vault capitals comply with the regular coursing of the piers and therefore do not mark an earlier level of a main arcade capital. Rather, the section of the column towards the presbytery would have continued above the level of the aisle vault capitals in the manner of a giant order, as at St Frideswide's, Oxford. As at St Frideswide's, the arches at St Davids would have been round-headed, as indicated by the trace of the round-headed wall arch in presbytery aisle. The alternating round and octagonal columns at St Davids recall Canterbury cathedral choir. The giant order was formerly used in the presbytery of Tewkesbury abbey and, under royal patronage, in the abbey churches at Romsey, Reading and Jedburgh.[19] After 1185 it appears in the Great Church at Glastonbury, possibly as a reflection of the Romanesque church there.[20] This would provide an iconographic association for St Davids because St David himself is reputed to have built an extension to the east of the *Vetusta Ecclesia*.[21] How the rest of the St Davids 1180s presbytery elevation was finished cannot be determined, except to say that there would certainly have been a clerestory and, given the evidence for a high vault in the nave, there must have been one in the presbytery.

The east wall of the presbytery is dominated by three richly ornamented, graduated lancet windows each with four orders, three of which are continuous and are framed by the outer order on shafts and capitals (Fig. 7). The inner order has a simple angle roll while the next two have varieties of 'gaping' chevron. The outer order has a filleted shaft flanked by thin rolls, a trumpet-scallop capital and thin filleted rolls and hollow mouldings in the arch. The outer jambs and the lower half of the two intermediate supports are of local grey sandstone while in the upper half of the intermediate supports and the arch heads local sandstone and Dundry stone are used to give an irregular polychrome effect. Moreover, the intermediate shafts and the lower halves of the

30

outer shafts are detached, filleted and have multiple shaft rings, while the upper halves of the outer shafts are coursed and are without rings. The capitals atop the outer shafts are trumpet scallops with square abaci while the intermediate capitals are stiff-leaf and have round abaci. These detail differences suggest that the windows are not the product of a single build. The 'gaping' chevron to either side of a roll moulding on the outer order of the windows is precisely the same as on the west crossing arch. This suggests that the windows belong in part to the 1180s, which would agree with the attribution of the east responds of the presbytery arcades to the first campaign of construction. Confirmation of this reading is supplied by the ornament on the string-course beneath the windows. Here the meander ornament may be compared with the east window in the west bay of the north nave clerestory, where it is used next to the 'gaping' chevron in the west window. Changes in details of the shafts and capitals are probably the result of rebuilding of the windows after damage in 1220 or 1248.

Given that the form of the east responds and the gaping chevron of the east windows relate to the western crossing arch, it is difficult to determine priority between construction of the nave and the presbytery. What is clear is that in 1220 the fall of the crossing tower caused major damage in the presbytery, so much so that the main elevation had to be rebuilt from just above the level of the aisle vault capitals. This was achieved, complete with a high vault, and in a remarkably conservative style in which details like trumpet-scallop capitals and chevron ornament conformed to the design vocabulary of the 1180s, even if the chevron of the main arcade arches generally lacked the gusto of that in the nave. Perhaps even more amazingly, this antiquarian attitude prevailed in the subsequent reconstruction following the 1248 earthquake, although this time a wood roof replaced a high vault.

The Transepts

As is often the case, the design of the east and west walls of the transepts seem unrelated. On the east there are three richly articulated, pointed arches in both arms while the west wall is plain, broken only by the plain surrounds of the doorways to the nave aisles and, in the north transept, a blocked window and adjacent blind arch above a door to the outside. The difference is simply to do with function, the rich east arches either mark entry into the presbytery aisle, frame an altar, or, in the case of the northern arch in the north transept, lead to the St Thomas Becket chapel. In each case the arches have three orders but the manner in which they are articulated varies from bay to bay.[22]

The unmoulded inner order of the pointed chamfered arch to the Becket chapel is carried on capitals atop triple shafts with the central one nibbed, as in the responds of the western crossing arch. The shaft group is set into an arced recess, which is a deeper version of this motif in the presbytery aisle responds. The capitals have no necking, and, on the south side, the cones of the trumpet-scallop capital have damaged foliage decoration. On the north side the capital has lost its symmetrically set foliage crockets but retains the plantain notches of the central leaf that recall in the nave capitals. Details of capitals in the other arches and on the high vault supports in the transepts, plus the use of nibbed shafts, indicate that the transepts were an integral part of the 1182 design of the cathedral.

Associations for the 1182 Design

The narrow bays of the presbytery allowed for a four-bay division in a relatively restricted space. Four bays would have been deemed desirable so as to conform to the tradition established in Anglo-Norman great churches at St Augustine's, Canterbury (1070); St Albans (1077), Winchester, Durham and elsewhere. It was also adopted by Bishop Roger of Salisbury, when he rebuilt the eastern arm of Sarum cathedral (1102–1139). It was never the norm in the south-west Midlands or West Country and, therefore, the four-bay presbytery at St Davids may be seen as a mark of superiority for the Welsh cathedral. For the much larger space of the nave, the use of bays the same size as the presbytery would have resulted in a cluttered appearance dominated by the masses of masonry of the main arcade piers and arches. As it is, large nave piers were deemed essential for a vaulted building but the dramatically wide bays impart a sense of openness lacking in the presbytery. Add to this the rich variations in the capital design and the chevron, then the public area of the church was to be by far the most opulent in Wales and intended to vie with the most prestigious churches in England. The transepts were not the place for such lavish displays. Their primary purpose was to house subsidiary altars for the canons and therefore rich displays of decoration deemed appropriate for location of the high altar in the presbytery, or in the public area of the nave, would have been excessive for the secondary liturgical spaces. Be that as it may, the different chevron patterns in the nave are matched by the variety in the shafts and arch designs of the eastern arcades the transepts.

The wealth of ornament at St Davids is associated with the most munificent patrons of architecture and the most prestigious churches of the twelfth century in England. The vogue for rich chevron ornament was established early in the twelfth century in the nave of Durham cathedral and the nave of St Peter's, Gloucester. A number of different chevron types are found at Hereford cathedral and in the Herefordshire School of sculpture, and in the nave arcades of Hereford cathedral the combination of chevron and roll mouldings foreshadows the arrangement in the St Davids nave.[23] The variety of rich chevron patterns was expanded to eighteen different types by Roger, bishop of Sarum (1102–39) in the rebuilding of the eastern arm, crossing and transepts of his cathedral. This aesthetic was followed by Henry of Blois, abbot of Glastonbury, 1126–1171, and bishop of Winchester (1129–71).[24] Most of Henry's work at Glastonbury perished in the devastating fire of 1184 but some idea of the richness can be gathered in his Church of the Hospital of St Cross at Winchester which he probably commenced after his return from France in 1158. Roger of Pont l'Eveque, archbishop of York (1154–81), used a wide variety of chevron in the windows of the eastern arm of York Minster.[25] The chapter house and gatehouse of St Augustine's, Bristol, also boast a lavish display of various types of chevron. And, it is on the southern arch of the St Augustine's, Bristol, gatehouse that we find the 'gaping' chevron as on the western crossing arch and the east window of the west bay of the north nave clerestory.[26] The same Bristol arch has an order of lozenge chevron similar to that used in the St Davids nave. Moreover, the plain inner order of the arch to the west range at St Augustine's has the unusual motif of a hollow chamfer as on the inner order of the main arcade arches at St Davids. Various patterns of lozenge and gaping chevron are further paralleled at Keynsham abbey and in the Lady chapel at Glastonbury abbey (1184–86/9).[27] An amazingly wide variety of chevron is encountered in Christ Church cathedral, Dublin.[28] It is also important to recognize that chevron, billet and dogtooth are used liberally in the aisle vaults of the eastern arm of Canterbury cathedral, 1175–84.

From the 1130s on, the most ambitious patrons of architecture showed a keen awareness of progressive contemporary church building in northern France. Bishop Roger of Sarum's cathedral almost certainly had a round window in the south transept *façade* like Abbot Suger's west front at Saint-Denis.[29] Connections with the sculpture of Saint-Denis are evident in the work of Henry of Blois.[30] The architectural vocabulary, and the sculpture and stained glass of Archbishop Roger of Pont l'Eveque's York Minster relate closely to work in northern France.[31] In each of these cases, reference to progressive elements from France was integrated with the rich ornamental tradition of English architecture of the twelfth century. This is exactly what is emulated at St Davids. On the one hand the majority of the detail and ornament is inherited from the well-established regional architectural school in the south-west Midlands and West Country. On the other hand, the use of high vaults throughout the church, the skeletal, hollow-wall treatment of the upper elevation of the nave, and the acanthus-related foliage capitals, all depend on recent French practice, if only through English intermediaries.

The 1180s work at St Davids belongs with the West Country School of masons, as defined by Sir Harold Brakspear.[32] The continuous quadrant roll on the inner order of the nave north doorway (Fig. 4) is ultimately derived from the wall arches in the late eleventh-century presbytery aisles of St Peter's, Gloucester. The motif was especially popular in the later twelfth century in the area around Worcester, so much so that Lovegrove labelled it the '"Worcestershire" sunk roll'.[33] In the west bays of the nave, and in the arch from the cloister to the western slype at Worcester cathedral, nibbed shafts and either trumpet-scallop or foliage capitals are used alongside an order with a continuous quadrant roll.[34] This work at Worcester probably dates immediately after the fall of the 'new tower' in 1175.[35] Other aspects of the north nave doorway at St Davids betray a West Country background. The label mask appears in the westernmost twelfth-century bay of the north nave arcade at St Peter's, Gloucester, at Sarum cathedral, in the nave arcades at Malmesbury abbey and elsewhere, while dragon's-head label stops appeared in Wales earlier in the twelfth century Wales at Llandaff Cathedral and Ewenny Priory. In addition, the shaft-swallowing-mask capital appears at Malmesbury abbey and elsewhere. Also from the West Country twelfth-century tradition is the use of doorways from the nave aisles to the transepts as at Ewenny Priory and Bishop's Cleeve (Glos.). The polychromatic treatment of the masonry as in the south transept and lancet windows of the east wall of the presbytery at St Davids recalls both the Romanesque and the post-1175 work at Worcester cathedral. The linkage between the false triforium and clerestory may be traced back to Romanesque Tewkesbury abbey in the original elevation of the presbytery and transepts as well as in the lantern of the crossing tower.[36]

The round-headed nave arcades on *piliers cantonnés* without vertical articulation in the spandrels at St Davids are presaged in the nave arcades of St James Priory, Bristol (founded 1144).[37] The *pilier cantonné* appears earlier in the West Country in the presbytery gallery of St Peter's, Gloucester, and if wall arches were used in connection with the original twelfth-century high vault in the Gloucester nave, they would have encompassed the triforium and clerestory as in the St Davids nave.

The capitals in the 1180s work at St Davids are either trumpet scallops or foliage chalice types or some sort of fusion of the two. Fully developed trumpet-scallop capitals are used at Keynsham abbey after 1166/67, and this is the most popular form in the west bays of Worcester cathedral. One capital from Keynsham is especially instructive in that it supplies a close parallel for the central south capital of the west crossing arch at St Davids in which the scallops begin to mutate into foliage.[38] An even closer comparison is with the left capital of the north nave doorway at St Mary, at Bitton (Glos.), where it carries an order of spaced, foliated-lozenge chevron in the arch similar to that in the second bay of the north nave arcade at St Davids. Bitton is located just a few miles north of Keynsham, between Bath and Bristol. Some fragments at Wigmore Abbey (fd. 1172, ded. 1179) are instructive, for in addition to a trumpet-scallop capital there is one with plantain notches and a ring beneath the abacus very similar to St Davids nave N3N. In these capitals we are dealing with an early stage in the development of the foliage capital that was ultimately derived from the classical Corinthian capital, and more immediately from examples from the third quarter of the twelfth century in northern France. They represent something radically different from the cushion or scalloped capital popular earlier in the twelfth century in that their basic form is an inverted bell, or chalice-shape, as opposed to a block shape with the lower angles cut as segments of a sphere. Aesthetically the cushion appears squat, heavy and bulbous, whereas the concave shape of the new capital is lighter and more elegant. The foliage capitals of the western crossing arch and the nave arcades are most instructive because they include specific details that are both unusual and can be dated with some degree of accuracy with reference to Wells cathedral, probably commenced in 1175, and the Great Church at Glastonbury abbey, commenced in 1185. At Wells cathedral in the eastern arcades and chapels of the transepts, and the eastern crossing arches, we find elegant capitals with plantain notches and upright leaves that blossom into profuse crockets, and even without necking, as at St Davids. In the capitals illustrated here from the eastern arcade of the Wells north transept we notice some very specific parallels for details in the St Davids capitals. There are trefoil leaves with a gouged middle lobe, trefoil leaves that grow from just above the necking of the capital, and even a small cluster of berries on the crockets. These details represent the beginnings of the so-called stiff-leaf capital, which was to become one of the hallmarks of Early English Gothic. The one inhabited capital at St Davids, N4S, may be paralleled generally with those in the western arcades of the Wells transepts and a fragment from Keynsham Abbey, although the setting of the figures on the trumpet-scallop faces is unique to St Davids.[39] A fragmentary figure from Keynsham also supplies a close parallel for the naturalistic drapery of the figure on the west side of the St Davids capital.[40] Like the details of the stiff-leaf foliage, this figurative naturalism is a mark of the most innovative artists of the 1180s, as is well illustrated in the sculpture of the Lady Chapel of Glastonbury Abbey.[41] The comparisons with Wells are instructive in that they demonstrate that the St Davids workshop was aware of motifs used in what is generally considered to be the most progressive building of its time in the West Country School. Yet, other progressive motifs at Wells, like finely moulded pointed arches and clustered piers, were not favoured at St Davids nave. Remarkably close parallels for St Davids capital N3N, including details like the ring beneath the abacus, plantain notches, and individual trefoil leaves on the lower part of the capital, are found in the arches from the transepts to the presbytery aisles in the Great Church of Glastonbury abbey. In addition, it should be noted that like St Davids, but in contrast to Wells, the Glastonbury arches are encrusted with chevron.

The large, upright trefoil leaves on the lower half of capital N2W at St Davids are not easily paralleled at either Wells or Glastonbury, but a similar form occurs on the only remaining early Gothic nave high vault capital at St Mary Redcliffe, Bristol. It will also be noticed that the central shaft is nibbed and that the hollows between the shafts approach those on the western crossing arch responds at St Davids.

What are we to conclude from these analogues for the work at St Davids? In the first place, the details accord happily with the start of St Davids in 1182. Secondly, the parallels have been made with some of the most prestigious works created by the West Country School of masons. This indicates that there was a desire to have the very best for the new cathedral. But what can we decide about the recruitment of the masons? The details of the hiring of the masons are unknown and are likely to remain so given the paucity of documentary evidence. The use of some Dundry stone at St Davids means that contact must have been made with that quarry, just south of Bristol. Perhaps masons could be hired directly from the quarry or information gathered as to the whereabouts of major building activity so that employers might be approached about the loan or release of masons. The many close comparisons between the late twelfth- and early thirteenth-century work at Wells Cathedral and Glastonbury Abbey strongly suggest that a number of the same masons were engaged on both buildings and the same, or approximately the same, time. Then there is the precious survival of a letter from the Abbot of St Augustine's, Bristol, to the Dean of Wells, written around 1218–20, requesting the loan of 'your servant L' – probably the mason Adam Lock – to design the Elder Lady Chapel at St Augustine's.[42] The close comparison between the architectural and sculptural details at Wells Cathedral and the Bristol Elder Lady chapel makes it clear that the Dean acceded to the request. The parallel between the 'gaping' chevron at St Davids and the gatehouse of St Augustine's, Bristol, was highlighted by Roger Stalley.[43] One wonders what other building might have been going on in Bristol in the 1170s and 1180s? Perhaps the completion of the church of St Augustine's, and certainly the large and prestigious St Mary Redcliffe from which we have just the one high vault capital.[44] Perhaps it was at Bristol that the St Davids masons were recruited.

Conclusion

With reference to the extravagant range of twenty-two different forms of chevron ornament at St Davids, Roger Stalley observed that the 'ostentatious display was evidently seen as a way of asserting the prestige of the cathedral at a time when the clergy still harboured ambitions for archiepiscopal status'.[45] Separation from Canterbury had been on the agenda of Bishop Bernard (1115–1148) and, although it was not subsequently the official episcopal position, the canons of St Davids boldly revived the claims in 1176.[46] A lavish rebuilding programme as an integral part of the promotion of a see would not have been unique to St Davids at this time. Between 1160 and 1162 St Andrews Cathedral Priory in Scotland began a massive new church in connection with their campaign for metropolitan status and independence from York.[47] The rebuilding of Wells is almost certainly associated with the claim to have the seat of the bishopric returned there form Bath.[48] While St Andrews and Wells opted for very progressive designs that appeared different from the regional architecture of the immediate past, at St Davids we witness something that embraces the traditional richness of the twelfth-century great church. The nature of the work is close in concept to the rebuilding of the choir of Canterbury Cathedral after the fire of 1174.[49] Here it is pertinent to recall Scott's assessment of St Davids as 'a wonderfully interesting and valuable landmark in architectural history, taking, in the extreme west, a position parallel to that held by Canterbury in the extreme east of the island'.[50]

It is clear from the contemporary account and analysis of the rebuilding of Canterbury cathedral after the fire, written by the monk, Gervase, that progressive elements in the new design were highly regarded.[51] Yet Gervase also records the monks' reluctance to destroy any of the old building and that reverence for the past was an important consideration in the design of the new building. Large sections of the aisle and eastern transept walls, and the north-east and south-east radiating chapels were retained from the old church, and the alternation of the choir arcade columns at Canterbury repeated that feature in Anselm's choir. What is so often overlooked at Canterbury is the use of chevron and billet ornament from a twelfth-century tradition to which is added dog-tooth, a north French detail that fuses so happily with the aesthetic of surface enrichment. This parallels the aesthetic of the new St Davids cathedral, something that would at once proclaim the history of the site and its status equal to that of Canterbury. Such a traditional aspect could only be enhanced with reference to Sarum cathedral and St Cross at Winchester, and Glastonbury abbey, products of the most munificent patrons of the day. The other side of the coin was the progressive one. Gervase seems to have been awestruck with the use of three triforia in the new work at Canterbury as opposed to one in the Romanesque cathedral. While there will always be debate as to the definition of 'triforium', there can be little doubt that at least in part Gervase was referring to passages in the thickness of the wall, that is double-skin or hollow-wall construction. This is precisely what we have in the hollow wall of the nave triforium/clerestory at St Davids. St Davids was vaulted throughout, like the new work at Canterbury, and throughout St Andrews and Wells cathedrals. Moreover, the sexpartite pattern of vaulting was used both at Canterbury and St Davids. While the main arcade at Canterbury uses pointed arches, as opposed to the round-headed arches at St Davids, round-headed transverse arches are used throughout the aisles vaults, and in the arches from the aisles to the eastern transepts at Canterbury. Round-headed arches were also used in connection with the progressive design of the Galilee chapel at Durham cathedral, and in the castle hall at Oakham (Rutland), *circa* 1180–90. It is perhaps most significant that both round-headed and pointed arches, and lavish chevron ornament, are used in both the Lady Chapel and the Great Church at Glastonbury Abbey, commenced two and three respectively after the start of St Davids.

To read the rebuilding of St Davids in light of the status of the cathedral raises the question of the patronage of the work. Bishop Peter de Leia (1176–98) is credited with the patronage in contemporary documents but what of the role of the canons? Peter Draper has argued that the canons were the prime motivators,[52] but if they were responsible for the new church it is difficult to understand why the eastern arm of the building is less than half the size of the nave? Whatever their role in the administration of the new operation, it is most unlikely that they had the deciding vote on the relative scale of parts of the church. Whether or not this means that the bishop contributed the majority of the funds is difficult to decide, and, in the absence of documentation, is likely to remain a moot point. Peter de Leia resigned as prior of the Cluniac priory of Much Wenlock before he moved to St Davids. The Cluniac taste for architectural richness is evident in the chapter house at Much Wenlock, yet that building does not display any close links with St Davids. It follows that, whatever Bishop Peter contributed to the rebuilding of St Davids, there is nothing to suggest that masons were recruited from Much Wenlock.

The burial of Lord Rhys of Deheubarth at St Davids in 1197 may indicate that he was an important benefactor for the rebuilding. He was a generous patron of religious orders; the Benedictines at Cardigan priory (as a daughter cell of Chertsey), and Llandovery; the Cistercian abbeys of Whitland and Strata Florida, and the Cistercian nunnery at Llanllŷr; the Premonstratensian foundation at Talley; and the Knights Hospitallers at Slebech.[53] He built castles at Cardigan, Dinefwr,[54] and Rhayader.[55] It has been suggested that it was under his influence that fonts were introduced in large numbers in Deheubarth.[56] He promoted the cult of St David and his court poet, Gwynfardd Brycheiniog, wrote the poem *Canu i*

Ddewi (Song to Dewi).[57] Numerous features of the Lord Rhys work at Strata Florida are closely paralleled at St Davids, including polychrome masonry, the *pilier cantonné*, Wells cathedral-related foliage capitals, and chevron and shuttlecock ornament.[58] With this in mind, David Robinson suggested that '[i]t is surely not improbable that this exceptional man (Rhys) was somehow the catalyst for the strong architectural links between the two buildings'.[59] The theory is most plausible. Moreover, given what can only be described as Rhys's great passion for building, it would be most unusual for him to be buried in a church where he had not been a major patron.

Notes

[1] For a summary and discussion, see M. Thurlby, *Romanesque Architecture and Sculpture in Wales* (Almeley, 2006), pp. 283–89.

[2] On the historiography of Romanesque, see T. Cocke, 'Rediscovery of the Romanesque', in G. Zarnecki, J. Holt, and T. Holland (eds), *English Romanesque Art 1066–1200*, Catalogue for Exhibition, Hayward Gallery London, 5 April–8 July 1984 (London, 1984), pp. 360–91; T. Waldeier Bizzarro, *Romanesque Architectural Criticism: A Prehistory* (Cambridge, 1992). For Gothic, see E. S. de Beer, 'Gothic: Origin and Diffusion of the Term: the Idea of Style in Architecture', *Journal of the Warburg and Courtauld Institutes*, 11 (1948), pp. 143–62; P. Frankl, *The Gothic: Literary Sources and Interpretation through Eight Centuries* (Princeton NJ, 1960).

[3] *Annales Cambriae*, Rolls Series, ed. John Williams ab Ithel (London, 1860), p. 55

[4] *Giraldi Cambrensis Opera*, ed. J. S. Brewer, J. F. Dimock and G. F. Warner (eds), *Giraldi Cambrensis Opera*, Rolls Series, 8 vols (London 1861–91), vol. vi, p. 110; Gerald of Wales, *The Journey through Wales/The Description of Wales*, trans. L. Thorpe (Harmondsworth, 1978), p. 169.

[5] *Giraldi Cambrensis Opera*, ed. Brewer, vol. i, pp. 84–5, vol. iii, pp. 71, 285.

[6] *Annales Cambriae*, ed. Williams ab Ithel, p. 61.

[7] *Annales Cambriae*, ed. Williams ab Ithel, p. 75.

[8] *Annales Cambriae*, ed. Williams ab Ithel, p. 87.

[9] For a detailed discussion of the crossing and other aspects of the twelfth- and thirteenth-century fabric of the cathedral, see Thurlby, *Romanesque Architecture*, pp. 283–338.

[10] Thurlby, *Romanesque Architecture*, Fig. 438.

[11] J. W. Evans and R. Worsley, *St Davids 1181–1981* (St Davids 1981), pp. 39–43, Figs 17–24. On Scott's restoration, see Orbach, below.

[12] For details, see Thurlby, *Romanesque Architecture*, pp. 300–2.

[13] M. Thurlby, 'The High Vaults of Durham Cathedral', in M. J. Jackson (ed.), *Engineering a Cathedral* (London, 1993), pp. 64–76; M. Thurlby, 'The Elevations of the Romanesque Abbey churches of St Mary at Tewkesbury and St Peter at Gloucester', in T. A. Heslop and V. Sekules (eds), *Medieval Art and Architecture at Gloucester and Tewkesbury*, British Archaeological Association Conference Transactions 7 (Leeds, 1985), 36–51: 49–50;

L. R. Hoey and M. Thurlby, 'A Survey of Romanesque Vaulting in Great Britain and Ireland', *Antiquaries Journal*, 84 (2004), pp. 117–84.

[14] The uninterrupted coursing of the rubble masonry above the high-vault capitals at Llanthony does not support Stalley's contention that stone vault springers have been removed at St Davids.

[15] On the use of tufa, see M. Thurlby, 'The Use of Tufa Webbing and Wattle Centering in English Vaults Down to 1340', in Marie-Thérèse Zenner (ed.), *Villard's Legacy: Studies in Medieval Technology, Science and Art in Memory of Jean Gimpel* (Aldershot 2004), pp. 157–72.

[16] R. A. Stalley, 'The Architecture of St Davids Cathedral: Chronology, Catastrophe and Design', *Antiquaries Journal*, 82 (2002), pp. 13–45, Fig. 19.

[17] Stalley, 'The Architecture'.

[18] Thurlby, *Romanesque Architecture*, pp. 315–27.

[19] M. Thurlby, 'Jedburgh Abbey Church: the Romanesque Fabric', *Proceedings of the Society of Antiquaries of Scotland*, 125 (1995), pp. 793–812; M. Thurlby and R. Baxter, 'The Romanesque Fabric of Reading Abbey Church', in L. Keen and E. Scarfe (eds), *Windsor: Medieval Archaeology, Art and Architecture of the Thames Valley*, British Archaeological Association Conference Transactions 25 (Leeds, 2002), pp. 282–301.

[20] P. Crossley, 'English Gothic Architecture', in J. Alexander and P. Binski (eds), *Age of Chivalry: Art in Plantagenet England 1200–1400* (London, 1987), 60–73: 69; P. Crossley, 'Medieval Architecture and Meaning: the Limits of Iconography', *Burlington Magazine*, 130 (1988), pp. 116–21.

[21] J. Carley, *Glastonbury Abbey: The Holy House at the Head of the Moors Adventurous* (Woodbridge, 1988), p. 111.

[22] The differences are analyzed in detail in Thurlby, *Romanesque Architecture*, pp. 327–34.

[23] M. Thurlby, 'Hereford Cathedral: The Romanesque Fabric', D. Whitehead (ed.), *Medieval Art, Architecture and Archaeology in Hereford*, British Archaeological Association Conference Transactions 15 (Leeds, 1995), pp. 15–28; M. Thurlby, *The Herefordshire School of Romanesque Sculpture* (Almeley, 1999; reprinted with additions 2000).

[24] M. Thurlby and Y. Kusaba, 'The Nave of St Andrew at Steyning and Design Variety in Romanesque Architecture in Britain', *Gesta*, 30 (1991), pp. 163–75.

[25] M. Thurlby, 'Roger of Pont l'Évêque, Archbishop of York (1154–81) and French sources for the beginnings of Gothic architecture in Northern Britain', in J. Mitchell (ed.), *England and the Continent in the Middle Ages: Studies in Memory of Andrew Martindale* (Stamford, 2000), pp. 35–47.

[26] For the Bristol gatehouse, see Thurlby, *Romanesque Architecture*, Fig. 106.

[27] B. J. Lowe, et al., 'Keynsham Abbey: Excavations 1961–1985', *Proceedings of the Somerset Archaeological and Natural History Society*, 131 (1987), pp. 81–156; B. J. Lowe, S. A. Harrison and M. Thurlby, 'Keynsham Abbey Excavations 1961–1991: Final Report, Part I, The Architecture of Keynsham Abbey', *Proceedings of the Somerset Archaeological and Natural History Society*, 148 (2004), pp. 53–102; M. Thurlby, 'The Lady Chapel of Glastonbury Abbey', *Antiquaries Journal*, 65 (1995), pp. 107–70.

[28] R. A. Stalley, 'The Construction of the Medieval Cathedral c.1030–1250', in K. Milne (ed.), *Christ Church Cathedral, Dublin: A History* (Dublin, 2000), pp. 53–74.

[29] M. Thurlby, 'A Note on the twelfth-century Sculpture from Old Sarum Cathedral', *Wiltshire Archaeological and Natural History Magazine*, 76 (1982), pp. 93–7.

[30] G. Zarnecki, 'Henry of Blois as Patron of Sculpture', in S. Macready and F. H. Thompson (eds), *Art and Patronage in the English Romanesque* (London, 1986), pp. 159–72.

31 C. Wilson, 'The Cistercians as "missionaries of Gothic" in Northern England', in C. Norton and D. Park (eds), *Cistercian art and architecture in the British Isles* (Cambridge, 1986), pp. 86–116; Thurlby, 'Roger of Pont l'Évêque'.

32 H. Brakspear, 'A West Country School of Masons', *Archaeologia*, 81 (1931), pp. 1–18. For an expansion of Brakspear's terms of reference for the west country school, see M. Thurlby, 'The early Gothic fabric of Llandaff Cathedral and its place in the West Country school of masons', in J. Kenyon and D. M. Williams (eds), *Cardiff: Architecture and Archaeology in the Medieval Diocese of Llandaff*, British Archaeological Association Conference Transactions 29 (Leeds, 2006), pp. 60–85.

33 E. W. Lovegrove, 'The Cathedral Church of St. David's', *Archaeological Journal*, 83 (1926), pp. 254–83: 260.

34 Brakspear, 'A West Country School', pls IA and XI.

35 C. Wilson, 'The Sources of the late twelfth-century Work at Worcester Cathedral', in G. Popper (ed.), *Medieval Art and Architecture at Worcester Cathedral*, British Archaeological Association Conference Transactions 1 (Leeds, 1978), pp. 80–90; P. Barker, *A Short Architectural History of Worcester Cathedral* (Worcester, 1994), 47–54; U. Engel, *Die Kathedrale von Worcester* (Munchen-Berlin, 2000), pp. 80–9, 93–111.

36 M. Thurlby, 'The Norman Church', in R. K. Morris and R. Shoesmith (eds), *Tewkesbury Abbey: History, Art and Architecture* (Almeley, 2003), pp. 89–108, Figs 9.9 and 9.11.

37 Thurlby, *Romanesque Architecture*, Fig. 462.

38 Thurlby, *Romanesque Architecture*, Figs 530, 533 and 572.

39 A. Gardner, *Wells Capitals* (Wells, 1956); Thurlby, *Romanesque Architecture*, Figs 450 and 451.

40 Thurlby, *Romanesque Architecture*, Figs 467 and 468.

41 M. Thurlby, 'Breaking Away from Formality (English Medieval Figure Sculpture)', *Country Life* (3 June 1976), pp. 1508–9; Thurlby, 'The Lady Chapel of Glastonbury'.

42 L. S Colchester and J. Harvey, 'Wells Cathedral', *Archaeological Journal*, 131 (1974), pp. 200–14; M. Thurlby, 'The Elder Lady Chapel at St Augustine's, Bristol, and Wells Cathedral', in L. Keen (ed.), *'Almost the Richest City': Bristol in the Middle Ages*, British Archaeological Association Conference Transactions 19 (Leeds, 1997), pp. 31–40.

43 Stalley, 'The Architecture', p. 32.

44 The inner north porch at St Mary Redcliffe, Bristol, probably dates from around 1200, but it has nothing in common with the work at St Davids.

45 R. A. Stalley, 'The Cathedral', in T. Lloyd, J. Orbach and R. Scourfield, *Pembrokeshire*, The Buildings of Wales (New Haven CT and London, 2004), p. 397.

46 P. Draper, 'St Davids Cathedral: Provincial or Metropolitan?', in Fabienne Joubert and Dany Sandron (ed.), *Pierre, lumière, couleur: Études d'histoire de l'art du Moyen Âge en l'honneur d'Anne Prache* (Paris, 1999), pp. 103–16: 106–9.

47 M. Thurlby, 'St Andrews Cathedral-Priory and the Beginnings of Gothic Architecture in Northern Britain', in J. Higgitt (ed.), *Medieval Art and Architecture in the Diocese of St Andrews*, British Archaeological Association Conference Transactions 14 (Leeds, 1994), pp. 47–60.

48 P. Draper, 'Interpreting the Architecture of Wells Cathedral', in V. Raguin, K. Brush and P. Draper (eds), *Artistic Integration in Gothic Buildings* (Toronto, 1995), pp. 114–31, Draper, 'St Davids Cathedral', p. 107.

49 R. Willis, *Architectural History of Canterbury Cathedral* (London, 1845).

50 G. G. Scott, *Report Made by the Order of the Dean and Chapter on the State of the Fabric of St. David's Cathedral* (London, 1862), p. 4.

51 Willis, *Architectural History of Canterbury Cathedral*, pp. 32–62.

52 Draper, 'St Davids Cathedral: Provincial or Metropolitan?', pp. 106–9.

53 J. E. Lloyd, *A History of Wales from the Earliest Times to the Edwardian Conquest*, 2 vols (London, 1912), vol. I, pp. 596–99; R. Turvey, *The Welsh Princes: The Native Rulers of Wales 1063–1283* (London, 2002), pp. 185–86; D. M. Robinson, *The Cistercians in Wales: Architecture and Archaeology 1130–1530* (London, 2006), pp. 28–9, 89, 94, 98, 99, 268, 294; D. M. Robinson and C. Platt, *Strata Florida Abbey/Talley Abbey* (Cardiff, 1998).

54 T. Lloyd, J. Orbach and R. Scourfield, *Carmarthenshire and Ceredigion*, The Buildings of Wales (New Haven CT and London, 2006), pp. 20, 178, 449.

55 John Edward Lloyd, *The Story of Ceredigion, 400–1277* (Cardiff, 1937), p. 66.

56 Thurlby, *Romanesque Architecture*, pp. 249, 256, 259, 260.

57 Turvey, *The Welsh Princes*, 188; N. A. Jones and M. E. Owen, 'Twelfth-century Welsh hagiography: the *Gogynfeirdd* Poems to Saints', in J. Cartwright (ed.), *Celtic Hagiography and Saints' Cults* (Cardiff, 2003), pp. 45–76; ed. and trans. A. Parry-Owen at 'Seintiau' (*https://saints.wales*)

58 Thurlby, *Romanesque Architecture*, pp. 249–56; Robinson, *The Cistercians*, pp. 89–99.

59 Robinson, *The Cistercians*, p. 98.

3.
BUILDING AND ORNAMENTAL STONES OF ST DAVIDS CATHEDRAL

Dyfed Elis-Gruffydd

This cathedral city . . . stands, with its restored market cross, on high ground, so that one's first view of the cathedral is the top of the 116-ft. tower. Only after passing through the S gate does the splendour of the building, built of local purplish sandstone, come into view . . .[1]

Yet so plain and unimposing [the cathedral] looks perfectly right for its setting in this frequently gale-swept place only a mile from the wild sea cliffs that were the source of its violet stones.[2]

There is no denying that the publication of *The History and Antiquities of St Davids* by W. B. Jones and E. A. Freeman in 1856 did mark '. . . a significant milestone in the study of the cathedral.'[3] However, in the same way that not all of its conclusions relating to the architecture and history of the cathedral stand close examination today, its reference to only four different building and ornamental stones, namely 'Caerfai stone' (Caerbwdi sandstone), 'a coarse species of oolite', 'a finer oolite' and 'Purbeck marble',[4] does less than justice to the great variety of material encountered within the fabric of the building and that of St Mary's College and Porth y Tŵr. Furthermore, although Jones and Freeman correctly identified Caerfai Bay – 'the prettiest creek on the coast' – as the probable source of most of the Caerbwdi sandstone employed, the relative importance of this particular building stone is grossly overstated: 'On the north-western side [of Caerfai] are the quarries of red and purple sandstone out of which the Cathedral is chiefly built.'[5]

Indeed, ever since the publication of Jones and Freeman and despite the appearance over the years of numerous articles dealing with the geology of the St Davids peninsula – from where the overwhelming

https://doi.org/10.16922/jrhlc.9.2.3

majority of the building stones were gathered – geologists, historians and other respected authors alike have been content to repeat, rather than critically examine or question Jones and Freeman's claim that the building is constructed almost exclusively of local sandstone. 'The cathedral . . . is largely built of purple Lower Cambrian sandstone, named after Caerbwdy [sic] Bay', wrote the distinguished geologist T. R. Owen in 1973.[6] Local author and glacial geomorphologist Brian John in 1995 reinforced this impression: '. . . the beautiful purple sandstones for St Davids Cathedral were quarried from the cliffs above Caerfai Bay.'[7] Although historian Dillwyn Miles in his book *Portrait of Pembrokeshire* does not refer to the stones of the cathedral *per se*, he too stresses that the purple sandstone '. . . for the building of [St Mary's] College . . .' was quarried at Caerfai.[8] Furthermore, with the exception of 'yellow oolitic [*sic*] limestone, imported from Dundry near Bristol' and a 'local grey sandstone', purple Caerbwdi sandstone is the only building stone, as opposed to ornamental stone, referred to in Roger Stalley's account of the cathedral in the Pevsner Guide to Pembrokeshire.[9]

Only Richard Fortey, a palaeontologist of distinction, appears to have recognised that the building stones are far more varied than other authors would have us believe. Fortey states that, 'The cathedral is constructed from the rock of the place . .', noting, tantalisingly, that in addition to 'Purplish sandstones . . . other hard building stones have ensured its endurance . .', and adding that, 'Beyond the cathedral the open countryside shows the occasional outcrop of those rocks from which the cathedral was built'. The building, he maintains, 'is truly part of the landscape. Such trimmings as there are inside the building from "foreign" parts, such as the Purbeck "marble", are like light touches of cosmetic which serve to heighten its native beauty'.[10]

Externally, only the imposing west front of the cathedral, completely rebuilt by George Gilbert Scott in 1877–1882, and the walls within which the clerestory windows are set, are faced either exclusively or for the most part with fine- to medium-grained, dull purple micaceous and felspathic Caerbwdi sandstone, the product of deposition in a shallow marine environment during the Cambrian period, some 540 million years ago.[11] This particular sandstone, which owes its colour to the presence of iron within the stone,[12] can, to some extent, lay claim to being the only local freestone available to the cathedral's builders. However, contrary to Stalley's claim, it is not a 'tough sandstone',[13] because the presence of laminations and a high interstitial clay-mineral content

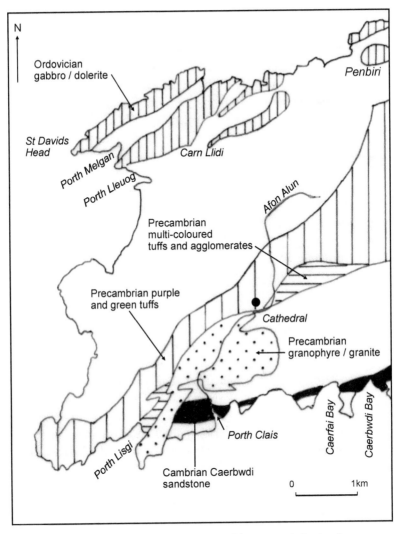

Figure 1: Simplified geological map of the St Davids Peninsula

render it susceptible to relatively rapid weathering, particularly granular disintegration and spalling. Such damage, the product of weathering over a period of some 130 years, necessitated the reopening of the quarry at Caerbwdi Bay,[14] immediately east of Caerfai Bay, for several months between autumn 1997 and spring 1998 in order to obtain some 500 tonnes of material to replace the most severely weathered stones of the west front and other parts of the cathedral, restoration work undertaken between 1998 and 2001.

Beyond the restored west front, dressed blocks of Caerbwdi sandstone are much in evidence in the exterior, south-facing wall of the south transept, and the same material has been extensively employed elsewhere to construct door and window jambs, and quoins and buttresses. Indeed, as in the adjoining Bishop's Palace, the subject of a comprehensive study by Rick Turner,[15] Caerbwdi sandstone is used for almost all the dressed exterior stonework of the cathedral, St Mary's College and Porth y Tŵr. However, Jones and Freeman were well aware of the fact that with the exception of the 'ragged ashlar' of the cathedral's west front and the north and south side of the clerestory, both of which were 'faced externally with ashlar, the rest of the external walls [were] ... chiefly composed of rubble'.[16] But what they and subsequent authors failed to recognise was that Caerbwdi sandstone does not form the bulk of 'the honest rubble' of which the external walls, including the tower, are largely constructed.[17]

As is the case in the Bishop's Palace, the stones used in the construction of the rubble walls of the cathedral, St Mary's College and Porth y Tŵr, which mainly date from the twelfth to the sixteenth century, are chiefly derived from local outcrops of various Precambrian pyroclastic and igneous rocks of the so-called Pebidian Volcanic Complex, many the product of land-based, explosive volcanic activity that probably took place between 650 and 570 million years ago.[18]

Particularly evident in the exterior walls of the south nave aisle (prior to the stonework being rendered with lime mortar), rebuilt in the fourteenth century,[19] are undressed blocks of fine- to coarse-grained Lower Pebidian lithic tuffs, i.e. consolidated volcanic ash, which are generally far harder and more resistant to weathering than the younger purple Caerbwdi sandstone (Fig. 2). These purplish-red and green trachytic and andesitic tuffs, '... which have a characteristic grittiness due to conspicuous grains of quartz and feldspar'[20] and contain a large number of small but conspicuous angular rock fragments, are truly local building materials for they, unlike Caerbwdi sandstone, outcrop in Glyn Rhosyn in the now overgrown Pen-rhiw (Pont y Penyd) quarry (SM 751258), situated near the banks of Afon Alun a short distance beyond the confines of the cathedral close, north of the site of Porth Boning (Fig. 1).

However, in addition to the purplish-red and green Lower Pebidian tuffs, the rubble walls also contain a colourful assortment of green,

Figure 2: Exterior wall, South Nave Aisle (Photo: Dyfed Elis-Gruffydd)

pale green, grey-green, grey, pinkish-grey, purple-brown, yellow and buff Upper Pebidian fine-grained tuffs and coarser agglomerates of the Pebidian Volcanic Complex. Indeed, in places, the purplish hue so characteristic of parts of the cathedral and Porth y Tŵr and attributable to the presence of both purple and purplish-red tuffs and purple Caerbwdi sandstone, is conspicuous by its absence. Precambrian tuffs impart a greenish hue to the east, exterior wall of the thirteenth-century Lady chapel (Fig. 3).

Similarly, the rubble walls of the upper two floors of the three-storey medieval building, that dominates the north-east corner of the cathedral and incorporates the earlier (fourteenth-century) chapel of St Thomas Becket on the ground floor, are built primarily of greenish Precambrian tuffs. At times, therefore, it would appear that green tuffs were deliberately selected and used in preference to other material. At other times, it seems that the colour purple was in vogue for above the basal section ($c.0.7$ metres in height) composed of irregular courses of Caerbwdi sandstone, a substantial part of the east-facing $c.$fourteenth/fifteenth-century

Figure 3: Exterior wall, Lady Chapel (Photo: Dyfed Elis-Gruffydd)

wall connecting the north transept to St Mary's College is constructed largely of purple tuffs.[21]

Many of the Precambrian tuffs, however, contain a high proportion of clay-minerals and consequently they weather very rapidly, disintegrating to a fine powder at the merest touch. This is particularly true of the soft, fine-grained, schistose sericite-chlorite, multi-coloured tuffs of the Upper Pebidian Ramsay Sound Group and amongst those that have fared the worst in the absence of what was once a protective coating of lime mortar are some of the pink, yellow and pale grey-green tuffs, whose deeply-hollowed surfaces are very evident in the east-facing, fourteenth-century exterior wall of St Mary's College, adjacent to the doorway leading into the cloister quadrangle,[22] and the south-facing, sixteenth-century wall of the vestry adjoining the south transept.[23] These tuffs are exposed in the cliffs of Porth Lisgi,[24] some two miles south-west of the cathedral, but they have also been mapped by the Geological Survey on the eastern slopes of Glyn Rhosyn, almost opposite Pen-rhiw quarry,[25] and the now completely overgrown quarries,[26] which scar the valley-side slopes above the lower section of Y Cwcwll (Quickwell Hill) were, in all probability, the source of the poorest quality rubble stones.

Hard green and purplish-red Precambrian tuffs were also mainly used to construct the rubble walls of Porth y Tŵr, built during the thirteenth century.[27] The dressings (quoins, window jambs), on the other hand, together with those dressed blocks of purple sandstone which would appear to have been incorporated into parts of the exterior wall during renovative work of more recent date, are chiefly of Caerbwdi sandstone, together with occasional dressed blocks of 'foreign', yellow Jurassic limestone.[28]

In contrast to the tower itself, however, the fourteenth-century fortified gateway attached to the south side of the structure is built primarily of undressed blocks of a hard, resistant and highly siliceous, light-grey granitic rock, which outcrops to the south-west of St Davids and forms the prominent headland immediately west of Porth Lisgi and the two small islands of Carreg Frân and Carreg yr Esgob. Described as an 'alaskite-granophyre' by Cox *et al.*, and as an 'alaskite' by Baker,[29] and more recently as an 'alkali-feldspar granite' by the Geological Survey,[30] this rock-type is well-exposed on the steep eastern valley-side slopes at the head of Porth Clais, the small harbour that once served the cathedral. Infrequent lumps of this crystalline, intrusive igneous rock of Precambrian age, are also encountered in the rubble walls of the cathedral (Fig. 1).

In addition to local Precambrian volcanic tuffs and agglomerates quarried from the flanks of Glyn Rhosyn, Caerbwdi sandstone won from quarries in the two neighbouring bays of Caerfai and Caerbwdi, and dressed blocks of yellow Jurassic limestone, irregular courses of weathered, angular to sub-rounded boulders also characterise the lower section of the tower and fortified gateway of Porth y Tŵr. On the basis of their nature and shape, there seems little doubt that these boulders of coarsely-crystalline dark grey/black gabbro and more finely-crystalline blue-grey dolerite are glacial erratics, derived from the Ordovician igneous intrusions of St Davids Head and the rugged hill mass of Carn Llidi-Carn Perfedd-Penbiri described by Bevins and Roach (Fig. 1).[31] After being transported in a southerly to south-easterly direction by the Irish Sea ice-sheet that crossed the St Davids peninsula at the peak of the Last (Devensian) Glaciation, some 21,000 years ago, the erratics were dumped and scattered across the area as the ice-sheet melted and retreated. Subsequently, the cobbles and boulders, a ready source of building stone, were utilized at least in part during early stages in the construction of Porth y Tŵr and the adjoining gateway, the south-facing wall of the cathedral's south transept (see below), for the stonework infilling the bays of the arches visible in the walls of St Mary's College, and in the Bishop's Palace '. . . in building phases prior to 1300 . . .'[32]

In addition to the boulders of gabbro and dolerite, transported from the vicinity of the rocky outcrops of St Davids Head, Carn Llidi and Penbiri, the occasional far-travelled erratic is also encountered. In his study of 'The glacial deposits of Northern Pembrokeshire', including the St Davids area, T. J. Jehu stated that 'The most striking fact in connection with the erratics is that so many of them can be traced to the south-west of Scotland ... The other region from which the [granitic] boulders have travelled is the north-east of Ireland, and its rocks are represented in Pembrokeshire by reddish granophyres, quartz-porphyries, and micro granites.'[33] In all probability the reddish-yellow granites amongst the local erratics within the walls of Porth y Tŵr are from one or other of these source areas (Fig. 5).[34]

Of particular note, also, are the large angular to sub-rounded boulders and cobbles of dolerite and gabbro set in the lower part of the south-facing south transept wall, built during the thirteenth century (Fig. 4). However, the two largest, sub-rounded boulders are of grey sandstone believed to have been derived from the Coal Measures of St Brides Bay: '... a thick mass of grey pennant-like sandstone ... is well-displayed in the cliffs of Nolton Haven ... From the haven the sandstone can be traced towards Nolton ...', where the stone was once quarried and '... wrought into tombstones, troughs, steps and flags'.[35] The two weathered boulders, perhaps gathered from the beach at Nolton Haven and transported as ballast in vessels carrying cargoes of coal from the Nolton area for fuelling limekilns situated at Porth Clais, may well have been carted up-valley – along with a load of lime for the production of lime mortar – and subsequently incorporated into the fabric of the south transept.[36] In this context, it is interesting to note that small lumps of Carboniferous Limestone, imported from south Pembrokeshire

Figure 4: Exterior south-facing wall, South Transept (Photo: Dyfed Elis-Gruffydd)

and burnt to produce lime, are occasionally encountered in the rubble walling, particularly in the c.fourteenth–fifteenth-century wall on the east side of the cloister quadrangle connecting the north transept to St Mary's College.

Three other rock types are also present, though poorly represented, in the ancient rubble walls: thin pieces of red cleaved mudstones which are well-exposed on the eastern and western side of Caerbwdi Bay, underlying the Caerbwdi sandstone; a fine- to medium-grained grey sandstone, probably derived from the beds overlying the Caerbwdi sandstone at the same location;[37] and thin slabs of dark grey/black fissile mudstone, similar to the fossiliferous mudstones of Ordovician age exposed at Porth Lleuog and Porth Melgan and into which the gabbroic rocks of St Davids Head and Carn Llidi-Penbiri have been intruded (Fig. 1).[38] The first two lithologies could well have been incorporated into loads of Caerbwdi sandstone quarried at Caerfai Bay and shipped to Porth Clais, whilst the pieces of mudstone, like the cobbles and boulders of gabbro and dolerite, are considered to be glacial erratics.

Unfortunately from an aesthetic point of view, renovative work undertaken during the twentieth century has resulted in the introduction of a further two building stones, not represented in the ancient walls. The stonework surrounding the door into the vestry, adjacent to the south choir aisle and south transept, consists of blocks of Forest (of Dean) stone, a grey-green Carboniferous sandstone, and red Hollington stone, a Triassic sandstone from Staffordshire. Repairs to the hood-moulds of the south choir windows have also been executed in Forest stone.

Interior Stonework

According to Jones and Freeman, 'Two kinds of stone were in use for the ashlar and enriched work throughout the fabric', namely Caerbwdi sandstone and a so-called 'oolite', '... probably brought from Gloucestershire or Somersetshire ...'[39] Inside the cathedral, Caerbwdi sandstone, the local freestone, has not only lasted well,[40] but is also much in evidence for it has been used to construct the twelfth-century nave arcading and associated carved capitals and decorative mouldings, and other notable features such as the splendid fourteenth-century *pulpitum*, considered to be '... Bishop Gower's most notable enrichment of his cathedral ...',[41] and the effigy of Bishop Henry Gower (d. 1347) himself. Slabs of purple sandstone also form the steps linking the north and south nave aisles with the north and south transepts, respectively.

Nevertheless, Precambrian tuffs of the Pebidian Volcanic Complex not only form the bulk of the material used to build the rubble walls (including the cores of the piers and the undressed, outward-facing walls above the arches, together with the twelfth-century wall behind the high altar and below the striking frieze carved in Caerbwdi sandstone) but dressed blocks (ashlar) of a fine-grained, brownish-yellow, foliated tuff also appear in the west wall of the nave between the arcading. Furthermore, a coarser tuff of similar colour was used as a springer within the arch between the south choir aisle and the south transept, and dressed stones of the same material appear in the adjacent arch between the south choir aisle and the choir, and elsewhere in the cathedral.

Amongst the tomb recesses, three are of particular interest. Two are located in the south choir aisle: that opposite the sixteenth-century screen leading into the chapel of the Holy Trinity, was described by Jones and Freeman as '. . . a Decorated recess with a cinquefoiled arch of Caerfai stone, having closed cusps . . ', whilst the other, opposite the reputed tomb and effigy of Giraldus Cambrensis (d. 1223), appropriately carved in Caerbwdi sandstone, is again described as a 'Decorated recess of Caerfai stone'.[42] In fact, both are of Nolton sandstone, described in 1603 by George Owen of Henllys as '. . . a kind of free stone [and] in colour a dark grey and of a grindstone grit . . . This stone is easily hewn and serves in buildings to make windows, doors, chimneys, arches, coignstones, water berges and wind berges or any other hewn work.' He also claimed that '. . . this stone endures all forces of the sea wind without fretting or wearing . . .'[43] Richard Fenton, on the other hand, whist conceding that the stone '. . . seemed to be in great demand for all sorts of work requiring the chisel', correctly cautioned that if '. . . taken from the most accessible part of the vein at Nolton . . . [it is] not to be depended upon.'[44] The second of the two arches, which is, indeed, very weathered, contains small clasts of dark mudstone, a characteristic feature of this particular Coal Measure sandstone formerly quarried in the vicinity of Nolton.[45] Beneath the arch lies an effigy of, presumably, an unknown priest which again is carved in grey Nolton sandstone incorporating small mudstone clasts and ironstone nodules. The figure lies on a plinth of Caerbwdi sandstone supported by large square blocks of Nolton stone.

According to Jones and Freeman, the tomb recess under the most eastern window of the south nave aisle is characterised by '. . . a canopy of a very peculiar form, which may be described as a semi-octagon with concave sides, the apex and the two adjoining angles being adorned with finials radiating from the centre . . . It contains the figure of a priest in Eucharist vestments . . . The whole is of Caerfai sandstone.'[46] The effigy is of Caerbwdi sandstone but the very badly-weathered canopy of Nolton stone, which crumbles and disintegrates at the slightest touch, incorporates conspicuous ironstone nodules and mudstone clasts.

However, it appears that not all the grey sandstone encountered in the internal fabric of the cathedral has been derived from the Nolton area. For example, atop the shaft at the north-west corner of the eastern ambulatory, constructed of alternating dressed stones of Caerbwdi sandstone and yellow Jurassic limestone, sits a bell capital of grey, foliated sandstone, possibly derived from the beds of 'Middle Solfa grey sandstone' exposed in the cliffs on the eastern side of Caerfai Bay, near the headland of Penpleidiau.[47] Alternating dressed stones of grey sandstone and yellow Jurassic limestone also appear in the pier to which the shaft is attached. Further work is required to confirm the provenance of this sandstone.

Two other ornamental stones are deserving of mention. The nave and north transept, for example, are floored with white and black marble tiles, laid during the late nineteenth century. The marble, acquired from the world-famous quarries in and around Carrara in the province of Tuscany in northern Italy, was originally a Permian limestone metamorphosed during the Alpine earth movements that gave rise to the Alps. But perhaps the most striking of all the various ornamental stones within the cathedral is the 'altar, tomb and reredos' in the chapel of St Edward the Confessor, vividly and aptly described by Stalley as 'a glistening, milky intrusion amidst the grey stone walls of the cathedral'.[48] The chapel was restored in the 1920s at the expense of the Countess of Maidstone, and the sculptured tomb, created under her own close supervision, is elaborately carved from slabs of richly veined and coloured alabaster (i.e. gypsum), a mineral found in association with rocks of Triassic age and probably derived from Derbyshire.

If the mineral gypsum is included as an ornamental 'stone', it is, in fact, one of twenty or more building and ornamental stones encountered in the cathedral, St Mary's College and Porth y Tŵr, and all three buildings owe their present character and colour, either wholly or in part, to the rich mix of predominantly local and locally-derived material whose native beauty, by and large, is in no way diminished by 'foreign' elements (Fig. 5). Furthermore, the stones, which span some 650 million

Period (million years)	Material	Source	Examples of use
Pleistocene	dark grey/black and white marble	Carrara, Italy	floor of nave and north transept
1.8			
Neogene / Palaeogene	yellowish-red granite	?north-east Ireland	rubble walling (Porth y Twr)
65			
Cretaceous	greyish-white chalk (Beer stone)	Beer, Lyme Bay, Dorset	tomb and effigy of Bishop Morgan †1504
	Purbeck 'marble' (limestone)	Isle of Purbeck, Dorset	tomb of Edmund Tudor †1456 and font
145			
Jurassic	greyish-white limestone (Portland stone)	Isle of Portland, near Weymouth	possibly incorporated in Nash's west front but not found
	yellow oolitic and bioclastic limestone (Dundry stone, Bath stone, Painswick stone)	Bristol, Bath, Gloucester	ashlar, dressings, window tracery and mullions, especially Chapel of the Holy Trinity; effigy of Rhys ap Gruffydd †1197 and Rhys Grug †1233
	greyish-white conglomeratic limestone (Sutton stone)	Aberogwr, Vale of Glamorgan	Chapel of the Holy Trinity screen
199	blue-grey Lias limestone	Severn valley, near Gloucester	effigy of Bishop Iorwerth †1231
Triassic	red sandstone (Hollington stone)	Hollington, Staffordshire	ashlar (vestry doorway)
251	alabaster (gypsum)	Derbyshire	tomb of Countess of Maidstone
Permian			
299			
Carboniferous	grey sandstone (Nolton stone)	Nolton — Nolton Haven	rubble walling (south transept); tomb recesses south choir/nave aisles
	grey-green sandstone (Forest [of Dean] stone)	Forest of Dean, Gloucestershire	ashlar (vestry doorway) and repairs to south choir aisle window hoodmoulds
359	Carboniferous Limestone	south Pembrokeshire	rubble walling (cloister quadrangle)

416	Devonian	yellowish-red granite	?south-west Scotland	rubble walling (Porth y Tŵr)
443	Silurian			
488	Ordovician	gabbro and dolerite	Carn Llidi — Penbiri and St Davids Head	rubble walling (Porth y Tŵr and south transept)
		dark grey / black mudstone	Porth Lleuog — Porth Melgan	rubble walling (south transept and south nave aisle)
542	Cambrian	grey sandstone	Caerfai Bay	rubble walling; in eastern ambulatory example of grey sandstone capital and grey sandstone in associated shaft
		red mudstone	Caerfai Bay	rubble walling (south transept)
		purple (Caerbwdi) sandstone	Caerfai Bay — Caerbwdi Bay	ashlar (west front) and dressings (including some effigies)
	Precambrian	granophyre / granite	Porth Clais	rubble walling (Porth y Tŵr gateway) and south nave aisle
		purple and green tuffs	Pen-rhiw Quarry, Glyn Rhosyn	rubble walling (cathedral, St Mary's College, Porth y Tŵr)
		multi-coloured coarse- and fine-grained tuffs and agglomerates	Y Cwcwll, Glyn Rhosyn	rubble walling (cathedral, St Mary's College, Porth y Tŵr) and limited use as ashlar and dressings (interior)

Figure 5: Building and ornamental stones of St Davids Cathedral, St Mary's College and Porth y Tŵr: age, nature, source and use

years of Earth history, are not only of great geological interest, for their use, at different periods during the development of the cathedral and its associated buildings, pose questions that deserve the attention of archaeologists, architects and historians alike.

Notes

[1] G. Boumphrey (ed.), *The Shell Guide to Britain and Northern Ireland* (London, 1967), p. 271.

[2] W. Condry, *Exploring Wales* (London, 1970), p. 241.

[3] J. W. Evans, 'Foreword' (1998), to reprint of W. B. Jones and E. A. Freeman, *The History and Antiquities of St. Davids* (London 1856).

[4] Jones and Freeman, *The History and Antiquities*, p. 125.

[5] grid reference: SM 759243; Jones and Freeman, *The History and Antiquities*, p. 12.

[6] T. R. Owen, *Geology Explained in South Wales* (Newton Abbot, 1973), p. 25.

[7] B. S. John, *Pembrokeshire Past and Present* (Newport, Pembs., 1995), p. 132.

[8] D. Miles, *Portrait of Pembrokeshire* (London, 1984), p. 98.

[9] R. Stalley, 'The Cathedral', in T. Lloyd, J. Orbach, and R. Scourfield, *Pembrokeshire*, The Buildings of Wales (New Haven and London, 1994), pp. 386–407. Dundry stone is a bioclastic as opposed to oolitic limestone. J. Wyn Evans, in the guidebook *St Davids Cathedral* (Andover, 2002), is much more circumspect in his choice of words (p. 23): 'Much [but not necessarily most] of the cathedral is built in a fine-grained sandstone . . .'.

[10] R. Fortey, *The Hidden Landscape: A Journey into the Geological Past* (London, 1993), p. 10.

[11] J. T. G. Stead and B. P. J. Williams, 'The Cambrian Rocks of North Pembrokeshire', in D. A. Bassett and M. G. Bassett (eds), *Geological Excursions in South Wales and The Forest of Dean* (Cardiff, 1971), pp. 180–98, esp. 188–90; B. P. J. Williams and J. T. G. Stead, 'The Cambrian Rocks of the Newgale-St David's area', in M. G. Bassett (ed.), *Geological Excursions in Dyfed, South-West Wales* (Cardiff, 1982), pp. 27–49; for a description of Caerbwdi sandstone, see pp. 38–40.

[12] R. Turner, 'St Davids Bishop's Palace, Pembrokeshire', *The Antiquaries Journal*, 80 (2000), pp. 87–194, esp. 'Cambrian Sandstones', p. 100.

[13] Stalley, 'The Cathedral', p. 390

[14] Grid ref: SM 765244

[15] Turner, 'St Davids Bishop's Palace'. The building stones were identified by Richard Bevins, Keeper of Geology at the National Museum of Wales. See also R. Bevins and R. Turner, 'Restoration of the Bishop's Palace, St Davids Cathedral', *Geology Today*, 7.4 (1991), pp. 125–6.

[16] Jones and Freeman, *The History and Antiquities*, pp. 52, 53. The two authors clearly imply that the west front which, at the time, was the work of John Nash, was constructed of Caerbwdi ashlar – see the drawing of its design, signed by Nash, reproduced in R. Suggett, *John Nash Architect/Pensaer* (Aberystwyth 1995), 20, and the photograph of Nash's west front, featuring Gilbert Scott, reproduced in Evans, *St Davids Cathedral*, p. 30. However, Richard Fenton (*Historical Tour through Pembrokeshire*, London, 1810, p. 87), was of the opinion that the sandstone employed may have been quarried at Nolton (SM 867182) near the shores of St Brides Bay: '. . . in Mr. Nash's work, it is but justice here to observe that the stone certified on the chapter books of St. David's by the architect employed to

put together the incongruous mass at the west end of that venerable fabric, to have come from Nolton, is either what came from the crumbling quarry of Carfai [sic], mistaken for, and too often confounded with, the other, or, for cheapness, was taken from the most accessible part of the vein at Nolton, by those who are acquainted with that stone rejected, as not to be depended upon'. In colour and texture Nolton stone, a grey Coal Measure sandstone often incorporating small clasts of black shale and ironstone nodules, is very different to the purple or greyish-purple Caerbwdi sandstone and it seems unlikely that Jones and Freeman would have failed to have identified Nolton stone had it have been extensively used in Nash's west front. That said, Nolton stone is encountered in the external and internal fabric of the cathedral but internally it was misidentified as 'Caerfai stone' by Jones and Freeman.

[17] Not all the external walling is constructed of 'honest rubble'. For example, courses of carefully dressed blocks of various lithologies, including gabbro, dolerite, purple and yellow tuffs, and grey sandstone, are encountered in the two bays (and partly in the third bay) of the external wall of the south choir aisle nearest to the vestries. It is presumed that this section of walling was rebuilt during or after George Gilbert Scott's programme of restoration and refurbishment. Portions of the east-facing wall of the Lady chapel and the walls of Porth y Twr also include courses of dressed blocks of tuff.

[18] J. W. Baker, 'The Pre-Cambrian Rocks of Pembrokeshire', in Bassett and Bassett, *Geological Excursions in South Wales*, pp. 170–79, esp. 176–7; J. W. Baker, 'The Precambrian of South-west Dyfed', in Bassett, *Geological Excursions in Dyfed*, pp. 15–25, esp. 22–3; Turner, 'St Davids Bishop's Palace', pp. 87–194, esp. 'Precambrian Volcanic Tuffs', pp. 99–100.

[19] Stalley, 'The Cathedral', p. 405.

[20] Baker, 'The Precambrian of South-west Dyfed', p. 23.

[21] Stalley, 'The Cathedral', p. 391.

[22] Bevins and Turner, 'Restoration of the Bishop's Palace', pp. 125–6.

[23] Stalley, 'The Cathedral', p. 391.

[24] Grid Ref SM 731236; Baker, 'The Precambrian of South-west Dyfed', p. 23.

[25] British Geological Survey, 1992. *St. David's*, Sheet 209, 1:50 000 provisional series.

[26] SM 753257.

[27] J. W. Evans, *Eglwys Gadeiriol Tyddewi*, Pitkin Pictorials (London, 1993), p. 11.

[28] For an account of the various types of Jurassic limestones and other Mesozoic rock-types encountered within the cathedral, see Tim Palmer's contribution, below.

[29] A. H. Cox, *et al.*, 'The Geology of the St. David's District, Pembrokeshire', *Proceedings of the Geologists' Association*, 41 (1930), pp. 241–73, esp. p. 249; Baker, 'The Precambrian of South-west Dyfed', p. 23.

[30] British Geological Survey, 1992: *St. David's*, Sheet 209, 1:50 000 provisional series.

[31] R. E. Bevins and R. A. Roach, 'Ordovician Igneous Activity in South-west Dyfed', in Bassett, *Geological Excursions in Dyfed*, pp. 65–80, esp. 'Itinerary 3 – St David's and Carnllidi [sic] Intrusions', pp. 73–9.

[32] Bevins and Turner, 'Restoration of the Bishop's Palace', p. 126.

[33] T. J. Jehu, 'The Glacial Deposits of Northern Pembrokeshire', *Transactions of the Royal Society of Edinburgh*, 41 (1904), pp. 53–87, esp. p. 82.

[34] In the absence of fresh, unweathered surfaces the exact provenance of the granites cannot be established.

[35] T. C. Cantrill *et al.*, *Geology of the South Wales Coalfield. Part XII. The Country around Milford* (London, 1916), pp. 136, 135 and 166. See also Bevins and Turner, 'Restoration of the Bishop's Palace, St Davids Cathedral'.

[36] Turner, 'St Davids Bishops' Palace', p. 101.

[37] Williams and Stead, 'The Cambrian Rocks of the Newgale-St David's area', p. 38 (Caerfai Bay Shales) and p. 40 (Middle Solva grey sandstones).

[38] Bevins and Roach, 'Ordovician Igneous Activity', pp. 74–6.

[39] Jones and Freeman, *The History and Antiquities*, p. 75.

[40] Here, the stone was not only '... protected from the weather, but also helped by the murals of the Middle Ages and the regular whitewashing it received between the 17th and 19th centuries'; see Evans, *St Davids Cathedral*, p. 23.

[41] H. Marriot, *St. Davids Cathedral* (London 1969), p. 8.

[42] Jones and Freeman, *The History and Antiquities*, p. 122.

[43] D. Miles (ed.), *The Description of Pembrokeshire: George Owen of Henllys* (Llandysul, 1994), p. 81.

[44] Fenton, *Historical Tour*, pp. 101, 87. Nolton chapel, at Nolton Haven, opened in 1858, is built '... of fast-eroding Nolton sandstone ...', in Lloyd, Orbach, and Scourfield, *Pembrokeshire, The Buildings of Wales*, p. 327.

[45] Bevins and Turner, 'Restoration of the Bishop's Palace, St Davids Cathedral'.

[46] Jones and Freeman, *The History and Antiquities*, pp. 109–10.

[47] Williams and Stead, 'The Cambrian Rocks of the Newgale-St David's Area', p. 40.

[48] Stalley, 'The Cathedral', p. 408.

4.
DUNDRY STONE AND OTHER LIMESTONES IN THE FABRIC, FITTINGS, AND MONUMENTS OF ST DAVIDS CATHEDRAL

Tim Palmer

Although St Davids is remote from other parts of Britain by the overland route, it has always been readily accessible by sea. Freestones, quarried and worked at faraway sites and typically transported by sea and river, are frequently encountered in medieval ecclesiastical buildings, where they were used for structure, decoration, and monuments. Polishable limestones (marbles) were similarly transported over large distances for a similar range of functions. With a little specialist knowledge these materials are usually readily identifiable. Hence they may give information about extraction, craft activity and supply routes, as well as about architectural practices and ownership links to source areas, at certain times in a building's history. This article summarises the variety of limestones and marbles that were brought from outside the area, doubtless by sea, to be used in the cathedral at St Davids, up to the time of the Reformation.

English Limestones in Monuments and Fitments

Much the best-known of the English limestones that was commonly transported over large distances for use in fitments, monuments, and decorative internal work is Purbeck Marble. Purbeck Marble comes from a single geological horizon of Lower Cretaceous age, that runs east-west across the Isle of Purbeck, Dorset. In medieval times it was worked on the Isle of Purbeck (at Corfe) and shipped out of Swanage, or from Ower on the southwestern coast of Poole harbour. Sometimes it was sent to London (and thence to the point of use) for brass inlaying work. It is a highly distinctive polishable limestone, dark greenish, bluish, or reddish

https://doi.org/10.16922/jrhlc.9.2.4

in colour, composed of a calcite-cemented mass of fossil pond-snails, each similar in shape to (but slightly smaller than) a winkle. Some blocks also contain scattered bivalve mollusc shells. The bowl of the font at St Davids is medieval Purbeck Marble (the supporting columns are the same material, but of much later date). However, the more spectacular use is in the chest tomb of Edmund Tudor, 1st Earl of Richmond, which dates from the late fifteenth century and was originally in the Greyfriars, Carmarthen. Sides, ends, and the brass-inlaid cover are in this material. The brass is a nineteenth-century replacement following seventeenth-century damage to the original.

Further westwards along the coast of southern England, just across the Dorset–Devon border, lies Beer. In Upper Cretaceous times, just under 100 million years ago, the sea that deposited the Chalk over much of southern England came to shore near here. Gritty and shelly sediment was deposited on the sea-bed which later consolidated into a limestone that has been used since Roman times. It was used in the fabric of Llandaff cathedral but tends to weather badly if exposed. However, its soft uniform texture made it very suitable for carving monuments, and the effigy and panels on the tomb of Bishop Morgan are made of it. Its fine-grained texture without obvious laminations is characteristic, and under the magnifier there are scattered dark green grains of the mineral glauconite – often helpful in distinguishing Cretaceous rocks from those of the older Jurassic Period. On the front panel a further characteristic geological feature can be seen: burrows of shrimps that excavated holes in the sea-floor and later filled them up by packing waste material behind them. The frame of this tomb appears to be of later date and is made of oolitic (probably Bath) limestone

Purbeck Marble and Beer Stone were taken eastwards and westwards around the British coastline as well as inland from their sites of origin. Purbeck in particular can be seen as far north as Yorkshire and Northumberland. The other English limestones that are seen at St Davids are of West Country origin and are more widely met in western Britain than they are to the east of the Cornish peninsula. They were probably shipped out of Bristol or from further up the Severn estuary. Particularly striking at St Davids are two rather similar reclining knight monuments attributed to the Lord Rhys (d. 1197) and Rhys Gryg (d. 1234). The style suggests a date shortly before 1400, long after the deaths of the subjects, and the stones are petrographically identical. They are made of a pale buff oolitic limestone; at the cut surface, the truncated ooliths are clearly seen with a lens and are surrounded with a natural cement of clear crystalline calcite. There is no strong sedimentary lamination and there are areas where fossils have been cut through. Brachiopods and high-spired gastropods are conspicuous. The stone is probably Painswick Stone of Middle Jurassic (lower part of the Inferior Oolite) age. Painswick Stone was produced during the Middle Ages from many sites in the vicinity of Stroud and Cheltenham, including the village of Painswick itself. The name is applied generally because it is not usually possible to tell the precise source in the absence of documentary records.

Two tombs, of Bishops Iorwerth and Anselm le Gras, lie side-by-side in the south aisle and are made of a rather similar blue-grey limestone. The more southerly (Iorwerth) is undoubtedly of Blue Lias, the Lower Jurassic muddy limestone that was sometimes used in medieval times as a low quality marble (there is also a Lias tomb in Llandaff cathedral).[1] Iorwerth's effigy contains an ammonite (poorly preserved and as yet unidentified) on the upper surface, just above the hem of the chasuble. It may be that an ammonite specialist would be able to identify this, in which case it could give a clue to the source of the stone. Lias effigies and inserts are common in south-west England, particularly Somerset,[2] but they are thought to come from beds of stone low in the stratigraphic sequence that do not contain ammonites (the Pre-*planorbis* Beds). Clearly, the Iorwerth stone is from another source and this may be in the Vale of Glamorgan where beds of Lias limestone are plentiful and well-exposed. Anselm's effigy is somewhat more problematical, and a Lias attribution is not absolutely certain. The stone looks siltier than that of Iorwerth and is pock-marked with small depressions (probably fossil burrows within the fabric of the stone). There do not appear to be any characteristic fossils. The stone of the plinth of Iorwerth is the same material, supporting the identification as Lias.

The badly eroded effigy of Archdeacon John Hiot and that of an unknown priest (against the outer wall of the south aisle) are made of Dundry Stone, which is by far the most important English stone used in St Davids Cathedral and in the adjacent Bishops' Palace.

Dundry Stone in the Fabric of the Cathedral

The cases described above point to medieval English industries that were based on local materials and which more rarely supplied customers in west Wales. However, the limestone from the village of Dundry, four miles south-west of Bristol, was sent to southern and western Wales (and further afield) in substantial quantities – much larger than for any other English stone in pre-Reformation times. Medieval secular and ecclesiastical buildings in Wales show extensive use of Dundry Stone in fabric, fittings, and monuments. Little is known of the industry that was based at the western end of Dundry Hill during the Middle Ages, but it must have been very substantial. Records suggest that the stone was taken to the port at Bristol, and archaeology proves that clients received it in large quantities, at least as far away as south-eastern Ireland.[3] In the cathedral at St Davids its use in monuments is almost anecdotal compared with its overwhelming importance as a freestone in the internal construction of the fabric of the building, where it is still plentiful and evident. Whether it was originally used for some external dressings and tracery as well is not known, but quite likely.

Today, Dundry Stone is most conspicuous as the pale buff component of the light-and-dark arches and pillars in the aisles of the eastern part of the cathedral, particularly in the early thirteenth-century arches leading out of the transepts. It is also the principal material used for the walls, vaulting, and tracery of Bishop Vaughan's Holy Trinity chapel (c.1520). The screens at the north and south ends of this chapel have a more complex construction of both Dundry and Bath stones and the southern one is described in further detail to illustrate some of the particular issues of identification'.

Description and Recognition of Dundry Stone

Dundry Stone is a marine limestone from the upper part of the Inferior Oolite Group, of lower Middle Jurassic age. It occurs over a very limited geographical area just to the west of Dundry village, and has been almost completely quarried away. The Dundry Stone that was extracted from the mid-nineteenth to the early twentieth century was considered by masons to be of lower quality than the medieval stone, which appears to have been more or less worked out by the Reformation.

Dundry Stone is easy to recognise and to distinguish from most other pale Jurassic freestones because it is not predominately oolitic in its lithology. Claims to the contrary in some accounts (particularly on websites) probably arise from misidentification, or from confusion by non-geologists between the meaning of the phrase 'oolitic limestone' when used in a petrographic, as opposed to a stratigraphic sense. Rather, it is made almost entirely of finely comminuted bioclastic (=shell) debris, largely worn down to such a fine particle size (<1 mm) that individual shell fossils are no longer identifiable. There are two rather different varieties of the stone:[4] in one, the insides of many of the bioclastic particles have suffered dissolution during the geological history of the rock, whereas their outer surfaces have become stuck to their neighbours by growth of small calcite (calcium carbonate) crystals. A lot of space remains in the stone, some between the original grains and some within their dissolved interiors. A close inspection of this variety reveals a porous and sugary texture, rather like a fine form of tufa. The other variety is much richer in the dissociated debris of echinoderms (sea-lilies, basket-stars, and brittlestars: zoological relatives of starfish and sea-urchins). The skeletons of this animal group are compiled from minute ossicles of calcium carbonate, and they have a crystallographic structure that is somewhat resistant to dissolution and which promotes precipitation of calcite on its surface. The spaces between the original particles in the soft sediment soon (after burial) became completely filled with natural calcite cement to produce a stone that is denser and less porous than the tufa-like variety. In some of the larger blocks of ashlar in the walls of the Bishop Vaughan chapel, both varieties are seen in the same block, in what were originally sub-horizontal bands, representing crinoid-rich and crinoid-poor layers on the accumulating Jurassic sea-bed. In examples of Dundry Stone that have been exposed to the weather, the crinoid particles tend to stand slightly proud of the surface (on the shaft of the cross in Cross Square, just uphill of the cathedral, for example). This may also have misled some people into describing the stone as oolitic.

These two varieties of Dundry Stone are long-lasting and resistant to decay by weathering in buildings. They are readily distinguished under the microscope or with a hand lens. Microscopy also reveals another characteristic feature: scattered grains of a darker, rusty brown colour, which is due to a higher iron concentration than in the surrounding rock. A few of these rusty grains are true ooliths with a concentrically laminated structure, but they are too few to permit the stone to be described as an oolite. On a larger scale, some blocks, probably as a result of pressure solution, have irregular seams of dark-coloured and slightly softer stone running through them, up to a few centimetres thick and roughly aligned with the sedimentary layering of the rock. Together, these features make Dundry Stone easy to recognise and unlike other stones that are likely to be met in medieval building.

Stone Use in the Holy Trinity Chapel

The light and delicate architectural character of the Holy Trinity chapel is closely tied to the properties of the material that was used to build it. The pale Dundry Stone is strong in compression, soft and easy to carve when first quarried, and readily given to the production of ornate mouldings and vaulting, as well as ashlar. The local liver-coloured Caerbwdy sandstone that was used so widely in other parts of the cathedral, was satisfactory for the chunkier Romanesque work but would probably have failed rapidly (by opening up along its geological cleavage as is seen in some parts of the building) if subjected to the engineering demands of the Perpendicular style. As far as can be seen from the ground, all the stone within the chapel is Dundry. However, the screens at either end, probably the last stonework to be built in St Davids Cathedral before the Reformation, are a mixture of stone from Dundry, Bath, and the Vale of Glamorgan (Sutton Stone). These screens and the aisles outside them were open to the air until the early twentieth century, and clearly suffered severe weathering and decay of some of the stones. Original stone can be distinguished from the new stone that was inserted as repairs on account of the remains of lichens or the scars that they etched into their limestone substrate on the original material. The replacement stone is all Bath Stone with traces of evenly-spaced saw marks from mechanical cutting on many of the flat surfaces.

Bath Stone (Fig. 1, right) is readily distinguishable from Dundry (Fig. 1, left) because it is strongly oolitic, and the ooliths tend to fall away from the enclosing calcite cement on the cut surfaces to leave a pattern of minute ($c.0.5$ mm) hemispherical depressions. Also characteristic in some stones are calcite-filled veins cutting across the stone matrix. However, the lichen bioerosion scars make it quite clear that some Bath Stone was mixed with Dundry in the material of the original structure – indeed many more than half the number of the individual pieces of stone of the original fabric of both north and south screens consisted of Bath Stone. This represents the earliest certain use of Bath Stone in St Davids and probably reflects a time when stone from the

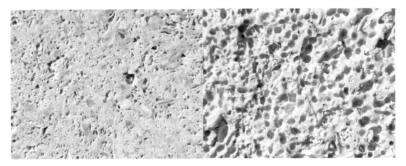

Figure 1: Cut surfaces of Dundry Stone (left) and Bath Stone (right) as seen with a magnifying glass

Bath quarries was starting to appear alongside that from Dundry on the quayside at Bristol.

Fig. 3 shows the distribution of individual stones in the southern screen, distinguishing the replacement (nineteenth-century) Bath, and the mixture of Bath and Dundry in the original sixteenth-century fabric. To the right of the doorway is an area where a third type of Jurassic

Figure 2: Southern screen of the Bishop Vaughan Chapel, showing pieces of original Bath, Dundry, and Sutton stones, and replacement pieces of Bath Stone from the late nineteenth-century repairs

limestone is used across four mullions (the third is a nineteenth-century Bath replacement): this is Sutton Stone from the Vale of Glamorgan, a pale non-oolitic freestone widely used in South Wales in the medieval period (easy to identify because of its pale colour and the small fragments of grey Carboniferous rock that it contains). The quality of the carving of this stonework is poor (Fig. 2), in contrast to that in the original fabric and the joints are in the wrong places, or marked by small inserts (probably repairs). These features suggest a partial dismantling (and subsequent patching) of the original screen at an early period, perhaps to take out from the chapel a large and heavy object that was too bulky to fit through the doorway. Could it have been a tomb, or an altar? Maybe the original stonework was damaged in the opening process and was repaired by a local mason (with less experience of working the fine mouldings of the Perpendicular style in Jurassic limestone), using a material that was easier to obtain than the original English stones.

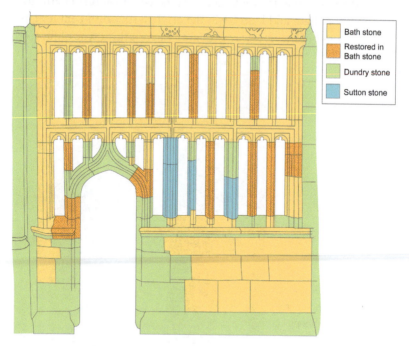

Figure 3: Sutton Stone early-replaced mullions in the Bishop Vaughan south screen

Dundry Stone in Wider Use in South and West Wales

This study has led on to an ongoing wider survey of imported medieval stonework in southern Wales. Previous work on particular sites has recognised examples of the use of Dundry Stone in Wales (e.g. Newport, Llandaff, Whitland, Strata Florida) and rarely there is even supporting documentary evidence of stone being shipped from Bristol (for the castle at Aberystwyth, for example). However, the scale and importance of Dundry to meet such Welsh needs is only gradually becoming apparent. Not only are extant medieval churches fruitful (Llangennith in western Gower, for example): so are ruins from which much limestone has been robbed (doubtless for lime-burning), because odd blocks that were difficult to extract may remain in a ruined structure (e.g. Haverfordwest Priory where lumps have been knocked off along a Dundry Stone string course) or in excavated material (e.g. St. Dogmael's Abbey). Fonts seem particularly promising, and often survived Victorian rebuilds of their churches. Examples are seen at Llanychaearn, near Aberystwyth; at Llanarth and Penbryn (Ceredigion); Newport (Pembs); Oystermouth, on Gower; and at Llanrhian, northeast of St Davids. Many more will doubtless be recognised in a systematic survey.[5]

Notes

[1] M. Gray, 'The Medieval Bishops' Effigies at Llandaff Cathedral', *Archaeologia Cambrensis*, 153 (2006), pp. 37–50.

[2] D. T. Donovan and R. D. Reid, 'The Stone Insets of Somerset Churches', *Proceedings of the Somerset Archaeological and Natural History Society*, 107 (1963), pp. 60–71.

[3] D. M. Waterman, 'Somersetshire and other Foreign Building Stone in Medieval Ireland', *Ulster Journal of Archaeology*, 33 (1970), pp. 63–75.

[4] T. J. Palmer, 'Limestone Petrography and Durability in English Jurassic Freestones', in P. Doyle (ed.), *England's Heritage in Stone* (Middleton by Wirksworth, 2008), pp. 66–78.

[5] Many thanks to Sally Badham and Mark Downing from the Church Monuments Society for advice on brasses and military monuments respectively; to the Right Revd J. Wyn Evans for advice on the history of the cathedral; to Arthur Price for samples of Painswick Stone; to the late David Pollard for information on the history of Bath Stone and Dundry Stone; to A. Smith for draughtsmanship, and to Caroline Palmer for photography.

5.
THE SHRINE OF ST DAVID

John Crook

Introduction

The monument traditionally identified as the 'shrine of St David' on the north side of the presbytery of St Davids cathedral (Fig. 1) was splendidly conserved and embellished in 2011–12, after years of neglect.[1] It appears to be a rare survival of the architectural core of a pre-Reformation saint's shrine, and it is therefore surprising that it has not been more fully studied.[2] The fieldwork for this report was done before the conservation programme, so the record photography shows the monument in its unembellished state, the advantage being that the stonework was then more accessible than it is today.

The question of whether the bones thought formerly to have been venerated at this monument were actually those of St David (d. *c*.589) is scarcely relevant to this study. His alleged relics had been miraculously discovered in 1275 after a period of loss, so they are inherently more dubious than those of saints such as Cuthbert, Swithun, Etheldreda, or Becket, the movements of whose bones may be traced from their death to the Reformation. Of course many other saints' cults (notably that of Alban) were, like David's, matters of faith, but as far as their shrines were concerned – and the activities that took place at those shrines – there is no difference between saints with provable physical remains and those whose authenticity might be challenged by the sceptical.

The Cult Since the Thirteenth Century

As discussed more fully below, the present monument would appear on stylistic evidence to date from the time of the rediscovery of the relics in

https://doi.org/10.16922/jrhlc.9.2.5

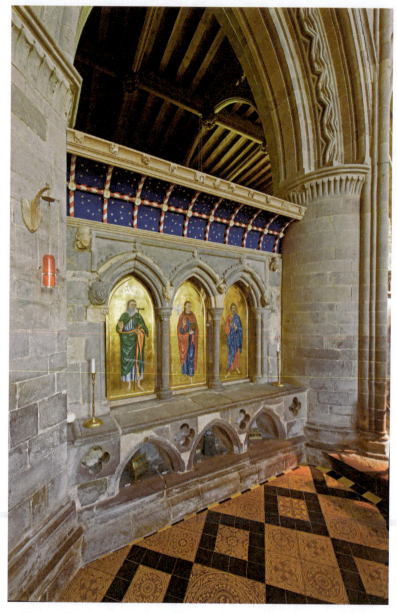

Figure 1: The shrine from the south-west after the conservation programme of 1911–12, showing its architectural context (Photo: John Crook)

Figure 2: The shrine from the south-west before conservation in 1911–12 (Photo: John Crook)

1275. Assuming that the traditional identification as St David's shrine is correct it cannot be earlier than that date, and so for the purposes of this paper it is unnecessary to trace in any great detail the previous history of the cult.[3] Before 1275, indeed, lies a gap of nearly two centuries. Relics, which presumably were thought to be those of St David, were available for veneration in 1081 when Gruffudd ap Cynan and Rhys ap Tewdwr 'proceeded together to the church of St David in prayer'. And there they became faithful allies through the pledge over his relics.[4]

However, the *Welsh Annals* state that in 1088, only ten years after William the Conqueror had also visited St Davids 'for the sake of praying',[5] the reliquary (*archa*) was removed from the church, stripped of its precious metal covering; the relics were presumably lost.[6] It was during this period (1091 × 1093 according to a recent study)[7] that Rhygyfarch ap Sulien wrote the earliest surviving Life of the saint,[8] and it is perhaps inconceivable that he would have omitted to mention the shrine or relics had they still existed – indeed his silence must cast doubt on whether the relics venerated by Gruffydd ap Cynan were those of St David. As Fred Cowley has noted, '[the Life] is silent about any shrine of the saint or miracles performed at his tomb'.[9] Rhygyfarch (and Gerald of Wales after him) merely says that '[David's] body . . . committed to the earth with honour, was laid to rest within his monastery'.[10] Some secondary relics – items purporting to have been associated with the saint (such as the portable altar, bell, staff, and coat allegedly given to David by the Patriarch of Jerusalem) – might, however, have been available for veneration in the late twelfth century.[11] Henry II called in at St Davids in 1171 on his way to Ireland; later this visit was characterised as a 'pilgrimage' and he was said to have offered a handful of silver.[12] On his return on 17 April 1173 he again visited the cathedral 'for the purpose of praying'.[13] On neither of these occasions are the saint's corporeal relics mentioned.

The inception of the present monument seems to have occurred in 1275 when John de Gamages, then prior of Ewenni,[14] was instructed in a dream to dig at a well-defined place a certain number of feet from the south door of the present cathedral church.[15] The detail is a somewhat stripped down version of a conventional *inventio* narrative; usually such miraculous revelations were made to third parties who experienced difficulty in persuading the church authorities of their validity. Following Prior John's vision a whole body was duly discovered and a *feretrum* was prepared;[16] it must have been complete by 1284 when Edward I and

The Shrine of St David

Queen Eleanor came to St Davids 'on pilgrimage'.[17] The king took various relics back to London with him, notably the saint's head, which in 1285 was borne in procession from the Tower of London to Westminster.[18]

A *feretrum* is of course not the same thing as a shrine, being merely – as the name implies – a container in which the relics could be transported. But by the late thirteenth century, following the example of the high shrine of St Thomas of Canterbury (1220), a *feretrum* would normally reside on a shrine-base, forming the ensemble which is conventionally called a shrine. The 1275 date accords well with the architectural and sculptural style of datable components of the monument that is the subject of this chapter. How far the monument in its present state conforms to what was erected in 1275 is of course a different matter which will be studied in due course.

The existence of the *feretrum* (though not, admittedly, the monument) in the early fourteenth century is confirmed by several references in the so-called 'Black Book of St Davids', an extent of the Bishop's lands in 1326. These state that in time of war the bishop's tenants were expected to follow the bishop bearing the saint's *feretrum* and other relics: the distance was restricted by a condition that they were to be able to return home the same night.[19]

Antiquarian Accounts of the Monument

Pre-Reformation descriptions of the monument are unfortunately lacking, and such antiquarian records as we have date from a period when the shrine had long ceased to fulfil its original purpose. The earliest account of the structure occurs in Browne Willis's *Survey of the Cathedral Church of St David's* (1717).[20] In fact Willis never visited St Davids and relied principally on drawings ('draughts') and descriptions provided by various people at St Davids, notably a certain 'M.N.', whose account is printed as a 'Memoir' within Willis's book. 'M.N.' may be identified as the disgraced antiquary, William Wotton, who was then living secretly in Caernarvon with the artist Joseph Lord.[21]

The account in the main part of Willis's text appears to be little more than a paraphrase of the relevant sentences of Wotton's memoir, supplemented perhaps by information from other sources. It tells us very little about what the monument looks like in 1715, being mainly concerned with its appearance at an unspecified earlier time ('formerly', 'anciently').

On the North Side of the Chancel, near the Steeple, under an Arch, is St. *David's* Tomb. Formerly it was all of one flat Stone, which is now broken into several Pieces : Above it, were anciently three Images ; St. *David's* in the Middle, St. *Patrick's* on the right Hand, and St. *Dennis's* on the left, as Tradition informs us.[22]

However, as the prolix title of Willis's monograph indicates, Wotton claimed to have had access to a manuscript written 'in the latter End of *Queen Elizabeth's* Reign . . .', and this source, if genuine, takes us closer to the Reformation. The text, as transcribed by Wotton, describes two coffins on the south side of the presbytery, then continues:

... on the other Side, is St. *David's* Shrine, between two Pillars of the Chancel, within a fair Arch of Timber-work painted. St. *David* himself is painted in his *Pontificalibus*; and on each Side of him, is a Bishop Saint ; one, by the Inscription, is known to be St. *Patrick*; the other is somewhat defac'd.[23]

Here then, recorded in the present tense of the source document, is the monument's appearance *c.*1600. This lost Elizabethan manuscript is the only authority for certain aspects of the monument, notably the wooden 'arch' and the paintings, and these will be discussed later in this paper. It is regrettable that Thomas Pennant's energetic journeys through Wales did not bring him to St Davids; nor did Archdeacon Edward Yardley (1698–1769) mention the monument in his *Menevia Sacra*,[24] though he may have been responsible for annotations in a copy of Willis's *Survey* in the National Library of Wales, collating it with the Elizabethan text.[25] The next description of the monument dates from the first decade of the nineteenth century, then the antiquary Richard Fenton (1747-1821) noted its architectural simplicity: 'the lower part consists of a plain tomb, with no other decoration than four quatrefoil openings in a row, two of which are stopped up. Above the basement are small divisions with columns, and on the spandrils of the arches, the heads of a king, a bishop and a monk.'[26] He also viewed the other side of the structure in the then roofless north aisle: 'at the back of David's shrine, observe a square niche between two quatrefoil openings as on the other side, and arched niches lower down'.[27]

Far more detailed is the excellent account of the monument by William Jones and Basil Freeman, writing in 1856. This was shortly before George Gilbert Scott embarked on his repairs, and the north presbytery aisle had just been re-roofed, having been open to the sky since the 1640s.[28] He had not yet started work on the shrine, however, so Jones and Freeman's description is evidence for the conservative nature of his repairs to the monument, and such changes as he did make are readily discernible. In general the authors' description could apply to the monument today:

> The front towards the choir consists of a table resting on three rather obtuse arches slightly chamfered, with four quatrefoil apertures in the spandrels chamfered inwards. The two outer ones of these are blocked internally: the inner ones have holes just large enough to admit a hand, and communicate with small lockers in the interior, which were in all probability receptacles for offerings. Above this rises a triplet of arches, backed with solid ashlar, and resting on detached cylindrical shafts, with engaged responds. As a matter of fact the shafts and their bases are lost, and have been supplied by wooden ones; but their caps remain, one of which has foliage tied by a band in a very peculiar manner. This is all of the original work remaining, on this side at least; but a late Perpendicular addition has been superimposed, consisting of crocketed hood-mouldings to the arches, of particularly shallow work, with a square label running over the whole ; on each side of the latter there is a corbel-head, removed from the back of the shrine at a recent period. [. . .] The back towards the aisle is now imperfect, but consisted of a composition of three low round arches, the central one larger than the others. Over each was a quatrefoil hole chamfered inwards ; and between the holes were two plain square niches.[29]

Location and Archaeological Context of the Monument

The monument (Figs. 1–2) is located on the north side of the four-bay presbytery in the second bay (counting from the crossing). It is inserted between two piers of the presbytery (one octagonal, the other a cylindrical column), a minimum width of 2815mm. This arcade undoubtedly forms part of the rebuilding which began in 1182 and was apparently still in progress when Bishop Peter de Leia, who had initiated the works, died in 1198. The presbytery must certainly have been complete before the famous collapse of the tower in 1220, for most of the new tower is clearly stitched into the existing fabric, and in any case the presbytery's quasi-sculptural features, such as the attic bases, multiple trumpet scallops, and chevron ornament, would have been decidedly out-dated by the 1220s.

Detailed Description

Viewed from the presbytery, the south side of the monument resembles a tomb-chest with an arcaded front, supported on a platform, with a high arcaded screen wall like a reredos rising behind it. The north side is somewhat differently articulated. The essential simplicity of the structure is confused by a multiplicity of niches, recesses, and other quasi-decorative features. It is important to try to understand the order in which the various components of the monument were assembled.

The lowest element is a basal course or platform (designated 'A' in the cross-section, Fig. 3), comprising the floor on which the 'table' (Jones and Freeman's convenient term for the body of the monument as seen from the south) is supported. The upper surface of the platform is concealed on the south side by the floor (C), but the cross-section indicates that it continues for the full width of the monument; the coincidence in level indicates that it was intended from the outset to form the floor of the lower niches on the aisle side of the monument. Its south edge is aligned to the ESE angle of the octagonal pier; on the north side it extends into the aisle, where it is approximately aligned to the bases of the engaged vault shafts. The platform is deeper at the west end so as to accommodate the eastward upward slope in the presbytery floor, suggesting that this deformation of the cathedral fabric (also evident in the nave) had occurred by the time the shrine was built – or rebuilt. The tiles of the present floor of the presbytery, about 175mm above that of the aisles, abut the platform. On the presbytery side the platform has a chamfered plinth, formed of seven sandstone blocks of varying widths. The blocks forming the plinth have diagonal tooling and might conceivably be recycled Romanesque stonework. The original masonry on the aisle side (including the floor of the round-headed niches) is less well finished.

The platform was built as the foundation for the east-west wall ('B') which completely blocks this bay of the arcade between the two flanking piers and forms the main vertical structural element of the monument.

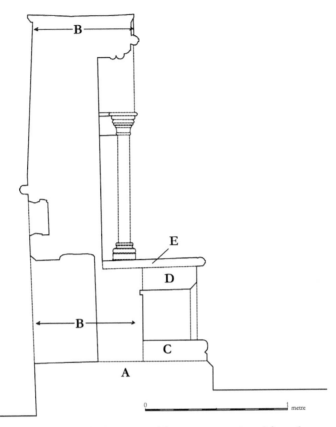

Figure 3: Cross-section through the centre of the monument viewed from the west

Its north face merely continues the line of the basal platform, without any articulation such as a chamfered offset. The wall is approximately 770mm thick in total, the position of its south face being determined by the ENE angle of the octagonal pier. Within this wall are contained the triple arcade of the 'reredos' on the south side and the round-headed recesses on the aisle side. The south face of the wall forms the rear of the niches in the main shrine-table and also approximately corresponds to the main face of the reredos, excluding the triple arcade.

The floor of the three niches (here numbered 1–3 from west to east) is formed of four slabs C, 142mm thick. These appear to have been set in place at the same time as the wall was under construction; for the floor extends beneath the coursed rear slabs of niche 1, though in the case of niches 2–3 the floor slabs abut wall B, with a wide mortar joint. The

Figure 4: Rectified photograph of the south side of
the monument (Photo: John Crook)

front edges of the three largest floor slabs are rounded off and defined by a deep quirk on the vertical face but the narrower slab between niches 1 and 2 is anomalous in also having a quirk on the horizontal surface.

The table D, built on top of the floor slabs C, abuts the face of wall B, which forms the rear of the niches, here numbered 1–3 from west to east. These niches are the largest features of the front face of the table, which is set back 59mm behind the front edge of the platform. The dimensions of the niches are slightly irregular: working from west to east they measure as follows (width × height): 535 × 340mm, 515 × 350mm, and 501 × 365mm. The eastward increase in height cancels out the advantage gained by bringing the platform to the level: the apexes of the niches match the eastward rise in floor level. Each niche is made up of just two long, gently curved voussoirs, chamfered on the front edge. They do not extend to the full 410mm depth of the niches, about half of each vault being of plastered rubble.

Between the niches, the spandrels are faced in vertical slabs in two courses. The upper course is the taller of the two and its four largest slabs are pierced with quatrefoils (also numbered 1 to 4 from west to east). All have double chamfers, steeper internally. However, the pair at either end (Nos. 1 and 4) were, probably from the outset, blocked with black slate backing slabs, perhaps to form a decorative contrast with the red stone of the quatrefoils. The slate backing of No. 1 has been damaged revealing the corework behind it; No. 4 was similarly damaged but has been repaired in lime mortar. This quatrefoil retains some red polychromy. Quatrefoils 2 and 3 have a rather less pronounced chamfer, and their upper lobes remain open, the slabs behind them only blocking the lower two-thirds of each quatrefoil. The backing slab of quatrefoil No. 2 has been cut in a curve matching the upper lobe, so as to form a circular hole. No. 3 was possibly also originally treated in the same way, and could have been modified during post-Reformation repairs. These holes give access to voids behind the backing slabs. Dish-like depressions cut into the horizontal surfaces of well-cut masonry forming the floor of the voids may be felt, and extra hand-room is provided by the dome-like hollowing of the stones forming the top of each void. These are the 'lockers' noted by Jones and Freeman – an inappropriate term as there is no obvious way they could be secured.

The table is topped by a *mensa* which is now composed of an untidy assemblage of stones of different shapes and sizes (Fig. 5). The slab, 59mm thick, has undoubtedly been broken and reassembled, calling to mind Browne Willis's observation that 'Formerly it was all of one flat Stone, which is now broken into several Pieces'. This is just one of many inconsistencies from this level upwards indicative of considerable reconstruction. The edge moulding of the slab has a fillet, which is consistent with the late thirteenth-century date proposed for the monument. To

Figure 5: Plan view of the *mensa* (Photo: John Crook)

east and west the slight gaps between the ends of the *mensa* and the flanking piers are filled with painted softwood; this survives at the east end but since 2011 has been protected by sheet metal at the west end. This use of softwood is highly unlikely to be medieval, though the gaps were presumably filled in some way from the outset.

Some of the fragments now incorporated within the *mensa* have mouldings: a rather shallow quirk which does not, however, appear to match that of the edge mouldings of the *mensa*; in any case there are enough moulded edge fragments to form the complete perimeter of the *mensa* in its present configuration. The provenance of these extra pieces remains uncertain. They might perhaps have come from the top slab of the reredos, which would be expected to match the *mensa*; the present capping is of nineteenth-century date, forming part of G. G. Scott's repairs.

The reredos also shows several anomalies of construction. The two ends of the main face, comprising as we have seen the main south face of the major wall 'B', have independent coursing. Nor does the coursing at either end continue into the masonry at the rear of the triple arcade. Furthermore, the latter masonry shows several disjunctions, and abuts the flanking walls and soffits of the arches above. Such anomalies are best explained as resulting from reconstruction.

The detailing of the triple arch is also a hotch-potch. The two shafts and their bases are introductions by Scott (as noted above, before the 1860s they were of wood). Their capitals are highly varied, but all could date from the late thirteenth century, though the use of limestone for the westernmost capital is anomalous. The arch mouldings are more regular and are consistent with a 1275 date. The label stops and intermediate head stops are more complicated (Fig. 6). The only one of the four heads which is properly integrated with its mouldings, having short projecting 'wings' of the same profile, is the left-hand head portraying a bishop. The angle of this head suits its position at the end of the series. The right-hand stop, portraying a monk, is not facing correctly inwards, is not integrated with the hood-mould which it supports, and is smaller than that of the king. Head No. 2 is also highly dubious. It is crowned, clearly intended for a king despite its gracile, feminine appearance, and must be the same as the king's head observed by Fenton *c*.1811. Again, this head is not integrated with the mouldings, and it is of a fine-grained yellow limestone. Finally, head No. 3 differs from the others in being a foliate type, again of limestone, and set much higher than the other three.

Figure 6: Head stops of the triple arcade (not to same scale) (Photo: John Crook)

Furthermore, the arch springer beneath it is an undoubted insertion, of yellow limestone like the anomalous corbels, and poorly aligned to the curvature of the main part of the arches.

True, there are some stylistic similarities in the portrait sculptures. They share several features such as the idiosyncratic rendering of eyebrows, the shape of the ears, the treatment of the hair, and the archaic smile. All could indeed be of late thirteenth-century date. But the cumulative evidence for a reconstruction of the reredos makes it highly unlikely that what is seen today is an unaltered medieval monument. Given that the reredos and the supporting shafts of its arches rest upon a *mensa* which is clearly a reassemblage, the best interpretation is that the upper part of the monument has been completely reconstructed, as discussed more fully below.

Finally, the reredos incorporates two alien elements: a length of arcading comprising crocketed panels, probably of the fourteenth century, which have been crudely adapted to fit the spandrels above the hood-mould of the triple arch, flanked by a pair of post-medieval corbel heads which are extremely weathered and the mouldings associated with them show they were formerly the label stops of an external window. They are set in different mortar from the crocketed panels, and seem to be later insertions. According to Jones and Freeman these originally adorned the north side of the monument (see above). They might be of sixteenth- or even seventeenth-century date.

The north side of the monument (Fig. 7) may be considered quite independently of the south. This side has evidently been much reconstructed, mostly by Gilbert Scott, and probably less than half of the visible masonry is medieval. Enough survives for one to be reasonably happy about Scott's reconstruction. The platform survives relatively unaltered, adapted as we have seen to the slope in the aisle floor. It forms the floor to three round-headed niches, that on the right side being by Scott. These niches are set in the main east-west wall, whose ashlar face is well represented at the east end of the elevation; the 'crazy paving' forming most of this face of the monument is of nineteenth-century date, as was previously clear from the distressing pointing in hard mortar with black gravel inclusions; this masonry has now mercifully been rendered. The

Figure 7: Rectified photograph of the north side of the monument. (Photo: John Crook)

three quatrefoil recesses are an authentic feature, though the one on the right is a replacement. These quatrefoils have a double chamfer, steeper on the inner edge. Only parts of the rectangular framed recess on the left are medieval. But assuming, as Scott did, that the monument was symmetrical, these elements are probably authentic.

The plan of the monument (Fig. 8) shows that the niches to north and south are completely independent in their spacing: they could never have gone right through the base of the monument as might be supposed at first glance. They are evenly spaced on either side, but the fact that the monument is off-set to the north of the centreline of the arcade means that the sides are of unequal length. Consequently, the niches on the north side are more widely spaced; furthermore, the north side of the monument is displaced slightly east of the centre of the piers, adding further to the lack of symmetry.

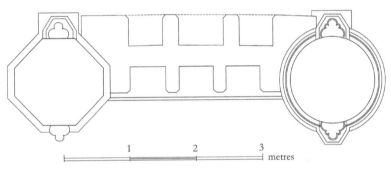

Figure 8: Plan of the monument (north at top) showing position of the niches

Petrography

The monument is almost entirely made of micaceous sandstones, varying in colour from purplish to green, most likely to be the local Caerbwdy sandstone, part of the St Davids (Caerfai) series of Lower Cambrian deposits. Many of the blocks have diagonal tooling resembling Romanesque work and could possibly be reused from an earlier period. However, as noted above, some fine-grained yellow limestone is also found within the monument, always in anomalous contexts, such as the apparently inserted heads, the poorly matched arch springer, and the uncharacteristic westernmost capital.

Polychromy

According to William Wotton's transcription of the lost Elizabethan manuscript the triple arcade on the south side contained images of three saints (including St David in the middle), but these had been destroyed by the early eighteenth century. The images are likely to have been painted on plaster rather than on the bare stone, but there are no traces at all of polychromy or of plaster. Some slight traces of whitewash occur on the pointing at the rear of the triple arcade. By contrast, evidence survives for the decoration of the lower part of the monument: there are traces of red paint at the top of the first block above the left-hand voussoir of the central niche. No polychromy has survived on the north side of the monument, but much of this was reconstructed by Scott. The recent introduction of painted panels by Sarah Crisp in the style of icons depicting SS. Patrick, David, and Andrew has brought new life to the monument; likewise on the north side, the inclusion of portraits of David's contemporary St Justinian and his mother St Nonna gives sense to the rectangular panels.

The Wooden Canopy

Another feature recorded only by the Elizabethan writer is the 'fair Arch of Timber-work painted' which in his day was above the monument. Like the episcopal portraits, it had vanished by the time Browne Willis began his investigations – the arch mentioned in his own description was the presbytery arcade. It is sometimes claimed that anomalies in the stonework above the monument reflect the previous existence of a wooden structure. A few of the trumpet scallops of the east pillar are damaged, and there is some small damage to the west pillar, but there is nothing to indicate that woodwork was attached here. Nevertheless, there seems no reason to doubt the Elizabethan author. Had such a canopy existed, it would have perished either during the Commonwealth, when the roof of the north presbytery aisle was stripped for the sake of its lead and the timbers removed,[30] or at the Restoration of 1660 when the arcade was filled in as a solid wall.

The modern coved canopy added in 2011–12 is a plausible guess, and it is possible that coving was what the Elizabethan author meant by an 'arch'.

Post-Reformation Reconstruction of the Monument

As noted above, the monument shows many signs of having been reconstructed from the level of the *mensa* upwards (and including the *mensa* itself); only the lowest parts of the base appear to be primary. There is, however, no written record either of such destruction or of the reconstruction – what follows must therefore be regarded as a best guess based on the available physical and historical evidence.

Obviously the most likely date for the spoliation of the monument is 1538, when the actual shrine containing the saint's alleged bones was destroyed.[31] But it is by no means certain that the monument itself was greatly damaged. The Elizabethan manuscript makes it quite clear that *c.*1600 paintings were still in place within the triple arcade of the reredos, portraying figures identifiable as saints. One explanation might be that during the short-lived Catholic revival under Queen Mary the shrine was hastily cobbled together again and paintings added at the rear of the triple niches. But the fact that such images were visible in around 1600 yet had disappeared without trace by the early eighteenth century, makes it more likely that both superstructure of the monument and the images painted on it were destroyed during that period. If the images had been painted in the 1550s *after* the reconstruction of the monument, some slight vestiges of plaster or polychromy might have been expected to have survived even to this day. Furthermore, the Elizabethan author's assertion that one of the images was 'somewhat defaced' might indicate that they were of pre-Reformation date and had suffered in the 1530s.

The other obvious period of destruction in the area of the shrine is the Commonwealth. It was then that the roof of the north presbytery aisle, above the monument itself, was removed, to be replaced only in the mid-nineteenth century.[32] Perhaps, therefore, it is more probable that the shrine fell victim to Puritan fanaticism in the 1640s and that the reconstruction seen today dates from soon after the Restoration of 1660. The superstructure of the monument might have been roughly reconstituted at that date, with the incorporation of alien elements (some of the corbel heads, and the fragment of fourteenth-century arcading), and served to support the wall which in this bay, as in the others on the north side of the presbytery, continued up to the apex of the arcade. The two post-medieval heads flanking the added arcading were added later still, having being transferred from the north side of the monument, perhaps at the time the north presbytery aisle was re-roofed and the inserted wall removed from the presbytery arcade, *c*.1856.

Parallels

As far as we can discern, after the reconstruction of more than half of the monument, the shrine of St David seems to have been very much *sui generis*. Nevertheless, some of its most obvious features have adequate parallels elsewhere. The triple niches on the south side have place in a long pedigree of *foramina* shrines, where the 'portholes' were intended partly to protect, partly to give access, to a relic which, more typically, was still *below* the monument. Here the archetype seems to have been the empty tomb of Christ in the Church of the Holy Sepulchre at Jerusalem, where perhaps in the eleventh century a *transenna* (pierced slab) containing three holes had been placed in front of the sepulchral bench. This arrangement gave pilgrims limited access to the most sacred contact relic of all, namely the actual sepulchral bench on which the body of Christ had been placed. The motif of three holes became a kind of icon for a shrine: similar designs were used for the tomb of Edward the Confessor (rebuilt 1163), the first tomb of St Thomas of Canterbury (*c*.1171), the tomb of St Hugh of Lincoln (1200-20), and many other examples besides, including the thirteenth-century tomb-shrine of Bishop Osmund in Salisbury cathedral, where the bishop's body, translated from Old Sarum, was reburied pending his long-awaited canonization.

Where St David's shrine seems to part company with these examples, is that it is clear that the relic could not have been within or below the 'table'. Yet But elsewhere the principle was also forgotten that *foramina* shrines were normally constructed *over* graves. At Whitchurch Canonicorum, for example (Fig. 9), the three vesica-shaped openings in front of the tomb of St Wita allowed pilgrims to crawl *below* rather than *above* the relics, which were entombed on top of the monument. The triple openings were the forerunners of prayer niches at rather more convenient level, such as adorned the sides of the high shrines of the later middle ages (St Alban, St Swithun). Their purpose was to provide a measure of privacy for the suppliant, insulating him from the world surrounding the shrine. Somewhat regrettably the openings at St Davids have now been glazed to allow them to serve as display niches for various items connected with the cult.

The Shrine of St David

Figure 9: Whitchurch Canonicorum (Dorset). Shrine of
St Wita in north transept (Photo: John Crook)

The closest parallel for the St Davids monument is of course the nearby shrine of St Caradoc (Fig. 10). This was probably created under the immediate influence of the parent shrine (it seems unlikely that this shrine of a minor saint was the exemplar for that of St David). In 1162 Gerald of Wales had successfully obtained from Pope Alexander III letters for Caradoc's canonization,[33] but the shrine was certainly not created for well over a century after that. It shares with the shrine of St David the provision of two-centred prayer niches, and quatrefoil openings for offerings.

How Did the Monument Function?

It is scarcely necessary to emphasise that despite its superficial resemblance to a *foramina* shrine, the alleged relics of St David could never have been placed below or indeed within the body of the monument. In any case, references like the account of his bones being borne in battle suggests that they were in an easily moved *feretrum*. The simplest

89

Figure 10: St Davids Cathedral. Shrine of St Caradoc. (Photo: John Crook)

solution is that the reliquary was small enough to be normally parked on top of the *mensa* in the central bay of the arcaded reredos, partly protected by the arcading above. This is a space only 600mm wide by 660mm deep, but there is no reason to suppose that the reliquary was more than a small casket. It is surely inconceivable that the reliquary could have been located on top of the reredos, the only other possible location, as it would scarcely have been visible at that height.[34] Furthermore, the niches in the front of the *mensa* were intended to allow pilgrims close proximity to the relics, which would not have been the case had the reliquary been other than on the *mensa* itself.

The recorded existence of flanking images of two bishop saints (one identified by William Wotton as St Patrick, the other 'by tradition' as St Denis) raises the possibility that their reliquary caskets were also displayed on the monument, in the other two bays of the superstructure. It is tempting also to associate these other relics with those which, together with those of St David, were paraded by the episcopal tenants in time of war as described above. But here we are deep into the realm of speculation.

Assuming then, that the reliquary normally stood on the *mensa* there were two possibilities for veneration. Some, presumably under supervision, could come into the presbytery and prostrate themselves within the niches below the *mensa*. More readily accessible were the round-headed niches on the north side of the monument, into which pilgrims might again be able to insert their heads, not being able to see the shrine, but knowing at least that they had got as near as possible.

As has long been recognised, the dish-like recesses behind the quatrefoil openings were probably intended for monetary offerings. They are unusual – no other extant shrine appears to possess such features. Being on the feretory side of the monument, rather than the presumably more accessible aisle side, they are perhaps unlikely to have been accessible to pilgrims for much of the time. They are also extraordinarily discreet; they only admit a single hand, rather like an old-fashioned ballot box, so truly the right hand would not know what the left hand was doing when it came to giving alms.

Finally, the notion that the monument was in fact an Easter Sepulchre should be dismissed. Admittedly the three-niche or three-hole motif was an iconographical shorthand for the tomb of Christ, but in no other ways does the monument resemble surviving Easter sepulchres.

The Shrine at the Reformation

In view of the uncertainties about the authenticity of the monument in its present form it is worthwhile looking at sources from the Reformation.

In the period immediately before the destruction of the shrine the bishop, William Barlow, a keen supporter of the reform, was actively petitioning Thomas Cromwell for his see to be removed to Carmarthen. St Davids he characterised as 'sytuated in soch a desolate angle and in so rare a frequented place (excepte of vacabounde pilgremes), that evill disposed persons, unwillinge to do good, maye lurke there at lybertye in secrete withowt reestraynte . . .'[35] The Welsh were superstitious and prone to idolatry. Most significantly, on St David's Day (1 March), despite his injunctions, the canons had responded to popular celebration of the feast by displaying certain relics, which he immediately confiscated. They comprised 'two heedes of sylver plate enclosinge two rotten skulles stuffed with putrified clowtes; Item, two arme bones, and a worme eaten boke covered with silver plate.'[36] Barlow does not state that the relics were those of St David, and obviously only one of the heads could have been identified as that of the patron; but the implication is that they were associated with the major cult, and would certainly have been placed on the shrine of the patron on his feast-day, if only as secondary relics.

There is no record of the destruction of the shrine, and its survival must be due to the fact that it was simply stripped of its jewels – and, presumably, of any relics that Barlow had not already purloined. Recovering the jewels proved a problem. On 29 September 1540 the privy council issued a commission for the Welsh Council headed by Lord Ferrers 'to examine what jewels have been embezzled from the shrine of St. David's, and to put what remain in surety to the King's use'.[37] Exactly four years later the value of the shrine was noted by the Court of Augmentations: 'Price of the sepulchre called le shryne of St. David in Wales, 66*l*. 13*s*. 4*d*'.[38] It rather sounds as though this did not reflect the price of all the decorative elements of the shrine, for in 1546 a reward of £40 was paid to James Leach who had sued for compensation for his pains in recovering 'plate and jewels which did belong to St. David's shrine in Wales'.[39] That such a large sum could be paid as a reward suggests that the value of the materials recovered was very much greater still. Until 2012 the monument remained a pale shadow of its pre-Reformation self – the new adornments have brought the monument back to life.

As a post-script to the story of William Barlow it is a curious irony that, ending his days as bishop of Chichester, his tomb was placed immediately to the north side of the former shrine-platform of another local saint, St Richard de Wych. Barlow might have been horrified to have been buried *ad sanctum*.

Notes

[1] The work was planned by the Cathedral Architect, the late Peter Bird, assisted by Cathedral Archaeologist Jerry Sampson to whom I am indebted for useful discussion.

[2] Published accounts of the shrine include Nona Rees, *The Mediæval Shrines of St David* (St David's Cathedral, 1998); Heather James, 'The Cult of St. David in the Middle Ages', in M. Carver (ed.), *In Search of Cult: Archaeological Investigations in Honour of Philip Rahtz*, University of York Archaeological Papers (Woodbridge, 1993), pp. 105–12: 110–11. E. G. Bowen, *Dewi Sant* (Cardiff, 1983), pp. 72–5, contains nothing significant about the actual monument.

[3] For the growth of the cult, see F. G. Cowley, 'The Relics of St David: the Historical Evidence', in J. W. Evans and J. M. Wooding (eds), *St David of Wales: Cult, Church and Nation* (Woodbridge, 2007), pp. 274–81.

[4] D. Simon Evans (ed.), *A Medieval Prince of Wales: the Life of Gruffudd ap Cynan* (Felinfach, 1990), pp. 36, 67. The Latin version in NLW Peniarth MS 434, which Paul Russell proposes

The Shrine of St David

may be a copy of the Latin text that was the basis for the Welsh Life, only mentions their praying in the church and not the relics: *Vita Griffini filii Conani: the Medieval Latin Life of Grufudd ap Cynan* (Cardiff, 2005), pp. 68–9.

5 '*causa orationis*': *Annales Cambriae*, Rolls Series, ed. J. Williams ab Ithel (London, 1860), p. 28.

6 *ibid.*, 28–9, *Archa* [*scrinium* in MS Domitian A.1 s. xiii^ex] *Sancti David ab ecclesia* [*sua*] *furata est, et auro argentoque quibus tegebatur spoliata est*; cf. J. Conway Davies (ed.), *Welsh Episcopal Acta*, 2 vols (Historical Society of the Church in Wales, 1946–8), vol. I, p. 234.

7 J. R. Davies, 'Some Observations on the 'Nero', 'Digby', and 'Vespasian' Recensions of *Vita S. David*', in Evans and Wooding, *St David of Wales*, pp. 156–60: 159–60.

8 For the difficulties surrounding the text, see R. Sharpe, 'Which Text is Rhygyfarch's Life of St David?', in Evans and Wooding, *St David of Wales*, pp. 90–105; J. R. Davies, 'Some Observations'. See also R. Sharpe and J. R. Davies (ed. and trans.), 'Rhygyfarch's Life of St David', in Evans and Wooding, *St David of Wales*, pp. 107–55.

9 Cowley, 'The Relics', p. 275.

10 Sharpe and Davies, Rhygyfarch's Life of St David', p. 151.

11 Though the altar was said to be housed at Llangyfelach, Sharpe and Davies, 'Rhygyfarch's Life of St David', p. 141.

12 Davies, *Welsh Episcopal Acta*, vol. i, p. 275: '1171. The Lord Rys . . . heard that the king had gone to Mynyv on a pilgrimage. At Mynyv, the king made an offering of two choral caps of velvet, intended for the singers in serving God and St. David; and he also offered a handful of silver, about ten shillings.' Cf. *Annales Cambriae*, s.a. 1172, ed. Williams ab Ithel, p. 53: *ad visitandum Sanctum David*.

13 *Annales Cambriae*, s.a. 1173, ed. Williams ab Ithel, p. 54.

14 From 1284, abbot of Gloucester.

15 *Historia et cartularium monasterii Sancti Petri Gloucestrie*, Rolls Series, ed. W. H. Hart, 3 vols (London, 1863–7), vol. i, pp. 39–40.

16 *Annales Cambriae*, s.a. 1274, ed. Williams ab Ithel, p. 104; quoting from MS Domitian A.1: *Inceptum fuit feretrum beati Davidi in ecclesia Menevensi*.

17 *Annales Cambriae*, s.a. 1284, ed. Williams ab Ithel, p. 109: *causa peregrinationis*.

18 Cowley, 'Relics', pp. 278–9 and references therein cited.

19 J. W. Willis-Bund (ed.), *An Extent of all the Lands and Rents of the Lord Bishop of St David's . . . usually called the Black Book of St David's* (London, 1902), pp. 51, 67, 125, 161: *Item dicunt quod tempore guerrae sequi debent dominum episcopum cum feretro beati Dauid et cum reliquiis ex utraque parte, ita quod illa nocte redire possint domi*.

20 Browne Willis, *A Survey of the Cathedral Church of St. David's and the Edifices belonging to it, as they stood in the year 1715. To which is added, Some Memoirs relating thereto and the Country adjacent, from a MS wrote about the latter End of Queen Elizabeth's Reign . . .* (London, 1717). In his preface Willis confesses, 'I fear the Gentlemen of *Wales* will pronounce me a very unfit and improper Person to engage in this Task, by Reason I have never been at *St. David's*'. His achievement recalls that of his namesake, Robert Willis, who more than a century later wrote a classic description of the church of the Holy Sepulchre, Jerusalem, relying entirely on information and drawings posted to him.

21 In Willis's own copy of his *Survey* he has written 'William Wotton' at the end of 'M.N.'s' Memoir: Bodleian Library Oxford, MS Willis 108, p. 90. Wotton is further identified elsewhere in Willis's papers (e.g. MS Willis 37, fo. 12, where correspondence is identified as 'Letters from Will: Wotton Esq who then absented himself out of Bucks & lived in Wales at Carmarthen with Mr Lord & took the name of Dr Edwards.'). Amongst other alleged vices,

Wotton had a drink problem and was heavily in debt; he took refuge at Caernarvon in 1714. See David Stoker, 'William Wotton's exile and redemption: an account of the genesis and publication of Leges Wallicae', *Y Llyfr yng Nghymru/Welsh Book Studies*, 7 (2006), pp. 7–106.

[22] Browne Willis, *Survey*, p. 13.

[23] Browne Willis, *Survey*, p. 69.

[24] E. Yardley, *Menevia Sacra*, ed. F. Green (London, 1927).

[25] Wyn Evans, *pers. comm.*

[26] Richard Fenton, *A Historical Tour through Pembrokeshire* (London, 1811), p. 79.

[27] Fenton, *A Historical Tour*, p. 87.

[28] As observed by W. B. Jones and E. A. Freeman, *The History and Antiquities of St David's* (London, 1856), p. 69, note 'h' (added whilst the book was in press); and by G. G. Scott, *Report made by Order of the Dean and Chapter on the state of the fabric of St. David's Cathedral* (Tenby, 1862), p. 20. Scott considered this new roof 'homely' and intended rebuilding it.

[29] Jones and Freeman, *The History and Antiquities*, pp. 102–3.

[30] Browne Willis, *Survey*, p. 16.

[31] The bones discovered in 1866 in a niche behind the high altar, where they remained in a modern reliquary casket until 2012 when the casket were placed in the central niche of the shrine, are emphatically not those of the saint, having been radiocarbon dated to the eleventh and twelfth centuries: T. F. G. Higham, C. B. Ramsey, and L. D. M. Nokes, 'AMD Radiocarbon Dating of Bones from St Davids Cathedral', in Evans and Wooding, *St David of Wales*, pp. 282–5.

[32] Browne Willis, *Survey*, p. 16.

[33] Giraldus Cambrensis, *De Jure et Statu Menevensis Ecclesiae*, Dictinctio II, in J. S. Brewer *et al.* (eds), *Giraldi Cambrensis opera*, Rolls Series, 8 vols (1861–91), vol. iii, pp. 101–404: 182–3. Gerald's Life of St Caradoc has disappeared (*ibid.*, preface, p. xlv), though the short account in John of Tynemouth's *Nova Legenda Anglie* may be a redaction of it: see Francesco Marzella, 'Gerald of Wales and the Life of St Caradog', in D. Parsons and P. Russell (eds), *Seintiau Cymru/Sancti Cambrenses: Studies in the Saints of Wales* (Aberystwyth, 2022), pp. 299–316.

[34] *pace* Cowley, 'The Relics', in Evans and Wooding, *St David of Wales*, pp. 274–81: 277.

[35] T. Wright (ed.), *Three Chapters of Letters relating to the Suppression of Monasteries*, Camden Society 26 (1843), pp. 207–8; letter 101, dated 16 Aug 1538.

[36] Wright, *Three Chapters of Letters*, p. 184; letter 93, dated 31 March 1538.

[37] J. Gairdner and R. H. Brodie (eds), *Letters and Papers, Foreign and Domestic*, Vol. XVI, ed. (HMSO, 1898), item 87.

[38] Gairdner and Brodie, *Letters and Papers, Foreign and Domestic*, Vol. XIX, pt. ii (HMSO, 1880), item 87.

[39] Gairdner and Brodie, *Letters and Papers, Foreign and Domestic*, Vol. XXI, pt. I (HMSO, 1908), item 1536; cf. Gairdner and Brodie, *Letters and Papers, Foreign and Domestic*, Vol. XXI, pt. ii (HMSO, 1910), item 775, recording the same compensation.

6.
FROM NASH TO SCOTT: THE MAINTENANCE OF THE FABRIC AND WORSHIP OF ST DAVIDS CATHEDRAL 1793–1862

Nigel Yates[†]

In its response to the visitation queries of Bishop Thomas Burgess in 1811 the chapter of St David's cathedral was very clear about the causes of the cathedral's decayed state and the problems which it faced in relation to the maintenance of the fabric:

> The North and South Aisles of the Chancel and Saint Mary's Chapel appear to have been stripped of the lead belonging to their roofs about the time of the Great Rebellion since which they have gradually fallen to decay. The roof of Saint Mary's Chapel was the last which remained and that fell down about the year 1775.[1]

The act of vandalism which had led to this state of affairs had taken place in 1648, at which time the lead was also removed from the roofs of both transepts. These were, however, re-leaded in 1696.[2] The precarious state of the rest of the fabric was such that there was a real danger that the nave would collapse and the cathedral fall into the sort of ruin that happened at Llandaff. Here the nave had become a complete ruin by the early eighteenth century and John Wood of Bath was commissioned to design what was described by contemporaries as a 'neat new conventicle' within the outer walls of the choir and the four eastern bays of the nave between 1734 and 1752.[3]

In 1791–3 the first major restoration of St Davids cathedral took place. John Nash (1752–1835), then operating from an architectural practice

---

† Nigel Yates died on 15 January 2009.

https://doi.org/10.16922/jrhlc.9.2.6

in Carmarthen, was employed to carry out this task. Nash's work was much criticised by later antiquarians and ecclesiologists:

> The west front is modern, in what would have been called the worst form of modern-antique, had not that of Hereford exhibited an example of a still lower depth.[4]

Hereford's west front was, of course, almost contemporary with that of St Davids, having been designed by James Wyatt following the collapse of the cathedral's western towers in 1786.[5] Contemporaries, however, were nothing like as critical. In the decade following Nash's restoration, St Davids Cathedral was complimented not just for the condition of its fabric but also for the quality of its worship:

> The whole cathedral church is in most excellent repair and its present neat appearance is attributed to the liberal attention of the chapter, who have vested the direction of the same in the present residentiary; knowing the rectitude of his heart to fill, conscientiously, and with dignity, the duties of his station . . . The great degree of attention paid to, and decorum observed in the service of this church, though in this remote corner of the Kingdom, where there are few to witness it, have been often acknowledged, and might put some of the proudest choirs to blush! There is one part of the service cannot be passed by in silence – the Responses to the Litany; which has a most pleasing, plaintive, and solemn effect; inspiring awe, and infusing the purest sensations of morality and religion.[6]

Doubts about the cathedral's architecture were, however, beginning to be expressed before 1820:

> In visiting this cathedral the mind is prepared, by the aspect of its desolate situation and miserable neighbourhood, by reflections on its antiquity and early dignity, to be satisfied with an edifice even of less pretensions; and forgetting the heterogeneous character of its western part, with some other discordances, it will rest with pleasure on the solemnity and massive grandeur of the nave, and be delighted with the lighter beauties of Trinity Chapel, the roodloft etc.[7]

Forty years later they were being expressed in much more open and vitriolic terms: 'there has been nothing to deserve the name of a restoration, nothing done with any ulterior view than that of rescuing the building from future ruin'. The blame for this was firmly placed on 'the general neglect of residence on the part of the so-called residentiaries, to which more than any other cause the cathedral owes its decay'.[8]

Such views, however, reflect more the spirit and prejudice of the age than actual reality and are an unfortunate slur on a chapter that was, with extremely limited finances, doing the best it could to maintain the functioning parts of the cathedral in a decent state of repair and which simply did not have the resources to rebuild those parts of the building which had fallen into ruin. It was unfortunate that the poorest Welsh diocese and cathedral chapter had by far the largest, and architecturally the most important, cathedral to maintain. Although Nash's restoration was condemned as tasteless, the evidence of the chapter minutes shows very clearly that it had been carried out following considerable debate and consultation. At the July Chapter in 1793 it had been:

> ordered that when the Drawings of the Intended Alterations in the Church are completed, that Mr Nash lay the same before the Society of Antiquaries, accompanied with a letter from the Master of the ffabric in the name of the Chantor and Chapter requesting their patronage in promoting the subscription for the purpose ... that Mr Nash be at liberty to show the Drawings to any persons he may think proper, and to any persons that either of the Members of the Chapter may direct ... that as soon as Mr Nash's estimate is received and the expenses of the past and intended repairs can be carefully ascertained that the Master of the Fabric make out an account of the same to be printed and delivers to each subscriber accompanied with a letter expressive of the Thanks of the Chapter for their kind Liberality and Solliciting their Interest with their friends to forward the accomplishing the design.[9]

The chapter records also make clear that the maintenance of the fabric and high standards of public worship were a priority for the chapter between the completion of Nash's restoration and the major restoration of the cathedral following the publication of Sir George Gilbert Scott's report in 1862.

At Bishop Burgess's visitation of the cathedral in 1811 the chapter reported that:

> the Chancel, the Nave and the Aisles of the Cathedral Church are in good and sufficient repair. That the Nave is entirely new flagged. That the walls of the Chancel and Nave are kept perfectly free from the green and the discolouring of wet and damp excepting the Altar Piece which the Canons are desirous of taking measures to remedy, if any proper method can be pointed out.[10]

The eastern part of the nave was fitted up with pulpit, reading desk and box pews for the parochial service in Welsh, and there was also a pulpit in the choir for preaching at the choral services in English.[11] However, by 1816, it was clear that Nash's rebuilding of the east front of the cathedral had not resolved the long-term problems of the fabric. A letter to the Master of the Fabric, Canon Payne, on 29 July 1816, recorded that:

> last week I happened to be at St David's. I saw the west end of the Cathedral much impaired by the weather; the stones seemed to be mouldering away; I made some enquiry there and was told that they thought it was to be repaired soon.[12]

The admission of Richard Richardson to the precentorship of the cathedral in June 1816 was to herald the start of a major effort to improve both the fabric and the services. One of his first priorities was the purchase of a new set of communion plate and ornaments for the altar, including a pair of candlesticks which cost £93 16s and a three-volume edition of the Bible, to be placed on the altar, which cost £88. When Richardson requested his fellow prebendaries to subscribe to this purchase, several voiced their objections to such large sums having been spent without previous authorisation by the whole chapter. Certainly there is no note of the purchase having been authorised in the Chapter Act Book and it must be assumed that Richardson had acted on his own initiative. Although some of the prebendaries contributed willingly, and others did so under protest, Richardson was obliged to cover the deficit of £26 10s himself.[13]

Richardson also took action to secure the fabric of the cathedral against further deterioration. On 8 July 1818 he was able to report that:

the roof of the Chapter-house . . . has been put, as I am informed, into a state of perfect security . . . It being observed at the last audit that there was a deficiency of cushions for the stalls, I have caused the want to be supplied . . . There was a very great want of accommodation both for the wives of the Canons, and other females connected with the establishment, which caused them to sit either in the Throne or the stalls, a practice highly indecorous and utterly unknown to any other Choir in the realm. To obviate a continuance of this novel practice, I have caused two Pews to be erected in a vacant spot in the Choir, for the decent accommodation of the parties to whom they are respectively appropriated . . . The space between the Pulpit and the Throne has been considerably enlarged by the removal of the pulpit to the north . . . The Pulpit, which was in great danger of being overset by the Preacher, has been completely repaired and rendered secure from any such apprehended disaster.

Richardson did, however, point out that a remaining requirement was 'a new Cloth for the Communion Table . . . the present one being very old and much worn'.[14]

At the annual meeting of the cathedral chapter in July 1820 it was:

ordered that the 2 seats now erected behind that appropriated to the families of the Canons be assigned to the use of the families of the Vicars and that a new seat be erected for the servants of the Canons.[15]

Three years later Canon Payne, who apologised for his non-attendance at the annual chapter meeting on account of his wife's serious illness, drew the attention of his fellow prebendaries to:

the East End of the Chancel of the Cathedral, which appears to me to be in a dangerous state, and also to the West Window over the door of the entrance into the nave, and to the roof of the chapter house.[16]

Four years later, in 1827, it was agreed to abandon the chapter house and convert St Thomas's chapel, on the east side of the north transept, into a new chapter room, though the actual work was not carried out until a year later. Part of the improvements included the purchase of 'a cast iron stove . . . for the proper airing' of the new chapter room. At the same time a small part of the ruinous north choir aisle was blocked off and roofed over to serve as a passageway from the choir to the new chapter room.[17] At the same time major repairs were carried out to the other roofs of the cathedral which Archdeacon Davies had reported his concerns about.[18] Further repairs were ordered to be carried out to the roofs of the south aisle and south transept in 1834.[19]

One of the major problems faced by nearly all English and Welsh cathedrals in the early nineteenth century was the cost of maintaining their choral establishments and the difficulties they faced in recruiting adequate personnel for the choir and of ensuring their attendance at the required number of choral services.[20] St Davids Cathedral was no exception; indeed its isolated location, and the fact that it was a parish church as well as a cathedral – a situation repeated in Wales at Bangor and Llandaff though not at St Asaph – made its situation particularly difficult. In 1825 the chapter had ordered that the

> gift of six Guineas to the Lay Vicars formerly given to them for Anthem Singing on Sundays be withdrawn no anthem having been sung for the last two years. And that the Organist be admonished to pay more attention to the instruction of the Choir than he has latterly done.[21]

Things had clearly not improved much by 1841 when 'the Dean was authorized to speak to the Lord Bishop of this diocese on the subject of reducing the services in the Cathedral'.[22] There were two choral services on Sundays,[23] in addition to the non-choral parochial service in Welsh, but the number of weekday choral services was considerably lower than that at most English cathedrals. Some improvements in the choir had been achieved by 1853 when the organist, W. P. Propert, reported to Dean Lewellin that in the previous year

> seventeen Anthems have been learnt . . . and committed to memory, together with fifty chants, and sixteen psalm tunes. The rudiments of music have not been neglected, and every boy is able, in some degree to read, or to find great assistance from, written music . . . The present number of adult voices is inadequate to the performance

of ordinary Cathedral Music. I propose, therefore, that three more be added . . . For forty five or fifty pounds I could get three voices for the year.[24]

The improvements do not appear to have been very long-lasting. In 1858 it was ordered that

> the Organist and the other Lay Vicars do attend the Service regularly every Wednesday and Friday morning and on Saturday evening; that the Choir Service be performed on these occasions; and that the Organist perform his duties in person, and not by Deputy, except after special leave given by the Dean or Senior Canon in residence . . . that the Organist and Lay Vicars attend the services regularly on all Saints' Days, when Choir Service must be performed.[25]

The order seems to have had little effect. In both 1861 and 1862 the organist was once again accused of 'neglect of duty'.[26]

In 1844 an attempt was made to improve the setting for the parochial service, previously conducted at the east end of the nave. The south transept

> was fitted up for the parochial service . . . and an altar placed at the south end . . . At the same time a pulpit was inserted in the splay of the west window, a plan of which one cannot help praising the ingenuity, whatever may be said of the taste: a staircase leading to it was constructed in the thickness of the wall.[27]

This was the start of a whole series of improvements to the building. In 1845 repairs to the roof and windows of the north transept were authorised; repairs to the roof of the north aisle, the insertion of a new window at its west end, and a new chest for the chapter room were approved in 1847; in 1848 order was given 'that a new Communion Rail be erected, and the Western Door of the Cathedral repaired'; in 1850 it was agreed that two more windows in the north aisle should be repaired and a new stove purchased for the chapter room.[28] Between 1846 and 1849 the rood-screen was restored and new tracery provided for some of the previously blocked windows under the overall direction of the distinguished architect, William Butterfield.[29] In the rows that later took place over the restoration of the cathedral under another distinguished architect,

George Gilbert Scott, this extensive work in the 1840s was conveniently forgotten and Dean Lewellin unfairly criticised for presiding over two decades of neglect.

At the annual chapter meeting in July 1856 it was 'ordered and decreed that Mr Richard Kyrke Penson be appointed consulting architect of this Cathedral Church'.[30] It is an intriguing resolution since there is no evidence that Penson ever carried out any work on the cathedral. He had been responsible for several new churches or church restorations in the diocese including four in Pembrokeshire: Amroth (1855), Angle (1856), St Petrox (1855) and Walton West (1854).[31] However, it is clear that by this time there was much division in the chapter over the restoration of the cathedral and it must be assumed that a vociferous minority simply thought that Penson was not up to the task required. The catalyst for the appointment of another architect was a letter from Bishop Connop Thirlwall, laid before the annual chapter meeting in July 1861.

> It appears to me that the time has come when the Chapter, as the official Guardians and Trustees of this venerable national monument, are bound to take steps for ascertaining its condition with regard to the repairs which may be needed, to secure it from serious danger. I think this could have been the case independently of any ulterior object. But it seems to me that such an investigation is the more urgently required in consequence of Mr Treharne's legacy, which may be expected to be placed before long at the disposal of the Chapter. I shall be deeply grieved and disappointed if that bequest is not applied to the restoration of some portion of the building, which may be a permanent monument to the donor's liberality. But it would be manifestly improper to determine its destination until all doubts are removed as to the general stability of the fabric. I therefore trust that the Chapter . . . will resolve to employ a competent professional man, thoroughly to examine the whole, and make a full report of it.

As a result the chapter resolved to appoint George Gilbert Scott to carry out 'a proper survey . . . without delay'.[32]

Although Scott (1811–78) was to become, over the next two decades, the restorer of many English and Welsh cathedrals, including those of Bangor and St Asaph, and to be knighted for his services to church architecture, he was at that time a more unknown quantity, having only been responsible, in respect of cathedral commissions, for the restorations at Ely from 1847 and Gloucester from 1857.[33] He immediately accepted this new commission, commenting that he was currently engaged on the restoration of Brecon Priory Church and would make his usual charge of five guineas a day plus expenses.[34] His eventual report, particularly his concerns about the safety of the central tower, did not make pleasant reading. He noted that after the Reformation all building developments belonged

> rather to the history of its degradation than to its construction, . . . consisting mainly of the lapse of certain parts into a state of ruin, the clumsy reparation of other parts, and alterations for modern convenience carried out without taste or feeling . . . [and] without that knowledge of the character of the building, which . . . satisfactory execution demanded . . . The walls, pillars and floor of the Nave are in a terrible state from damp . . . As to the floor, it must be wholly relaid with better material laid hollow upon a stratum of concrete . . . The South Transept has been much disfigured by being converted into a separate church . . . The South Aisle of the Choir is partly a ruin . . . It must be brought back to its ancient form, re-roofed and restored . . . The miserable pews, which now disgrace the choir, must, of course, be done away with, and any seats which may be necessary, in addition to the stalls must be of a very light and moveable character, showing plainly that they are introduced from necessity alone, and not as a permanent portion of the arrangement . . . the fittings of the part allotted to the Welch Services must be new, and of appropriate character and arrangement.

Scott described the Lady chapel as 'having been long in a state of unmitigated ruin' and pointed out that the installation of proper heating and lighting were essential to counteract the prevailing dampness of the building.[35]

An extraordinary meeting of the cathedral chapter was called for 20 February 1862 to discuss Scott's report. It was agreed that the report should be printed at the chapter's expense and that an application should be made 'to the Exchequer Loan Commissioners for the amount and the terms in which they would advance a sum of money . . . on security of the tithes of Uzmaston and Knelston'. The chapter also agreed to send a copy of Scott's report to the Ecclesiastical Commission with a request

103

for financial assistance. It was clear from a further letter from Bishop Thirlwall that there were strong episcopal concerns that the Chapter was simply not competent to deal with the seriousness and urgency of the situation.

> If they were able without assistance from without to provide for that which is absolutely necessary it would rest simply with themselves, whether they chose to attempt anything more. But if they are obliged to appeal to the public, they must consider what is to be the object for which the appeal is to be made. If it were not to go beyond the indispensable repairs . . . I doubt very much whether they will find a general readiness to relieve them from what many will consider as a mere duty incumbent upon them, and I think it very questionable whether Mr Treharne would or ought to consent to such an appropriation of the £2000, as I feel sure that if the Testator was now living, he would not have given it without a clear prospect of its being applied to a much more extensive restoration.[36]

It is clear that opinion within the cathedral chapter was firmly polarised between those who agreed with the bishop and those who despaired of even being able to raise the money for essential repairs, such as securing the central tower. A letter from the bishop's chaplain expresses the concern that divisions within the chapter will delay the implementation of any restoration programme; Scott's 'report on the condition of the Tower is very alarming, and it will require much skill and no small degree of courage to commence the formidable work which he so able describes as necessary'. Neither Dean Lewellin nor Prebendary George Harries appeared to have the necessary courage; the latter wrote 'I have only to wish we had the means of accomplishing all he suggests. In my opinion it is quite a hopeless affair'.[37]

It was at this point that the attacks on Dean Lewellin began in earnest. Prebendary Sir E. N. G. Williams expressed the view that 'the Dean had better die, then he will be spared the bitterness of rebuilding which he has done his best to destroy' but it was clear from his later remark that if St David's College, Lampeter, of which Dean Lewellin was the principal, 'was swallowed up whole, there would be no loss to old Cambria',[38] that other issues were the real cause of Lewellin's unpopularity. It was perhaps unfortunate for Lewellin that the cathedral's crisis should have occurred at the same time that his own vice-principal, Rowland Williams, was being prosecuted for heresy for his contribution to *Essays and Reviews*, and the view was being widely circulated within the diocese that Lewellin had presided over an institution which promoted unorthodox theology in its students, who would pass on such opinions to their future parishioners. Since the majority of Lampeter ordinands were licensed to curacies in the diocese of St Davids this was clearly a matter of concern to many of the local clergy who were prebendaries of the cathedral. Lewellin called another extraordinary meeting of the cathedral chapter for 10 April 1862. There were present the dean and three of the four residentiary prebendaries: William Richardson, W. H. Thomas and Sir E. N. G. Williams; the fourth, George Harries, was represented by proxy. The meeting was subsequently described as a farce by Williams: 'what was done was nothing and we ought to have another meeting'. There was a further attack on Lewellin.

> It is quite wrong that the Dean, 70 miles absent, and so little here, should take upon himself to order the Service to the great disgust of the Resident Canons. It is truly unworthy of any Cathedral.

The meeting appears to have done no more than authorise the setting up of a restoration fund and it was followed immediately by an appeal from the Chapter Clerk to all members of the cathedral establishment to 'advance any and what sum to enable them to make certain repairs to the Cathedral Church of St David's now in a sad state of decay'.[39]

Lewellin refused to call another meeting and expressed the view that, without a favourable response from the Ecclesiastical Commission, it would be impossible to undertake even the most essential repairs. At exactly the same time the Chapter Clerk was informed that Scott's report had been tabled at the Ecclesiastical Commissioners' meeting on 27 March 1862, but that no further action had been taken.[40] Lewellin's response was, perhaps predictably, rather negative.

> We appear now to be at a dead stand. What is next to be done, I know not. Talk and brag and grand words won't do. Under the circumstances it seems to me advisable to send the Bishop a copy of the substance of the replies ... from the Ecclesiastical Commissioners and the Loan Office. It will at least show him what we have tried to do, and may perhaps induce him to press the matter upon the attention of the Commissioners.[41]

The response from Prebendary Williams was equally predictable.

> It is uncourteous – stronger adjectives might be used – to Mr R[ichardson] and myself, two of the Chapter who wish the work to go on, not to call a Chapter, to say nothing of the Breach of Word. I have no intercourse with Thomas, or I should write to him to join with Mr R and myself to compel the Dean to call a Chapter . . . The Dean will have the finger of scorn pointed at him by the Public if he jibs any more . . . This cursed love of money is the bane of all righteousness, and the Dean has it in perfection. Between ourselves R thinks nothing will be done unless the Bishop visits the Chapter. It really is quite horrible . . . The Dean's reluctance to move at all, after the many thousands he has drawn from this cathedral. There was an epitaph on a person in these words
>
> > 'Whether he lives, or whether he dies
> > Nobody laughs and nobody cries
> > When he is gone and how he fares
> > Nobody knows and nobody cares'.
>
> It is not inappropriate to another who shall be nameless . . . We are a shabby lot.[42]

Despite these serious divisions within the cathedral chapter, the annual meeting in July 1862 did agree to launch a cathedral Restoration Fund and the chapter also agreed to donate a thousand pounds towards it.[43] The long restoration programme begun by George Gilbert Scott had made a modest beginning.

Whilst a number of contemporaries were highly critical of the slowness and lack of enthusiasm with which the St Davids cathedral chapter approached the matter of the cathedral's restoration, it is important that this should be set in context. Among the Welsh cathedrals only Llandaff, in a state of much greater ruin than St Davids, had begun its Victorian restoration earlier, in 1841, initially under T. H. Wyatt, and from 1843 under a young local architect and son of one of the vicars-choral, John Prichard, and the whole programme of restoration was not completed until 1869.[44] In England the process of cathedral restoration was extremely slow: one of the first cathedrals to begin a restoration programme was Ely, from 1843, with Scott taking over supervision of this programme four years later, but the situation in others was as bad as that at St Davids. The restoration of Lincoln cathedral did not begin until the 1870s and the choir of Norwich cathedral was described as being 'in a deplorable condition' with blocked windows and flaking plaster as late as the 1890s. Partly this was the result of cathedrals having no proper relationship with the dioceses in which they were situated. It was not until well into the second half of the nineteenth century that a determined and eventually successful campaign was waged to make cathedrals venues for major diocesan services and to open them to the ordinary worshipper, as distinct from the families and servants of the residentiary canons, and to the growing number of potential tourists.[45]

We also have to treat with caution the particular criticisms of Dean Lewellin. Part of the problem was that Lewellin was seen as a representative of the pre-reform established church, a pluralist who drew income from three positions: dean of St Davids, vicar of Lampeter and principal of St David's College. By the 1850s the established church in Wales was trying to rescue itself from the allegations made against it by nonconformists. Many of these allegations, especially in relation to the wealth of the church and its clergy, and the evils of pluralism, were at best exaggerated and at worst spurious.[46] They were, however, widely believed and those like Lewellin, who appeared to lend them credence, were much despised and regretted by the younger clergy. Lewellin's position was not helped by the belief that his vice-principal was inculcating heresy among the students at St David's College, or the charges made against the college that its curriculum was old-fashioned and not suited to the new attitudes towards ministerial training being promoted at the newly-established theological colleges in England at Chichester, Cuddesdon, Salisbury and Wells.[47] Lewellin's problems were, one suspects, more a case of being in the wrong place at the wrong time, rather than being actually guilty of some of the charges made against him.

Looked at in the wider perspective of British cathedral history, the condition of St Davids cathedral before Scott's restoration was very much in line with that of most other English and Welsh cathedrals at the time. In the early years of the nineteenth century they were seen by many as something of an anachronism, a survival of the pre-Reformation church, large buildings whose sole function was the saying or singing of Morning and Evening Prayer every day by a handful of residentiary canons and other members of the cathedral establishment and, except where they were also parish churches, frequently minute congregations even on Sundays and festivals. The big question for the reformers of the established church was what were cathedrals for? The answer was eventually discovered in the later nineteenth century when, led by St Paul's in London, they began to become spiritual centres for their respective dioceses and major players in the growing tourism industry. But that was not their function before 1860, in St Davids or anywhere else.

Notes

[1] National Library of Wales (hereafter NLW), SDCh/8/8 (Chapter Act Book 1768–1829), p. 349.
[2] T. Lloyd, J. Orbach and R. Scourfield, *Pembrokeshire*, The Buildings of Wales (New Haven CT and London, 2004), p. 389.
[3] J. Newman, *Glamorgan*, The Buildings of Wales (London, 1995), p. 240.
[4] W. B. Jones and E. A. Freeman, *The History and Antiquities of Saint David's* (London, 1856), p. 52.
[5] N. Pevsner, *Herefordshire*, The Buildings of England (Harmondsworth, 1963), p. 146.
[6] G. W. Manby, *The History and Antiquities of the Parish of St. David* (London, 1801), pp. 40–1.
[7] J. Storer, *History and Antiquities of the Cathedral Church of St. David's* (London, 1817), p. 16.
[8] Jones and Freeman, *The History and Antiquities*, pp. 177, 355.
[9] NLW, SDCh/B/8, pp. 199–200.
[10] NLW, SDCh/B/8, p. 347.
[11] Engravings of both in Storer, *History and Antiquities*.
[12] NLW, SDCh/LET/117.
[13] NLW, SDCh/Misc/90 and SDCh/LET/171–185.
[14] NLW, SDCH/LET/150.
[15] NLW, SDCh/B/8, p. 457.
[16] NLW, SDCh/LET/189. This letter also records that Payne had 'subscribed £5 5s 0d to the plate procured by the Precentor'.
[17] NLW, SDCh/B/8, pp. 518, 531–2; Jones and Freeman, *The History and Antiquities*, p. 177.
[18] NLW, SDCh/LET/219–220 and 224–7.
[19] NLW SDCh/B/10 (Chapter Act Book 1830–79), p. 39.
[20] See P. Barratt, *Barchester: English Cathedral Life in the Nineteenth Century* (London, 1993), pp. 166–75.
[21] NLW, SDCh/B/8, p. 495.
[22] NLW, SDCh/B/10, p. 103.
[23] Barrett, *Barchester*, p. 115.
[24] NLW, SDCh/LET/320.
[25] NLW, SDCh/A/8081.
[26] NLW, SDCh/B/10, New Book, pp. 97, 105.
[27] Jones and Freeman, *The History and Antiquities*, p. 98.
[28] National Library of Wales, SDCh/B/10, pp. 135, 139, 144, New Book, p. 10.
[29] Jones and Freeman, *The History and Antiquities*, p. 178.
[30] National Library of Wales, SDCh/B/10, New Book, p. 60.
[31] Lloyd, Orbach and Scourfield, *Pembrokeshire*, pp. 121, 123, 446, 492.

From Nash to Scott: The Maintenance of the Fabric and Worship

[32] NLW, SDCh/B/10, New Book, pp. 96–7.
[33] A. S. B. New, *A Guide to the Cathedrals of Britain* (London, 1980), pp. 149, 221.
[34] NLW, SDCh/LET/413.
[35] G. G. Scott, *Report on the State of the Fabric of St. David's Cathedral* (London, 1862), pp. 8–9, 18–21, 23, 27, 32.
[36] NLW, SDCh/B/10, New Book, p. 99.
[37] NLW, SDCh/LET/420–422.
[38] NLW, SDCh/LET/424.
[39] NLW, SDCh/LET/425–427; SDCh/A/92.
[40] NLW, SDCh/LET/428–429.
[41] NLW, SDCh/LET/430.
[42] NLW, SDCh/LET/431.
[43] NLW, SDCh/B/10, New Book, p. 105.
[44] Newman, *Glamorgan*, pp. 240–1.
[45] Barrett, *Barchester*, pp. 233, 242, 252–71.
[46] See especially A. J. Johnes, *An Essay on the Causes which have produced Dissent from the Established Church in the Principality of Wales: to which the Royal Medal was awarded at an Eisteddfod of the London Cambrian Institution, held in May 1831* (London, 1835).
[47] See D. T. W. Price, *Bishop Burgess and Lampeter College* (Cardiff 1987), pp. 67–9; W. M. Jacob, 'The Diffusion of Tractarianism: Wells Theological College, 1840–49', *Southern History*, 5 (1983), pp. 189–209.

7.
LLEWELYN LEWELLIN AND THE CONDITION OF ST DAVIDS[1]

J. Wyn Evans

Barchester had Anthony Trollope. St Davids had 'Peter Pipps'. Although the well-known novelist and the anonymous pamphleteer were poles apart in attitude and culture, nevertheless they were both in their different ways highlighting problems facing the Church of England in general and cathedrals in particular during the first half of the nineteenth century. Trollope, as far as is known, did not visit and was not aware of the troubles affecting St Davids Cathedral in the 1840s;[2] nor did he begin writing *The Warden* until July 1853;[3] nor was the book published until 1855. In both the imaginary Barchester and the real St Davids, however, the Cathedral and its clergy were attempting to cope with problems brought about by the ecclesiastical legislation of the 1840s. The tale, related in this article, about the quarrel between the Schoolmaster and the Dean at St Davids is quite as dramatic as any told by Trollope. It sheds light on the complicated circumstances underlying the restorations of the Cathedral fabric in the nineteenth century. The readers of the *Pembrokeshire Herald* during July and August 1853 were to gain a close acquaintance of how that collision was affecting St Davids Cathedral and its clergy.

The 1 July issue of *The Pembrokeshire Herald*, under the heading *Cathedral Trusts*, advertised the publication of the first of five pamphlets:

> this day, price sixpence of *Notes on The Cathedral Church of St David's* by Nathaniel Davies MA of Pembroke College, Oxford, Prebendary and Minor Canon of the Cathedral and Master of the Chapter School, of St David's.[4]

Dean Lewellin responded with four pamphlets and a 'Peter Pipps' offered a riposte to Davies and the Dean. The cast of characters – pamphleteers

https://doi.org/10.16922/jrhlc.9.2.7

and correspondents both – is every bit as entertaining as any in Trollope's novels. The *dramatis personae* ranged from the Bishop,[5] the Dean,[6] through the Canon Treasurer,[7] the Subchanter,[8] the Bishop's Vicar,[9] the Junior Minor Canon, as he styled himself,[10] and to Ebenezer Williams (who, or someone close to him, may have been the pseudonymous 'Pipps').[11] Pipps does not seem to have had any direct involvement with St Davids Cathedral, but took a close interest in the doings in the Cathedral close and was well informed about church – and Dissenting – life at St Davids Cathedral and the surrounding parish. He commented pungently and with little sympathy for the sensitivities of personalities caught up in the situation. It is Pipps, however, who not only removes the whole exchange into another sphere, but goes to the heart of the matter.

Notes is twenty-eight pages long. Within that compass, Davies raises several *gravamina*, directly or indirectly relating to the school. His focus is, as would be expected from the Master, on the school and the difference of opinion about the funding and status of the school between him and Dean Lewellin. A study of the School and the problems affecting it and its Master, brings into sharp focus the problems facing the Anglican Church in England and Wales in the 1850s. Davies was well aware of the wider implications of his campaign, and the issues – the abuses as he saw them – which lay behind it, hence his stated desire to lay the matter before 'the Imperial Parliament'. The peroration of *Notes* reveals the breadth of his concerns on p. 19:

> yet still nothing is done by the Dean and Chapter to mitigate such abuses. They go on in their old course, refuse redress, and calculate upon the poverty of the Master and the Scholars ... Can the Church flourish when such things go on, and there is no one found to effect a reform of such crying evils as are to be found at St David's? A splendidly endowed cathedral with a gross Corporate Revenue of £6,000, besides the separate Income of the various members, yet the Canons for years non-resident, and grudging payment to those who have done their duties; – a magnificent pile of building, the glory and the ornament of the place, fast falling into ruins, yet an annual revenue of above £200 appropriated to its repairs, by our pious ancestors; –

At first sight, the dashes separating each assertion give the impression that this is an inchoate scattergun rant. Closer examination, however, reveals that Davies had constructed a coherent argument, buttressed by statistics and historical evidence together with calculations as to what current income should be. His case revolved around his discovery that there was property specifically set aside for the support of the school with the entry fines on the renewal of leases being been 'almost entirely swallowed up' into the general fund of Dean and Chapter – 'their corporate revenue'. Their diversion of funds towards themselves was causing damage to other areas of Cathedral life, literally in the case of the fabric of the Cathedral and the city walls, which were in a parlous state. This unacceptable state of affairs was due not only to their greed, but to their pluralism and non-residence.

It was the School and its perceived problems, however, which furnished the *casus belli* – and the impression given by the four pamphlets is that this was open warfare between Master and Dean. The issue threw light on larger perspectives, masked both by personal animus and locality. The state not just of Menevia but of the church to which both Cathedral and diocese belonged was implicitly but vividly illuminated. The problems facing the School had exercised Davies over the previous eleven years. He was implicitly blaming the Cathedral and in particular, the Dean for the unfavourable circumstances in which School, Choristers and Master found themselves in 1853. The Master's grievances about the condition of the school are summed up, thus: 'a School, endowed by pious Bishops of the See, with an *apparent* revenue of £182 . . . receiving with the Bishop's Vicar, only £41 per annum'.

Davies draws his readers' attention to evidence he had discovered about churches appropriated several centuries before, which, in his view had been and still were unambiguously specific endowments of the school and its Master, and not of the Cathedral. He traced the genesis of the school to its foundation, or re-foundation by Adam Houghton, bishop of St Davids between 1361 and 1389.[12] He seems to have had access to a copy of MS Harley 6280, folio 133.[13] His case is based on the Statute of Houghton. He concluded that the church of Silian, held in plurality with Llanwnnen, was part of the endowment but directed towards the stipend of the Master rather than the support of the Choristers. Davies had discovered all this after his appointment to the post as Master on 25 July 1840.[14] He was informed in 1841 that the tithes of Llanwnnen, worth £100 per annum, belonged specifically to the School and also that certain lands and houses in the parish of St Davids were the property of the Choristers, but that they were let at very small rents. His discovery prompted Davies to present a Memorial to the Dean and Chapter at their Annual Meeting in July 1842, laying the matter before them; drawing to their attention that Master and Scholars together were getting less than the salary of a Master of a National School who was earning about £40 a year; and requesting that a committee be called to look into the matter. Davies was astounded by the discovery that in 1849 the leases had been renewed on the same terms. As his figures show, he considered that the School and the Master should be in receipt of £182.13.6, rather than the £41 that he and the Bishop's Vicar and the Choristers were actually receiving. For Davies this was a result of mismanagement – 'grosser mismanagement than that of Rochester School'.[15] He got no answer from the Dean, but nothing daunted, he presented a Memorial to Bishop Thirlwall, who 'immediately commanded the Dean to summon a Special Chapter' to consider the matter. He got an answer from Canon Philipps who asked his consent to put off the matter until St Jamestide. Davies in reply, agreed but also asked whether he might examine the Statutes 'in order to prepare his case more accurately'. He got a chilling response. Philipps refused. If Davies wanted to see the Statutes, the Dean would have to call a Special Chapter to gain the unanimous consent of Chapter. Davies found this a 'pitiful stretch of authority: a Canon of the church refusing a Prebendary of the same ecclesiastical body access to the Statutes'. He reminded his readers that Thomas Burgess (bishop of St Davids 1803–25) had, in his Visitation Charge to the Cathedral in 1811, stated a wish to reduce into one body the statutes and ordinances of the church, 'for the use of all who became members of the church, and who had to swear to observe the statutes'. It was understood that Canon H. T. Payne had done just that by compiling his *Collectanea*, in response to the Bishop's wishes. Davies notes that the canons had not responded with the same openness and had raised 'jealous and odious surmises' in the minds of 'inferior members of the church'.[16] From then on, matters deteriorated. 'The Special Chapter' of 1844 had seemed to Davies to have established the right of the Choristers to Llanwnnen and the lands in St Davids, which were in any case called Chorister's Lands.[17] He thought he had secured a promise – his words, perhaps ill chosen, are:

> he demanded of them a promise that they would never more renew these leases so that at some distant time, the School would be in

possession of a fitting income. To this they assented at once and with pleasure.

As Bishop Thirlwall was not present at the special chapter, Davies immediately sent him a full account of proceedings. He had not just done that on account of his personal concerns about the chapter's diversion of income to their general funds; he had placed the matter, as Thirlwall's rather non-committal reply makes clear, in a wider context: that of possible confiscation of the School's endowment by the Ecclesiastical Commissioners.

Dean Lewellin's *Reply* to the charges that Davies was laying against him and the Cathedral went straight to the point:

> Mr Davies asserts that the Choristers are 'oppressed' and 'defrauded' by The Chapter. That we divide between ourselves certain sums of money which belong to The Choir. That is to say, that we are guilty – knowingly guilty – of a scandalous breach of trust in our character of Trustees of a Charitable Endowment.' This is his Indictment against us. If proved, we deserve to be driven out of all decent society, and to be branded with every mark of a public contumely and scorn'[18]

He denied Davies's charges, section by section. When he comes to section VII, the School, he makes the telling point that the Master did not always observe the distinction between School and Choristers but, conceded that he and Davies were in agreement on the sum 'annually paid by the Chapter to the Choristers and Master'. From then on, they were at issue (*Reply*, p. 10).

Lewellin pointed out that under a statute of Bishop Bek, Silian had been gifted by Edward I to the Bishop who had appropriated it to the Chantor and Chapter.[19] The issues of Llanwnnen, which like Silian is near Lampeter, are noted by Lewellin as being divided thus: one third to the vicar and the remainder for the maintenance of the Choristers who were to be under the Bishop's Vicar. There was no mention of the endowment being directed toward paying a Master, who as a teacher was paid by ten pounds a year by Chapter. As far as the property within St Davids claimed by Davies as belonging to the endowment of the School 'as an indisputable fact', Lewellin found no evidence for that either. He did, however, make the point that he had advised Chapter to discontinue leasing property within the parish, a suggestion to which they had acceded.

This is a telling sidelight on the way Chapter operated. The eighteenth and early nineteenth century Chapter Act Books are full of attempts by the Precentor as the president of Chapter to exercise jurisdiction over his five colleagues. Each time he was rebuffed and reminded that authority lay with the Chapter collectively and with the Senior Canon in particular. In terms of Davies's bringing the matter of the school and its endowment before Chapter, the Dean not only denied that the Chapter of 1844 was a 'Special Chapter' but queried Davies's detailed knowledge of what had gone on there, since as prebendary he had no access to Chapter meetings which only the five Canons attended. By the same token, Davies would not have had access to the record of the meeting in either the Chapter Act Book or the Chapter Order Book.[20]

Lewellin, who had, of course, been present, denied that any promise had been made – with pleasure or otherwise. He also noted that the Chapter Order Book shows that the Llanwnnen lease was renewed. To Davies's further assertion that 'he found in 1849 that we had made no entry in our Chapter Book' Lewellin reminded his readers that they had made the same entry in the same book every year until 1853. He then turned to statistics in answer to the use made of them by Davies. He put together out of the Chapter Books a statement of accounts relating to the School. It began in 1813, and extended over thirty one years. His calculations meant that the Chapter had over that period *overpaid* (my italics) the Choristers by £344.0.0. This is somewhat of a contrast with Davies's accusation that the Chapter had *underpaid* (my italics) the School and the Master by £140.00. Davies, in reply states not only that the Dean's account was fallacious, but that the Chapter had underpaid the Choristers' Fund, as he now called it, £78, 17s, 0d.; it was also due 47 years of the reserved rent (£0, 11s, 8d *per annum*) of the 'Town Lands, belonging to the Choristers; in total, £306.5.4d.' Davies also insisted that the Master's salary was derived not from general Chapter funds but from the tithes of Silian.[21]

Lewellin, perhaps unwisely, observed that the style of Davies's remarks served only to inflame the prejudices of 'the lowest class of Political Dissenter',

> whose only religion is hatred of Establishments, or a class of men almost as worthless, the frequenters of low Taverns and readers of Sunday Newspapers – people who enjoy with infinite zest a course

(sic) joke at the Parsons, just as 'Ravens scream, however vainly, at the noble eagle.'[22]

The most unwise thing he had done, perhaps, was quoting Pindar, since that gave Pipps the title of the fifth pamphlet.

At this point, we move into a wider sphere, both personal and ecclesial,[23] as the Dean failed to resist the temptation to set Davies's plea of poverty in a wider context. He tells his readers that the Master was not a 'fossil Welsh curate':

> ... you shall see a gentleman with all the unmistakable external signs of great wealth and prosperity, whose POVERTY consists in a freehold house of residence – one of the most comfortable and pleasant in the district, with gardens and pleasure grounds and lands adjoining –, farms in the parish of considerable value, – mortgages – lands at Narberth – the advowson of a valuable living in Norfolk. . .[24]

And regarding the School and its Master, Lewellin takes up Davies's complaint that as a second-class man of Oxford he deserved more than a 'miserable pittance' of £20 a year:

> ... but what say you, gentle reader, to the fact that he has under his charge, twenty-five or thirty boys, on an average, at sums of £40 a year each (some I believe at £60) the sons of the aristocracy of the three counties – the Owen's, the Brigstockes, the Leaches, the Higgons, the Massies, the Lloyd Prices,&, &. This truly may be called the 'High' School of the country, a sort of Pocket Eton, Harrow, or Rugby.

Lewellin spoke whereof he knew, not least about the fees and the families from which the pupils were drawn, since his son George had been a pupil of Davies.[25] Moreover, he also reminded his readers that he

> truly had a right to rejoice in these results for I certainly had no small part in placing him in that position in which he has been able to realize his fortune.

Davies, however, in *Strictures*, firmly denies that Lewellin had anything to do with his appointment (*Strictures*, p. 11), but Archdeacon Richard

Davies's letterbook tells a different story.[26] There, Lewellin having been installed as Precentor, on 21 March 1840,[27] brings to Archdeacon Davies's notice <u>one matter</u> (underlined) in which Lewellin takes the deepest interest: the Mastership of the grammar school at St Davids. Although he was aware that Chapter had promised the appointment to Mr James (Propert) Williams, nevertheless he urged them to reconsider in favour of Nathaniel Davies.[28] Lewellin had secured Williams's withdrawal.

Davies, had been educated at the Haverfordwest Grammar School under the Revd James Thomas, and had been among the first entrants to St David's College Lampeter in 1827. Lewellin, as Archdeacon Davies's Letterbook reveals, had urged him to go to Oxford; which he did and became a member, and Bible Clerk, of Pembroke College. And, says Lewellin, 'I proved to be right for he took a tip top second and was very near a first class . . .' Indeed in his *Observations* on Davies's *Strictures*, the Dean reminds the Master that the Archdeacon of Brecon had made it clear that it was the Dean who was responsible for bringing him to St Davids (*Observations*, pp. 19–20). Moreover, Davies was not to know, at that time, that his response to the Cathedral Commission had been fruitless – unless perhaps he had sight of the Appendix to their Report. Bishop Thirlwall had praised the excellence of his school and its standards since Davies had taken it over, but thought it 'very doubtful whether its efficiency would be increased by an addition to its present endowment'.[29] There also survives in the Chapter Archives a transcript of a part of a report on the Chapter School of St Davids by a Mr Bryce,[30] and seems to be an account of the school under Nathaniel Davies. According to the transcript, now at the NLW, after Davies had sent his memorial to the Cathedral Commissioners, 'a chilling reply was received, and so the matter rests'. That, together with the fact that it was, after the advent of the Great Western Railway to Pembrokeshire easier for the local gentry to send their sons to school in England, led to the comparative slump in the numbers and quality of those attending the school. The Chapter School came to an end with the opening of the St Davids County School (now Ysgol Penrhyn Dewi, Dewi Campus) in 1895.

In 1854, Davies left St Davids for West Lexham, the parish in Norfolk whose advowson he had purchased in 1849, 'that I may not have to labour as a teacher all the days of my life'.[31] The implication was that he had not been offered a Chapter living as was customary in the case of Minor Canons. He was, however, as will be seen, offered a living which was near to St Davids by Bishop Thirlwall.[32] Lewellin's response was that no living in Chapter patronage had become vacant since Davies's appointment; hence there was no living that he could have been offered. Moreover, Davies's obituary in the *Pembrokeshire Herald* states that Bishop Thirlwall had offered him Mathry but that Davies had turned it down because he could not serve a Welsh-speaking parish since he could not speak Welsh. Lewellin's attitude in the matter was to write that it 'was a great pity that Mr Davies has not applied his acknowledged talents to the acquisition of the noble old language, just as many Englishmen have successfully done, without a tithe of his advantages'.[33]

This response to the needs of the 'Saxon souls' of St Davids shows that the grievances embraced more than dissatisfaction with the finances, governance and status of the Chapter School of St Davids. They were about the general state of Menevia in the mid-nineteenth century. The dissatisfaction which Davies felt was shared by the Dean and by Peter Pipps, but their responses were however entirely different. Any discussion of the rights and wrongs of the state of affairs relating to the School and the Dean and Chapter of the Cathedral has to take account of the problem which underlay the whole situation: funding; and the means by which that funding was obtained. It is a matter which underlies other aspects of the *gravamina* with which Davies buttressed his arguments in relation to the school, for example pluralism, non-residence and repairs to the Cathedral fabric and the Close walls. Both School and Cathedral were reliant on a system of the leasing of property, including tithes to provide the income upon which they depended to carry out their work, that was generally agreed to be unsatisfactory: 'absurd and deplorable' are Geoffrey Best's comments.[34] In his view, before the advent of the Ecclesiastical Commissioners, advantage lay with the lessees.[35] It took the Commissioners until the 1880s to complete a process which gave due regard to the long-term interests of the church.[36]

In the case of St Davids Cathedral, the greater part of its corporate income was drawn from the rectorial tithes of appropriated churches from across the diocese.[37] Among the exceptions are, ironically, the small pieces of land claimed by Davies as the property of the Choristers. The major ecclesiastical landowner in St Davids was not the Dean and Chapter but the Bishop. The income from individual prebends, however, tended to derive from estates such as the Treffgarne Estate, attached to the Precentor's stall. It is interesting that Lewellin had, presumably in the interest of securing a regular stipend rather than a fluctuating income, had handed over the Treffgarne estate (part of the Precentorial Estates) to the Commissioners.

The following quotation expresses Lewellin's views in this matter of church property. He did not

> feel called to enter into any explanation or defence of the system of Leasing, adopted by, I believe, all Chapters. For two hundred years this system has been the rule, and *manifestly*, the only *necessary* rule. The Chapter finds a 21 year's lease subsisting. The only right they possess in it is the *reversion* and the *reserved* Rent. For the *necessary* purpose of obtaining *funds for carrying on the objects of their trust, and for liquidating present demands*, they renew annually, that is to say, they agree to the *postponement* of the reversionary right from the expiration of twenty years to that of twenty one.[38]

It is therefore worthy of remark that Lewellin, who on the one hand had clearly accepted the role of the Ecclesiastical Commissioners, and therefore a case for change in the administration and finances of church property, was on the other, giving a firm impression of speaking on behalf of the lessees of that same church property. The interest in his remarks lies in the way he implies that church property is in effect irrecoverable by the church. In his *Observations* he suggests to Davies that the only answer to the dilemma is:

> Confiscation. – The lease is *only two hundred* years old. Let us re-enter. How the Honourable and Reverend Gentleman; who is our lessee, may relish this remedy, it is not difficult to imagine.[39]

What makes Lewellin's observations more striking is that the Canons of St Davids Cathedral in the earlier nineteenth century had been assiduous in commissioning fresh surveys of their lands and tithes; raising entry fines considerably; and when sitting tenants forbore to accept those raised fines, the Chapter issued concurrent leases, of which some were substantial, as the pages of *Collectanea*, reveal.[40] Given that Lewellin had access to Payne's work, it is remarkable that he had not taken up the torch from his predecessors. The clue may be in the perception that Lewellin in the words of his obituary in the *Welshman*: 'ably and faithfully discharged the duties of a country gentleman of the olden type and continued to do so until the very last'.[41] That perception of the Dean as country gentleman as well as being a thorough going Tory, as the obituary again reminds us, is of a piece with his service as a magistrate, serving in the Commission of the Peace for the three counties of Cardigan, Carmarthen and Pembrokeshire and as chair of Lampeter Petty Sessions. It also accords with the picture which his daughter paints in her memoir of him where he is described as the 'King of Lampeter'.[42] He was also related to many of the squirearchy of the Teifi Valley around Lampeter. This may account for his implicit defence of the tenants of the tithes of Llanwnnen and Silian, both of which parishes adjoin Lampeter.[43]

It is a fair inference from Davies's attitude, persistence in pursuit of his goal, possession of his house and school, and from his general remarks, that had he been in receipt of the prebendal income from St Nicholas Penyffos, small though that was, he would have been more satisfied with his lot. Thus, both Lewellin and Davies were highlighting the underlying problem, namely that of church property and the income deriving from it.

It was not only Davies and Lewellin who were aware of the significance of property in sustaining the work of the Cathedral and its clergy. So was Peter Pipps but in an entirely different way. Thus it is to his pamphlet that we now turn. Pipps's pamphlet is shorter at only twelve pages than its four predecessors. It takes the form of a meditation by Pipps, from the heights of Carn Llidi, overlooking a very Old Church, 'founded by one DAVID, in my opinion a very good old soul', and is expressed in terms of an Aesopian fable complete with moral covering the last half-page. It also contains a dialogue between Pipps and Mrs Pipps, who had accompanied him to Carn Llidi; a lament from the figure of St David, himself a tall and venerable old Man. It is not only the Church which Pipps could see, but that a 'great many very voracious RAVENS, nestled around it'. Pipps has a knowledge of the Book of Common Prayer for he quotes from the Litany this was 'unity peace and concord' with a vengeance!

> About a month ago, one of them – *a fat little Raven* (Pipps's italics.) – perhaps of the best that do fly around, did make a great big scream about his not having all his share of some *Carrion* . . .[44]

As he develops his narrative, he characterises the *dramatis personae* as Eagles, Doves and Ravens. One of the Doves, who nestled in the 'old ruins' is either Philemon Appleby, the Senior Lay Vicar, or James Roberts, the Junior Lay Vicar listed among members of the Lower

Chapter.[45] The dove then 'took wing' to the ruins of Pembroke Castle to 'mutter' to a Raven who lived there what the fat little Raven had been doing. The Pembroke Raven is Charles Philipps, Canon Treasurer. Back at St Davids there was a skirmish between the Pembroke Raven and the fat little Raven which the latter won. This was a signal for two other birds to get involved, a Cock Raven and a Bull Raven. These two are William Richardson and James Propert Williams and the fracas between the little Raven and the two, which Davies is perceived as winning, is a clear reference to the correspondence in the *Pembrokeshire Herald* between Davies and Williams and Richardson; and also between Davies and Philipps.

At this point the Eagles enter. The little Eagle is a reference to Dean Lewellin's son, David, who had written to the *Herald*, explaining that his Father had not responded because he had been laid up as a result of an accident (copied in *Reply*, p. 19). The big Eagle, whose scream 'an unearthly sound' was that of Lewellin himself. The latter's arguments about 'jealousies', 'distress' and 'distrust' and 'blasted and dishonoured name' sickened Pipps who states that everyone else around was sickened too. He speaks well of the 'good and kind English Doves who lived in new habitations (?)'.[46]

Pipps's tone is a moral one. Instead of Lewellin's frequent use of Latin tags, one of which had given Pipps the title of his pamphlet, equally frequently, Pipps quotes scripture '*Money is the root of all evil*'. Nor was that all. There was also a Magpie 'who alighted and settled in the chimneys of certain houses'. It has not been possible yet to identify the Magpie. Pipps also refers to the argument made by Davies that Sunday dinners which were once given to the inferior members of the Cathedral staff had been discontinued. The Dean's argument was that the money once spent on dinners had now been expended on sermons. Pipps, in a classic expression of puritan Sabbatarianism, castigated the Birds for looking forward to the Sunday when instead of a day of 'fast and solemnity' they looked on it as a day of 'feast and jollity'. Pipps then summons the figure of St David, who laments the loss of his original vision of St Davids as a 'place wherein might nestle some gentle Doves, to become bearers of the olive leaves of peace and good will among men and whose grief at its infestation by Ravens more numerous than the Doves; and that *Enmity* had usurped *Love*'.

Then the scene changes. He looks now not down on the Cathedral below him but turns his eye to the North, East and South. There he finds a great number of Blackbirds – who did not scream but sang melodiously the 'new song in their mouths, even praise'. And thousands stood around them delighted with their melody. Pips embellishes this with a quotation from a seventeenth-century proverb: 'Birds [who] in their little nests agree',[47] making a contrast between 'their superiors in the Vineyard who agreed not they did their appointed work with earnestness and humility'.

The moral with which the pamphlet closes takes its tone from Davies's peroration in *Notes*. Pipps exhorts the Cathedral's clergy not to waste time in squabbles for perishing Carrion, but as successors of Christ's Apostles they are called to deny themselves; their calling, their meat and drink was to do the will of his Father. Was Pipps punning: the usual designation for a prebend being 'corpse'? They are called, first- and second-class men, graduates, undergraduates, not to demean themselves, but to obey the New Commandment: that they love one another. This is indeed speaking of God at the Bazaar. Pipps's view of church property is that it was a distraction, since the clergy spent all their time quarrelling about what constituted a fair share.

Dean Lewellin did not think much of the pamphlet: 'low minded and scurrilous remarks' is his response.[48] On the other hand it was clear that Lewellin's intemperate remarks about Political Dissenters, 'whose only religion is hatred of establishments', coupling with them 'the frequenters of low Taverns and readers of Sunday Newspapers' had triggered this response.[49]

Given Davies's stated intention in the Preface to *Notes*, to lay the situation before Parliament, his pamphlet campaign was really a failure. There is an ineptness, compounded by misinformation, about his efforts. His attitude to the Bishop, and the relationship between Bishop and Chapter, is proof of that. Had he been really serious, he would surely have asked the Bishop to hold a Visitation of the Cathedral. After all he had a friend at court; Thirlwall's Chaplain in the 1840s had been the Revd William Beach Thomas, with whom Davies claimed a cousinship and who had held the prebend of Clydey since 1845.[50]

In conclusion, the episode of the Schoolmaster and the Dean sheds a sidelight on the sometimes bald narrative of Victorian reform and reconstruction and the formal records of Chapter. We see in the grey literature of pamphleteers – who included in their number senior clergy – a fragile record of the highly personal and contentious debates that formed the context within which the reconstruction and repair of the Cathedral fabric was undertaken. Setting the poisonous personal relationship between Davies and Lewellin aside, important though it is as a factor in the disagreement, both men found themselves caught up in the slowness of change. Both the 1840 and 1843 Acts insisted that current vested interests were to be respected; i.e. that existing office holders who had a freehold remained in post until they died or resigned their office.[51] Davies, because he had come into post as vicar choral a month before the 1840 Act came into force, could not benefit from the stipend of £150 for Minor Canons. Nor was he able to enjoy an income from his prebend which had been suspended under the Act. Lewellin, having been appointed to the Precentorship prior to the passing of the Act in August 1840, remained on the old pre-Ecclesiastical Commission foundation. Davies's claim, therefore, that the Dean was paid £350 per annum from his prebend was nonsense. Indeed, the Dean could not have claimed his decanal income under the new arrangements unless he resigned and was reappointed. He remained Precentor and was, under the Act only styled Dean. On the other hand, he was aware enough of the potential for a settled rather than a fluctuating income to have handed over the Treffgarn Estate to the Commissioners.

Trollope's fictional cathedral of Barchester, too, had to cope with the uncertainties consequent upon the piecemeal implementation of the 1840 Act. Hence, we might characterise the situation at St Davids in the 1850s as the world of Jane Austen colliding with the world of Anthony Trollope. Or perhaps more fairly, it is one of surviving Hanoverian attitudes, exemplified by Dean Llewelyn Lewellin, colliding both with the modernising Victorians, exemplified by Nathaniel Davies, and the Victorian Nonconformist conscience, exemplified by 'Peter Pipps'. We may also make some comparisons with Trollope's *dramatis personae*. Nathaniel Davies embodies some attitudes of both John Bold and Obadiah Slope: but without the persistence of Bold and the hostility of Slope – but with the latter's ignorance of cathedral life and liturgy. William Richardson can be compared to Mr Harding, Lewellin to Archdeacon Grantly, not least in their Toryism. If Lewellin, however, would not – I suspect on cost grounds – tackle the dangerous condition of the north-west tower pier, he had been moved to make improvements to the Cathedral. He allowed the transformation of the South Transept into a Parish church in 1844; and also, ironically, manoeuvred to secure the appointment of a new Master for the School in 1840 – none other than Nathaniel Davies. And it is to that same Nathaniel Davies that Dean Lewellin pays a compliment when he says that the first window in the nave was done by 'himself, (Davies) and his friends'.

The future of the Cathedral fabric, however, lay neither with Davies nor Lewellin. In any case they disagreed about the parlous state of the north-west pier of the tower and the expedient employed in the adjoining north transept to deal with the ingress of rain. That future lay with another, who had already gained Dean Lewellin's approbation, 'our excellent friend, The Revd Basil Jones, whose name is for ever associated with St David's'.

Dean Lewellin's prophecy was correct – and in a far fuller sense than he could have imagined. Basil Jones's connection with St Davids went back to the 1840s, when with his Oxford (and Trinity) contemporary E. A. Freeman, he collaborated in a detailed study of the history and architecture of the Cathedral. The culmination of their joint efforts appeared in 1856 as *The History and Antiquities of St David's*.[52] Not only was the book a groundbreaking account of the developments and the personalities which had affected the building over the centuries but also a description of the structure as it was at that point in its existence. It therefore furnished a sound guide to Sir Gilbert Scott when he commenced his thoroughgoing restoration of the Cathedral in 1863.[53]

Thus, Jones bridges the interlude between the 1840s and the 1870s, by which time he had become bishop of St Davids. In the 1840s Dean Lewellin made a substantial contribution, to which Nigel Yates has rightly drawn attention (*supra*) to the restoration and adaptation of the building – with the help of Nathaniel Davies and his friends. From the 1860s, as is described by Julian Orbach (*infra*), Scott's endeavours, both rescued the building from both long running structural problems and what was perceived as previous lapses in taste, thus incidentally removing much of the construction for which Lewellin had been responsible in the first half of the nineteenth century.[54]

Notes

1   This paper has gone through many changes since it was first delivered to the Fishguard Historical Society on 18 January 2006. I first came across *Notes on The Cathedral Church of St David's by Nathaniel Davies MA of Pembroke College, Oxford, Prebendary and Minor Canon of the Cathedral and Master of the Chapter School, of St David's* (London and Haverfordwest, 1853 – henceforth cited as *Notes*) in 1971 as a newly minted curate in the Cathedral parish of St Davids and was astonished, as I still am, at the daring of a mere minor canon, schoolmaster notwithstanding, who had challenged the Dean and Chapter in such vehement terms. I later came across Dean Lewellin's *A Reply to the Rev N. Davies's Notes*

on the Cathedral Church of St David's by Llewelyn Lewellin MA DCL, Dean of St David's (London and Haverfordwest 1853 – henceforth *Reply*); Davies's *Strictures on a Reply to the Rev Nathaniel Davies's Notes on The Cathedral Church of St David's by Nathaniel Davies MA of Pembroke College, Oxford, Prebendary and Minor Canon of the Cathedral and Master of the Chapter School, of St David's* (London and Haverfordwest 1853 – henceforth *Strictures*) and Lewellin's riposte *Reply to the Rev N. Davies's Notes on the Cathedral Church of St David's* (Second Edition) *with Observations on a Second Paper lately published by the Author entitled Strictures on a Reply etc. by Llewelyn Lewellin MA DCL, Dean of St David's* (London and Haverfordwest 1853 – henceforth *Observations*).

I was originally unaware of the existence of a fifth pamphlet, *Observations on the Screams of the Eagles and Ravens of St Davids* (Solva, n.d. – henceforth *Ravens*). Internal evidence suggests it was published in August 1853. Its publication was advertised in *The Pembrokeshire Herald* on 26 August 1853 in the same column and just below Dean Lewellin's *Observations*. As far as I can ascertain, only one copy survives, among Bishop Connop Thirlwall's papers deposited in Trinity College Cambridge.

2   Trollope was in the West of England and South Wales between early 1851 and September 1853: Anthony Trollope, *An Autobiography*, ed. N. Shrimpton (Oxford, 2014), pp. 62–4. His wife and children lived in Llansteffan in Carmarthenshire, and he date-lined letters to his mother from Haverfordwest in September and October 1852: F. E. Trollope, *Frances Trollope* (London 1895), p. 241. He might then have heard something of the troubles at St Davids Cathedral.

3   Trollope, *An Autobiography*, p. 294.

4   Davies dated his Preface as 28 June 1853. The copy held at the National Library of Wales (Dyb 2005 A 320) was deposited by C.A.H. Green, archbishop of Wales 1934–44. The inscription on the cover reveals that it had been owned by his father, 'A.J.M. Green Caius College Cambridge', who had been Davies's pupil at the Chapter School, and was himself Master 1867–74: Francis Green, his nephew, describes the School and its Masters in 'Pembrokeshire Parsons', *West Wales Historical Records* 6 (1916), pp. 21–5.

5   Connop Thirlwall, bishop 1840–74.

6   Llywelyn Lewellin was Precentor, 1840–78, and styled Dean from 1840, following the Ecclesiastical Commissioners Act (3&4 Victoria, *c*.113; The Dean and Chapter Act). He was also Principal of St David's College, Lampeter, 1827–78 and Vicar of Lampeter 1833–78. He was technically not a pluralist in Canon Law, because Cathedral dignities did not carry Cure of Souls.

7   Charles Philipps, Canon Treasurer from 1823 to 1854, had been Bishop Burgess's Chaplain. He was Vicar of Pembroke, 1809–54; and perpetual curate of the family living of Llangynin until his death in 1854.

8   James Propert Williams, Subchanter 1840–74 and vicar of Whitchurch, the parish adjoining St Davids 1840–74. His father, Thomas, had been a vicar choral from 1786–1831 and Schoolmaster 1802–10. Williams had been offered the Mastership of the School; but withdrew at Dean Lewellin's request in favour of Nathaniel Davies.

9   William Richardson (1791–1876) had been Schoolmaster 1810–29, vicar choral 1804–54, Bishop's vicar from 1817–54; Prebendary of Llangan 1820–76 Perpetual Curate (Parish Priest) of St Davids 1820–76. He was also vicar of Jeffreyston 1826–54, and simultaneously vicar of Henfynyw in Cardiganshire. There is a memorial plaque to him in the Dean's Vestry in St Davids.

10 Nathaniel Davies 1808–86, a native of Prendergast, was educated at Haverfordwest Grammar School under James Thomas – with whom he claimed cousinship. He entered

Llewelyn Lewellin and the Condition of St Davids

into St Davids College Lampeter as one of the first students in 1827, but was advised by the Principal, Llywelyn Lewellin, that he ought to go to Oxford. He matriculated at Pembroke College in 1830, graduated with a second class honours in 1834, became Curate of Grappenhall, where he kept a school, then became Curate of Steynton where he also kept a school, from which he was headhunted for the St Davids post by Dean Lewellin. He became Prebendary of St Nicholas Pen y Ffos in 1842, and held it until his death in 1886. By this time he had, after moving to West Lexham in 1854, become Rector of Mount Bures in 1873 where he died on Thursday 2 December 1886 at the age of 78. I owe this information to the kindness of his great-granddaughter, Mrs Sheila Anstead, who gave me copies of several documents relating to Nathaniel including a family tree. His family had no knowledge of his difference of opinion with Dean Lewellin nor of the pamphlets.

[11] Ebenezer Williams, 1813–57, was a grocer and druggist at St Davids, besides having considerable interests in land, shipping and insurance. He was a Welsh Calvinistic Methodist and worshipped at Tabernacle. He made the return for Bethania Calvinistic Methodist Chapel at Treleddid Fawr to the 1851 Religious Census: I. G. Jones and D. Williams, *The Religious Census of 1851: A Calendar of Returns Relating to Wales, Vol I South Wales* (Cardiff, 1976), p. 437. He was declared bankrupt in 1855 and died not long after aged 44. He was the brother in law of Nathaniel Davies's predecessor as Master of the School, the Revd Jonah Owen: P. Davies, *The Footsteps of our Fathers* (St Davids, 1994), pp. 30; 43–6.

[12] For an outline of Houghton's life, see J. W. Evans, 'From Chapel to Cloister', in H. James, and P. Moore (eds), *Carmarthenshire and Beyond: Studies in History and Archaeology in Memory of Terry James* (Llandybie, 2009), pp. 174–91.

[13] In particular he wished to consult H. T. Payne's *Collectanea Menevensia,* but Philipps refused him sight of it. Dean Lewellin denied him access because Payne had dedicated the collection to the Precentor and Canons Residentiary of the Cathedral church (NLW, SDCh/B/27, ii).

[14] 25 July was the date of the annual Chapter Meeting and Audit. Davies was also appointed as vicar choral at that meeting. The date is noteworthy since it predates the coming into force of the Ecclesiastical Commissioners Act (also known as the Dean and Chapter Act or the Cathedrals Act) on 11 August 1840. Thus when Davies became Prebendary of St Nicholas Penyffos on 4 Jan 1842, the income from the prebend which had lain suspended since 1839 had passed to the Ecclesiastical Commissioners; and his prebend was honorary. Moreover as he was already in post as vicar choral before when the Act was promulgated he could not benefit from the stipend of £150 which only came into force for Minor Canons appointed subsequent to the passing of the Act.

[15] The Chapter were paying the school and Master what they were statutorily obliged to do, but no adjustment/increase had been made to take into account inflation over several centuries. Note also that the commutation of Chapter estates to the Ecclesiastical Commissioners did not happen until 1866 (NLW, SDCh/LET/540); the estates of the Lower Chapter we not handed over to the Commissioners until March 1876: Green, 'Pembrokeshire Parsons', *West Wales Historical Records*, 5 (1915), p. 236

[16] Payne's *Collectanea Menevensia,* remains unpublished within the archive of St Davids Cathedral Chapter (NLW, SDCh/B/27 and 28) and can be viewed online.

[17] Lewellin, *Observations* (pp. 13, 27) denies that the Choristers had any right to the lands in St Davids termed *Terra Choristarum,* and made sarcastic reference to Dr Hewson's *Classical Exhibitions.* William Hewson (1782–1845) was Chancellor, 1825–45: Green, 'Pembrokeshire Parsons', *West Wales Historical Records*, 4 (1914), pp. 291, 294. He and Davies had been discussing the meaning of *Terra Choristarum*; both Davies and Lewellin were classicists.

J. Wyn Evans

18 *Reply*, p. 3

19 Thomas Bek was bishop of St Davids from 1280 to 1293. Edward I had in 1284 granted him Silian, a parish on the outskirts of Lampeter in Ceredigion.

20 The matter of access to Chapter records looms large in the dispute; which led to accusations and denials of lying; and which deepened the personal animosity between Dean and Master.

21 *Reply*, pp. 12–13. It is worth noting that the salary of the contemporary headmaster of Cowbridge School was £20 *per annum*, comparable to Davies £20, 10s (*Notes*, p. 13); however the Master of Cowbridge was a Fellow of Jesus College Oxford, and in receipt of dividend thereby. Even so, it was said that a headmaster of Cowbridge needed private means. The headmastership and the fellowship were separated in 1853. See Iolo Davies, *A Certaine Schoole* (Cowbridge, 1977), pp. 94 and 97.

22 Pindar, *Olympian* 2:88, ed. D. Svarlien *http://perseus.tufts.edu/* Pipps clearly knew what the reference was. Had he been a pupil in the Chapter School?

23 The matter had already moved from the local to the national. In an article on St Asaph Cathedral, it is noted in passing 'that the state of things with regard to the cathedral of St David's, exceeds anything yet brought forward, except the case of Christ's College, Brecon. . ', *Morning Advertiser*, 28 July 1853.

24 *Notes*, p. 15. The house is the present Grove Hotel at St Davids. The advowson was that of West Lexham in Norfolk, whither Davies moved in 1854.

25 In 1851 Wales Census, George Smith Lewellen (sic) aged 14 was a Scholar at Nathaniel Davies's school at Grove House, St Davids. The surnames of the other pupils bear out Lewellin's observations about gentry families from the three counties sending their sons to Davies's school.

26 Now held at Powys Archives as B/D/ACA/2/366/P. 9. I am grateful to Charlotte McCarthy, County Archivist, for allowing me to take a copy of the relevant letters in the book – which reveals from its singed edges that it was saved from a bonfire.

27 B/D/ACA 2/66/P, 15. Green (*West Wales Historical Records* 4, pp. 286, 288) notes that Lewellin was installed in 21 March and admitted Canon Residentiary on 24 July 1840. Furthermore Nathaniel Davies was admitted to his vicar choralship on the 25 July 1840; and James Propert Williams to the Succentorship on the same day, Green, *West Wales Historical Records* 6, pp. 6, 17; Mastership, 23 and 26. All these appointments occurred before the Ecclesiastical Commissioners Act came into force in August 1840. Thus Lewellin remained Precentor under the old dispensation.

28 Whose father Thomas, we have already noted, had been Master.

29 *Appendix to the First Report of the Cathedral Commissioners, appointed November 10 1852*, London, 1854). Davies's Submission is on page 752; that of Thirlwall on page 595.

30 This is James Bryce, later Viscount Bryce. The transcript, which is written on House of Commons notepaper is dated February 1870. The situation he is describing seems however, to relate more to the period when Nathaniel Davies was Master than afterwards, since Davies left St Davids in 1854: NLW, SDCh/Misc 161.

31 *Strictures*, 12.

32 as had been the case with Richardson and J. P. Williams. Whitchurch with St Elvis was a chapter living; Henfynyw was in episcopal patronage but the dean and chapter were appropriators of the tithe.

33 *Observations*, p. 26. Lewellin was a fluent Welsh speaker as I shall show in *Y Traethodydd* (forthcoming). Both Alfred Ollivant, Lewellin's Vice-Principal at Lampeter and subsequently bishop of Llandaff, and Connop Thirlwall, both Englishmen, had learnt Welsh and could preach in it.

34 G. Best *Temporal Pillars* (Cambridge, 1964), p. 370.
35 Best, *Temporal Pillars*, p. 369.
36 Best, *Temporal Pillars*, p. 380.
37 NLW, SDCh/Accts/1–144 (running from 1724 to 1873).
38 *Reply*, p. 11.
39 *Observations*, p. 15. The Honourable and Reverend Gentleman was the Revd Sir Erasmus Henry Griffies-Williams. He became Chancellor of the Cathedral in 1858, and proved a thorn in Lewellin's side during Scott's campaign to restore the Cathedral. See R. Hellon, *The Saving of St Davids Cathedral* (St Davids, 2012), p. 18.
40 NLW, SDCh/B/28, 278–96, *passim*, dealing with the years 1814–27. Lewellin became a Prebendary in 1827.
41 *The Welshman*, 29 November 1878.
42 E. Nares, *Pleasant Memories of Eminent Churchmen* (Carmarthen, n.d.), p. 3, furnishes a lengthy list of the positions he held.
43 I deal with Lewellin's connexions with the local squires in *Y Traethodydd* (forthcoming).
44 *Ravens*, pp. 4, 9, 12.
45 Philemon Appleby served as a lay vicar choral from 1830 to 1859, when he was dismissed for insobriety; James Roberts, became lay vicar choral in 1833–86: Green, *West Wales Historical Records* 6, pp. 6, 17.
46 *Ravens*, pp. 7, 8.
47 *Ravens*, p. 10; *Oxford Dictionary of Proverbs* (Oxford, 2009), online version.
48 *Observations*, p. 30.
49 *Reply*, p. 9. It had certainly moved Ebenezer Williams to write a long letter in protest to *The Pembrokeshire Herald*, 9 September 1853.
50 For Beach Thomas as Thirlwall's chaplain, see, John Connop Thirlwall, *Connop Thirlwall, Historian and Theologian* (London 1836), pp. 134 and 135; and as prebendary of Clydey: Green, *West Wales Historical Records* 5, pp. 176, 179.
51 Section 75 of the 1840 Act; Section Eleven of the 1843 Act.
52 J. W. Evans, 'Victorian Vignette', in H. James and T. Driver (eds) *Illustrating the Past in Wales* (Llandysul 2021), 54–6.
53 G. G. Scott, *Personal and Professional Recollections*, ed. G. Stamp (Stamford, 1995), p. 312.
54 See also Hellon, *The Saving of St Davids Cathedral*, *passim*.

8.
GILBERT SCOTT AND THE RESTORATION OF ST DAVIDS CATHEDRAL

Julian Orbach

I am sure that the name of Mr Scott is a sufficient guarantee that not a single superfluous stone will be added to the building – nothing more than is absolutely necessary to bring out its genuine original character.[1]

When George Gilbert Scott was asked to consider the restoration of St David's Cathedral he was the leading specialist and indeed, at the age of 51, leader of the architectural profession in England since the death of Sir Charles Barry in 1860. He was the only British architect with a European reputation, as the first to win laurels in European competition, for the Nikolaikirche in Hamburg in 1844 and the Rathaus in the same town 1854. It was almost inevitable that the Dean and Chapter would turn to Scott, although there were others in the field. Already old-fashioned were Anthony Salvin who had worked at Norwich, Durham and Wells (and Scott had already replaced him at Durham), Sydney Smirke at York, and Edward Blore at Norwich. Of the advanced Goths, R. C. Carpenter had secured Chichester but had died young, Benjamin Ferrey, the biographer of Pugin, had recovered Wells from Salvin, and, the most fortuitously successful appointment of the era, John Prichard had Llandaff, in whose precincts he had grown up. But Carpenter, Ferrey and Prichard did not make careers of cathedrals, and Scott secured so many in his lifetime that his name is still synonymous with Victorian cathedral restoration.

Scott had begun his architectural career with workhouses in the 1830s, discovered the true Gothic with Pugin around 1840 and erected one of its early monuments with the Martyrs' Memorial at Oxford in 1841–4. His earliest notable church restoration had been at St Mary, Stafford in 1841–4 and from the very first Scott was in baffled conflict with the

https://doi.org/10.16922/jrhlc.9.2.8

antiquarians.[2] Here it was the Rev. J. L. Petit who in Scott's words wrote a 'very important and talented letter' objecting that the restorations were not 'sufficiently conservative'. The several strands of Scott the restorer appear in this first crossing of swords. Scott, always sensitive to criticism, affected a disarming modesty about his own expertise, and was painfully eager to explain the circumstances that had led to his decisions, whether right or wrong. He was always careful not to be offensive to his critics, saying of Petit and Stafford:

> I differed from him, not in principle, but on the application of the principles to the matter in question. I wrote stoutly, and I think well, in defence of my own views, and the correspondence was, by mutual agreement, referred to the Oxford and Cambridge Societies, who gave their verdict in my favour.[3]

This is from Scott's *Recollections*, jotted erratically in notebooks and edited for publication after his death by G. Gilbert Scott Jr. It is one of the most delightful of architect's memoirs for the way in which the man, the most successful architect of his day, but still uncertain, vulnerable and also a little vain, continually argues old cases as if still facing an uncomprehending or hostile jury.

At Stafford Scott rebuilt the south transept in an Early English at variance with the late Gothic external character of the church, but in harmony with a single surviving south lancet, and he was able to pronounce that

> the result was a happy one, for embedded in the later walling we found abundant fragments of the earlier work, which enabled me to reproduce the transept with certainty, and a noble design it is.[4]

The story of Stafford shows up Scott's strengths as a restorer as well as the problems. He followed Pugin into the path of the true Gothic, and shared in the reverence for the Gothic of the early fourteenth century, the Decorated, over the later Perpendicular and therefore favoured the restoration of originals of this period or earlier, over the retention of late Gothic work, even where it determined the character of the whole building, as at Stafford. He was therefore careful in his dismantling of old work to find clues as to original form, but having found these they governed enthusiastic reconstruction. It is important to emphasise how much Scott's anxious and self-critical character pushed him to a greater care than that exercised by most of his contemporaries and not just in the 1840s but throughout his career. He wanted any new work to be supported by archaeological evidence. At Stafford, and we must remember that how exceptional this is in the early 1840s, he says

> the pains we took in uncovering old forms and details were unbounded, and though too little actual old work was preserved, I believe that no restoration could, barring this, be more scrupulously conscientious.[5]

Here for the first time Scott had to tackle a collapsing tower, and his strictures on the means are thoughtful and practical, concluding with the recommendation: 'Above all, have a thoroughly practical clerk of the works, neither too young not too old.'[6] Edwin Gwilt here was the first-mentioned of a line of Scott's assistants whose role was critical in the general absence of the architect.

This has always been the question asked about Scott. How could he ever have been there? Scott's workload was prodigious, David Cole estimates some eight or nine hundred jobs in a career of forty years,[7] and besides there were the books, the reports, the lectures, the committees, the meetings and the other trappings of a career at the heart of British architecture, not to speak of the European study tours (seventeen in

Figure 1: St Mary Stafford, prior to Scott's restoration

Julian Orbach

Figure 2: St Mary Stafford in 1852, after Scott's restoration

twenty years) generally taken without his family, and the annual family holiday. The account of the office given by Sir T. G. Jackson who was there just before the St Davids period, in 1858-61, is of rush and confusion, twenty-seven employees, and the principal barely available, indeed hardly ever there. But the essential Scott is not absent, as Jackson is careful to say, in that the office produced: 'something of a continuous style that passed for Gilbert Scott's and which one can always recognise wherever one meets it'.[8] This is no small thing, for Scott was no middle ranking Victorian, but the man who did most to steer Britain into the path of the Gothic Revival, and the man whose office trained more than a generation of British architects.

It is awesome to realise that in the years of his major church restorations Gilbert Scott fought and lost the battle for the Gothic government buildings in Whitehall (1856-9), picked himself up and re-designed them in Byzantine in 1860, redesigned them again in Italianate in 1861-2, and then began the construction of what was the most important government building contract since the Houses of Parliament, a job that was to be coterminous with the work at St Davids. In the decade from 1856 Scott designed country houses that established modern Gothic as a style for great houses: Kelham Hall, Notts, 1858-61, followed in 1861 by Hafodunos, Denbighshire. At the same time he was promoting secular

Gothic for college libraries at University and Exeter Colleges at Oxford, for town halls at Preston, and banks and hospitals at Beckett's Bank and the General Infirmary, both at Leeds. And as Scott started to think about St Davids, on 16 December 1861, Albert the Prince Consort died. For a decade Scott and Albert's memory were synonymous and Scott's knighthood in 1872 was bestowed by the Queen for the Albert Memorial built 1863–72. Scott also refitted Wolsey's chapel at St George's Windsor as a kind of Albert cenotaph, the empty tomb and effigy to compensate the public for Albert's actual interment in the inaccessibly private Frogmore mausoleum.[9] He competed for the Albert Hall in London and designed the Albert Institute at Dundee. Within this schedule (and just when the two western piers supporting the tower at St Davids were being removed) Scott set aside six months in 1866 to plan a vast complex for the new Law Courts, then a further month at the seaside to work exclusively on the elevations, an abortive work of which Scott said in a wonderfully typical remark:

> I do not know that my general architectural design was of much merit, though I think that it was fully as good as any recent work I know of by any other architect.[10]

In the same decade Scott's new church work was at its most intense with major churches at Doncaster, Halifax, Richmond, Crewe Green, Stoke Newington, Leafield, Ranmore, Nocton, Sandbach Heath, Rhyl, Wanstead, Southgate, Sherbourne, Bromborough, Taunton and Shackleford, as well as the college chapels at Exeter College Oxford, Wellington College, Harrow School and St John's, Cambridge. There were many smaller works too and while some of Scott's work can be pedestrian no-one who has visited All Souls, Haley Hill, Halifax or Exeter College can doubt that Scott designed some of the noblest interiors of the age. Scott only designed one outstanding cathedral, Edinburgh (1871–93), but was involved in a surprising little list of others: Dundee and Glasgow for the Scottish Episcopalians, and overseas at St Johns, Newfoundland; Shanghai; Christchurch, New Zealand; and Grahamstown, South Africa. His son Oldrid completed some and himself designed cathedrals for Lahore and Port Stanley. But by 1865 the ecclesiastical side of Scott's practice had shifted heavily towards restoration, some eighty jobs in the following seven years, as opposed to 29 new churches. Eventually Scott was to work in every county of England and Wales bar Cardiganshire.[11]

Scott was probably asked to look at St David's Cathedral with some urgency in 1861 as on 21 February that year the tower and spire of Chichester cathedral collapsed, inspiring alarm in chapters all around the country. The condition of the tower at St Davids was the worst that Scott had yet seen, and his report of 1862 identified critical failure of two of the four piers carrying the tower, and emphasised the extreme urgency of the rescue attempt. In that year, 1862, Scott was also engaged at Ely, Westminster Abbey, St Albans, Hereford, Lichfield, Peterborough, Salisbury, and most recently of course, Chichester, as well as at the abbey or priory churches at Dorchester, Malvern and Pershore, and at several of the greatest parish churches including Boston, Wakefield, Hull and Ludlow. In the course of that year he added Brecon and Ripon, Bath and Worcester followed in 1864, Bury St Edmunds and Selby Abbey in 1865, Gloucester, Beverley Minster and Jarrow in 1866, the year that the St Davids tower was saved. St Asaph followed in 1867, Bangor and Chester in 1868, Oxford, Exeter and Durham in 1870, Rochester in 1871, Dunblane in 1872, Tewkesbury Abbey in 1874, Canterbury and Winchester in 1875, and Bridlington in 1876, the year that Scott designed the west front at St Davids. Then in 1877 Scott's career as a restoration architect was called into question by William Morris in his attack on the Tewkesbury job, an essentially unfair attack which Scott attempted to counter in the last notebook. He died in March 1878 leaving the practice to his two sons George Gilbert and John Oldrid. They were to work together for two years, but fell out, and it was John Oldrid who continued the restoration practice, overseeing St Davids until his death in 1913.

The work at St Davids began early in 1865 under a resident clerk of the works, J. B. Clear, whom Scott had already employed on a collapsing crossing tower at St Cuthbert, Darlington.[12] Scott's clerks of the works were crucial to each operation, supervised perhaps by an assistant architect under Scott himself. The clerks of the works were not trained architects in general. The best known of them, J. T. Irvine came from humble background to become the best church archaeologist of the era. We know the names of the clerks for two of the main phases at St Davids, for the 1865–6 rescue of the tower and repair of the choir, Clear is named, and called 'resident architect' in *The Builder*,[13] though Scott does not use the term. Scott's praise for Clear is unstinting and he emphasises that for much of the time Clear worked without supervision.[14] For the work from 1872 including the rebuilding of the West

Figure 3: Elevation of the south side of St Davids Cathedral by A. W. Pugin (Courtesy of Pembrokeshire County Council)

front William Cook replaced Clear, who had died suddenly in 1870.[15] The builders for the whole period of Scott's involvement were Joseph Wood & Son of Worcester.

Clear oversaw an operation of monumental complexity.[16] The wholly shattered west piers were partly supporting 124 feet and 4,000 tons of tower above and would have to be removed and entirely replaced. This type of work had been done before at Hereford, by Cottingham in 1841–7, and by Scott at Salisbury and Darlington, and was being done at Bayeux. Clear braced the whole upper structure with iron, screwing the sides some three inches closer before building enormous wooden shoring against the west and north side, on which the whole weight rested for a period of time. The ends of the pulpitum or screen were removed entirely together with the tomb of Bishop Gower, to make way for the shoring. The supporting structures were basically timber infill of the west and north arches, the south arch being already blocked in stone, and horizontal baulks threaded through the lower tower walls carried on massive vertical supports 3'6" square at the base and 36' long, assisted by raking shores at various heights.[17] Three of the four crossing arches had long been blocked, shown as such on a plan of 1770. William Butterfield in 1847 opened the upper part of the west arch,[18] confusingly shown open in John Parker's 1836 view,[19] which must be idealised. Scott gives an alarming description of the river of loose material flowing from the tower as the holes for the horizontal members were made, and the continuous emergencies that occurred as each portion of each pier was removed. Few stones survived unshattered in the two piers but Scott was able to return to the nearby Caerbwdi cliffs from whence the original purple stone had come.[20]

The tower piers were complete in May 1866, and work proceeded to the upper part of the tower, followed by the choir and choir aisles.

The fifteenth- or sixteenth-century wooden tower ceiling cut across the fourteenth-century windows of the tower. Scott felt free to raise this ceiling to expose the windows, and re-coloured the painted woodwork. Then Scott turned to the presbytery, and here faced the Stafford problem. The upper walls, ceiling and upper east window were a late Gothic addition (as at St Mary, Haverfordwest), and the original lower wall height and steeper roof pitch were clearly visible. Scott strongly desired to replicate the earlier upper east window, whose stones he could see reused in the six feet of additional side wall and was tempted to remove all the fifteenth-century work and attempt a vault, at least in oak, on the original vaulting piers. In the 1869 report Scott explains why this procedure was not followed. Jones and Freeman, Scott says, had laid down a principle – that he endorsed – that

> when ancient alterations had become stereotyped as part of an historical monument, all change in them not included under the term *restoration* is set down as to be in itself reprehended. . . This rule would certainly demand the repair and retention of the later roof, and even, at first sight, of the later window . . .[21]

Writing the *Recollections* in 1872 he says

> Mr E. A. Freeman says he would either have retained the perpendicular window or else have 'gone the whole hog' and restored the high roof.[22]

Scott vacillated painfully and chose a middle way, he kept the fifteenth-century roof, though he had to dismantle it, but gave himself permission to replace the fifteenth-century upper east window. He had found the sills of the original and fragments in the side walls which, as he put it, he worked *as a mine*, in dismantling them for useful stones. Scott's quartet of richly shafted and deeply set lancets sit better with the great triplet of blocked windows below. Filled with the Hardman stained glass of 1870, they return the east wall to a side-lit gloom where previously it was flooded with light.

Scott's report of 1869 still reads as a remarkably astute analysis of the complicated story of the presbytery with its reconstruction after the tower collapse of 1220 and the conflicting evidence as to the vaulting. While there may be reason to disagree with his decision to replace

Gilbert Scott and the Restoration of St Davids

Figure 4:
Presbytery,
St Davids Cathedral,
prior to Scott's
restoration

Figure 5 (*below*):
Presbytery,
St Davids Cathedral
in the late
nineteenth century

139

the east window, the process to the decision is admirably set out,[23] and the care with which he repaired the fifteenth-century ceiling, which he would prefer to have lost, is also admirable. The choir aisles also were repaired in 1867–9 and re-roofed. It is important to remember just how derelict they were. The south aisle was roofless with no tracery at all, and the west bay had been cheaply rebuilt in 1843–4 as part of the fitting up of the south transept as the parish church.[24] The north aisle had been poorly roofed in 1828–9 solely to shelter the access to the Chapter House (in St Thomas's chapel) and only fragments of tracery remained, on which Scott based his new work.[25] Within the church, Scott's restoration of the woodwork of the choir and stonework of the pulpitum was exemplary and he curiously remarks

> I am aware that the conservative manner in which they have been dealt with has provoked some criticism of those who undervalue these relics of ancient workmanship.[26]

This may be a reference to the bane of Scott's first period at St Davids, Canon Sir Erasmus Williams whom he describes with some pleasure as:

> a most eccentric man, aristocratic and gentlemanly by nature, but, as one must suppose, somewhat touched in his mind. His monomania was hatred of the Dean and of most of the Canons . . . Next to that came hatred of all that is Welsh, though a Welshman himself; and lastly a general hatred of the human race.[27]

Williams's running joke was that it would be better to pull the cathedral down and build a new one, which Scott found more tiresome than amusing after a while, and it was with relief that Canon James Allen succeeded him, and put his own fortune into restoring the north transept.

The new fittings are reticent apart from the mosaic infill of the blocked east lancets, made by Salviati & Co. of London and Venice from designs, like the stained glass above, by John Hardman Powell of Hardman. Scott was a great advocate of Salviati's work, using it in the Westminster Abbey reredos of 1866 but *The Builder* thought the St Davids work '*outré* and unsatisfactory, not the sort of thing the nineteenth century should be doing'.[28] The mosaics are rather good, with a static early Gothic drawing style and muted subtle colours that do not shout against the rich chevron of the surrounds. Scott designed the simple Gothic altar rails and

Gilbert Scott and the Restoration of St Davids

choir seating, all in oak and very nicely restrained, such that they pass un-noticed. Scott placed all the available ancient tiles in the sanctuary (regrettably bedded in concrete) and had the designs reproduced by Godwin of Lugwardine for the rest of the presbytery and the choir aisles.

By the time of the 1869 report restoration had extended to two and a half bays of the nave walls and had begun work on the approach to the chapter house (now the cathedral library). Scott stressed that the nave was still in dreadful condition with water coming down 'in cataracts' such that the congregation approaching the restored choir would need umbrellas. He had begun to repair the ceiling and hoped to restore the south aisle timber roof and match it on the north. St Thomas's chapel and the chapter house above it were in such dilapidation that the roof was likely to fall in. He finishes the report with a ringing appeal for funds for the '*Mother Church*' and a stirring appeal for services in Welsh to be given equal weight to those in English,

Though an Englishman, I am ready to cry heartily, *Wales for the Welsh*, and to add, the *Church* of Wales for the Welsh and, a fortiori, the *Cathedral of St David* for the Welsh.

It is hard not to admire Gilbert Scott.

In 1870 Scott suffered his heart attack at Chester, which was so serious that he could not be moved from there for five weeks. But work carried on. Around 1871 Charles Baker King became Scott's principal assistant at St Davids. William Cook was clerk of the works after James Clear died in 1870. King estimated in 1872 that £21,460 had been spent and that another £12,500 was required to finish the transepts, nave and nave aisles.[29] The nave and south aisle were almost finished towards the end of 1872, the corbelled parapet of the nave replicated from found details and the north transept was re-roofed to the original pitch with a groined oak ceiling. The roof of Bishop Vaughan's chapel east of the presbytery was redone, and in 1873 the north aisle and the Chapter House were repaired.[30] Much of this work was personally financed by Canon Allen.[31]

The final phase of Scott's work was the replacement of the late eighteenth-century west front designed by Nash, derided by even the cheap guide-books, and said to be failing structurally.[32] The proposal to make this the memorial to Bishop Connop Thirlwall, who had died in 1874, was agreed before a meeting in April 1876 of Scott, the new bishop Basil Jones and his co-author of 1856, Edward Freeman, to discuss how the pre-Nash front might be recreated.[33] Its much-altered final form was known from the elevation by the elder Pugin and there were some unreliable earlier views from which Scott was able to base his design.[34] The massing of the facade was relatively straightforward, Scott had to invent the spired tops to the four framing piers and a new great west door. His crowning gable was to the steep original pitch known from the outline on the tower, this requiring the replacement of the whole nave roof to match. However the Chapter decided to cut the cost by half by preserving the existing nave roof, lowering the window lights to keep within the original nave west arch and omitting some ornament.[35] This suggests that Scott intended significantly taller upper lights that would have cut through the internal arch putting the window heads above the nave ceiling. The loss of Scott's crowning gable is to the detriment of the composition, which while consonant with the original Romanesque detail, is more massive than lively, and overwhelmingly purple from the Caerbwdi stone. The tender of Wood & Sons for the work was accepted in 1877 and work continued until 1882, by which time Scott was four years dead and buried in Westminster Abbey.

It would seem that among the works completed after Scott's death was the south transept groined oak roof, recorded as finished just before the west front, in 1882.[36] The porch was restored perhaps later as label-stops of the porch with heads of Queen Victoria and Bishop Basil Jones were

Figure 6: Cathedral from south-east, showing Scott's restoration of tower and east end

put in only in 1889.[37] The Italian marble paving of the nave was not laid until 1882–3 and so perhaps the pews, which look like G. G. Scott's work, are a design of his son.[38]

George Gilbert Scott's restoration of St Davids cathedral ranks as one of the best that he did, considering the fragility of the original, the extreme difficulty of the solution adopted for the tower, and indeed the careful thought that animated each decision. When under attack from the Society for the Protection of Ancient Buildings in 1877, it was his work at St Davids that Scott offered in his own defence as a restorer pointing out that in the whole work he had only altered one medieval window and that from Perpendicular Gothic to Early English. The wonderful photograph of Sir Gilbert Scott on his last visit to the cathedral in 1876, in the roofless NE chapel aisle, with Bishop Basil Jones, Dr Edward Freeman and Dean James Allen, is a touching memorial to the four men through whom the cathedral was recorded, interpreted and finally saved.[39]

Figure 7: Photo of G. G. Scott, E. A Freeman and others at St Davids, 1877 (image courtesy of RCAHMW)

Postscript

When Scott died the eastern chapels remained roofless, and although some restoration continued under his son, J. Oldrid Scott, work proceeded slowly. A payment book for 1893–7 shows that five men, paid between £1/10/0d and 10/0d a week, were employed on the eastern chapels, frequently diverted to repair the Dean's house or other pressing works.[40] They seem to have been in Bishop Vaughan's chapel mostly, where Tudor windows were found in the east wall in 1897[41] and may have restored the windows of the three roofless chapels. At the end of 1897 Oldrid Scott made an appeal for the completion of the work,[42] which was taken up, the whole restoration to cost £6–7,000.[43] The first part, a memorial to Bishop Basil Jones, Dean Allen and Dean Phillips, was to be the restoration of the stone-vaulted Lady chapel and vestibule. This was achieved in 1900–1.[44] Both Sir Gilbert Scott and his son wanted to put stone vaults on the two outer chapels, following the medieval evidence, but expense precluded this and the roofs are of oak. The NE chapel of St Nicholas was restored in memory of Dean Howell in 1904[45] and the SE chapel of St Edward the Confessor was restored at the expense of Lady Maidstone in 1909–12,[46] completing the process begun half a century before with the 1862 report.

Figure 8: Photo, *c.*1890, of roofless East End of St Davids Cathedral

Oldrid Scott died in 1913 leaving designs for the fitting-out of the SE chapel and it was left to his unfortunate successor W. D. Caröe to deal with the impossible Lady Maidstone and her penchants for the Book of Revelation and Greek key pattern.[47] The alabaster tomb with the beautifully-carved effigy by Brooke Hitch, the alabaster altar and reredos and the marble floor make this a modern version of the medieval chantry chapel, to a wealthy lady whose only connection to the cathedral was that she was grand-daughter of an earlier nineteenth-century bishop: 'the programme reveals how much the dean and chapter . . . were prepared to concede in return for much needed cash'.[48]

The work occupied Caröe from 1916–22. He restored the detached bell-tower at Porth y Twr in 1929–30 and designed the hanging Rood in the nave in 1930–1. His plans for restoring St Mary's Hall and rebuilding the late medieval cloisters date from 1934 but went no further. Caröe, his son, grandson and their successors continued as architects to the cathedral into the twenty-first century. Alban Caröe designed the inner nave porches in 1947, put the vestries into the south transept in 1953, and brought the roofless St Mary's Hall back into use in 1965–6. Martin Caröe designed the modernist gates to the Lady chapel, made by Frank Roper in 1977–8. Alban Caröe's organ case of 1953 was enlarged in 1999 by Peter Bird, of Caröe & Partners, who restored the Porth y Twr to use as exhibition spaces in 2002, and designed the new oak-framed cloister buildings, finished in 2007, completing the long story of the restoration of St Davids Cathedral.

Notes

[1] *Restoring St David's Cathedral. Speeches by the Lord Bishop of the Diocese and Geo. Gilbert Scott Esq RA at Carmarthen October 1863* (London, 1863), pp. 13–14.

[2] Chris Miele '"Their interest and habit": Professionalism and the Restoration of Medieval Churches, 1837–77', in C. Brooks and A. Saint (eds), *The Victorian Church* (Manchester & New York, 1995), pp. 151–72, at 152–3.

[3] Sir George Gilbert Scott, *Personal and Professional Recollections, edited, introduced and restored by Gavin Stamp* (Stamford, 1995), p. 98.

[4] Scott, *Recollections*, p. 99.

[5] Scott, *Recollections*, p. 99.

[6] Scott, *Recollections*, p. 100.

[7] David Cole, *The Work of Sir Gilbert Scott* (London, 1980).

[8] Sir T. G. Jackson, *Recollections of Thomas Graham Jackson* (London, 1950).

[9] E. Darby and N. Smith, *The Cult of the Prince Consort* (New Haven CT & London, 1983).

[10] Scott, *Recollections*, p. 274.

11 Even there his former partner William Moffatt seems to have used the Scott & Moffatt name for his National Schools at Cardigan and Lampeter of 1847 and 1850.

12 James Bulley Clear (1829–70), from Norwich, worked for Scott at Darlington, 1864–5, before St Davids, where he died young in 1870.

13 *The Builder*, 23 June 1866.

14 G. G. Scott, *A Second Report on the state of the fabric of St David's Cathedral* (London, 1869), p. 11.

15 William Cook was in St Davids in 1871 as his name is on the advertisement for tenders for the new schools in *The Welshman*, 29 December 1871.

16 Specification in NLW, SDCh/Misc/238.

17 W. Evans and R. Worsley, *Eglwys Gadeiriol Tyddewi/St Davids Cathedral 1181–1981* (St Davids, 1981), p. 94

18 Miscellaneous Notes: 'St Davids', *Archaeologia Cambrensis* (1848), pp. 80–1, at 81.

19 Evans and Worsley, pp. 50–1.

20 Sir G. G. Scott, *St. David's Cathedral: Extracts from the First and Second Reports* (London, 1873), pp. 13–15.

21 Scott, *Second Report*, p. 14.

22 Scott, *Recollections*, p. 314.

23 Scott, *Extracts*, pp. 18–22.

24 W. B. Jones and E. A. Freeman, *The History and Antiquities of Saint David's* (London, 1856), p. 178.

25 Jones and Freeman, *History and Antiquities*, p. 177.

26 Scott, *Second Report*, p. 23.

27 Scott, *Recollections*, p. 316.

28 Quoted in *The Welshman*, 3 March 1871.

29 *The Builder*, 28 September 1873.

30 Scott, *Extracts*, pp. 28–31.

31 Scott, *Recollections*, p. 316.

32 *Pembrokeshire Herald*, 28 April 1876.

33 *Dewisland and Kemes Gazette*, 12 January 1876.

34 Illus. in Evans and Worsley, *Eglwys Gadeiriol Tyddewi*, pp. 40–1; National Monuments Record for Wales, 9400047/1.

35 *The Welshman*, 1 September 1876.

36 *Carmarthen Journal*, 1 September 1882.

37 *Pembrokeshire County Guardian*, 28 September 1889.

38 A photograph of the nave with no furnishing but the pulpit is in Haverfordwest Library PO32 LQ/N745.

39 Evans and Worsley, *Eglwys Gadeiriol Tyddewi*, p. 126.

40 NLW, SDCh/B/45.

41 *Pembrokeshire County Guardian*, 11 September 1897.

42 NLW, SDCh/Misc/243.

43 *Tenby Observer*, 13 January 1898.

44 *Tenby Observer*, 22 August 1901.

45 *Haverfordwest & Milford Haven Telegraph*, 21 September 1904.

46 Pembrokeshire Record Office, HDX/894/22-7.

47 NLW, SDCh/Misc/351–403.

48 Roger Stalley in T. Lloyd, J. Orbach and R. Scourfield, *Pembrokeshire*, The Buildings of Wales (New Haven and London 2004), p. 408.

9.
'THE GLOW AND THE GLORY': CONTEXTUALIZING AND INTERPRETING THE STAINED GLASS OF ST DAVID'S CATHEDRAL

John Morgan-Guy

I

The title of this paper comes from an observation made by the artist John Piper, in his *Stained Glass. Art or Anti-Art*, published in 1968.[1] This is a provocative work in which Piper was critical of 'the tide of the browns and mauves and plentiful dirty whites, and the demoralized Gothic, of establishment Edwardian windows'[2] and also of the conservatism of both patrons and clergy which had encouraged that tide to flow.[3] Stained glass had fallen into 'the clutches of the archaeologists and the clergy. They are', he asserted, 'the two gangs that make the whole subject seem such a bore.'[4] Together they had turned churches into:

> imitation art galleries, with odd and hopelessly divergent examples of different personalities in the windows – not placed as a gallery is hung, in helpful relation one to another, but arbitrarily, in the mere order of commissioning.[5]

Piper agreed with Christopher Whall, the *doyen* of the revival in the design and manufacture of stained glass associated with the Arts and Crafts Movement, who in his classic 1905 text-book reminded students that theirs was an art:

> which soars to the highest themes, which dares to treat, which is required to treat, of things Heavenly and Earthly, of the laws of God, and of the nature, duty and destiny of man. . .[6]

https://doi.org/10.16922/jrhlc.9.2.9

It was this calling, sincerity of purpose, and vocation of the artist that Whall and Piper both regarded as paramount. 'All stained-glass gathers itself up into this one subject', Whall taught, 'the glory of the heavens is in it and the fullness of the earth, and we know that the showing forth of it cannot be in words.'[7] Piper echoed Whall when he wrote that he believed

> on the whole, the stained glass lover is not looking for art history, or even for masterpieces. . . but for *the glow and the glory* [my italics], and the general pattern of the art.[8]

Piper would have known Whall's work; there would have been few stained-glass artists of his generation who did not.[9] The revival of the art of stained glass in the mid-nineteenth century, inspired and led in particular by A. W. N. Pugin and the firms that he used, such as John Hardman of Birmingham, had the same understanding. Stained-glass, Pugin and his disciples believed, was more than representational art, more than merely decorative. It had to be epiphanic. Of prime concern to the artist had to be the glory of and in the salvation-history of the Bible. The purpose of the artwork was to communicate the gospel message of love, and to call man to God. That call and communication came through and in the community of faith, and was mediated through the work of the artist. It was not made through the medium of words but in and through the beauty of the image.

II

Sadly, there are only fragments of the 'glow and the glory' of the medieval glass at St Davids, fragments now gathered into one of the north aisle windows. Today the earliest glass in the cathedral dates from 1870–71, and it is with the story and the interpretation of this glass, and its associated glass-mosaics, that this study begins. The east wall of the presbytery is meant to be seen as a unity; Gilbert Scott's restoration gave it the general appearance that it has today. The four lancet windows which form the upper part of the east wall of the presbytery were inserted during that restoration undertaken in the late 1860s. They replaced a large, Perpendicular, window, which was, somewhat controversially, removed by the architect, who claimed to have rediscovered enough evidence of earlier windows to restore them as a quadruplet of lancets.[10] These were glazed in 1870, a year before the mosaics in the great Romanesque lancets below were put in place, but it is necessary to read the glass and mosaics together; there is one donor and one artist involved, even though the work had of necessity to be undertaken by two different companies.[11] The unifying *motif* can be seen in the head of each lancet, both in the glass and the mosaic; the towered and turreted vision of the heavenly Jerusalem, recalling Paul's words in the epistle to the Galatians (4:26). However, the key text is rather Revelation chapter 21, John's vision of the new Jerusalem, accompanied by the 'great voice out of heaven' which proclaims 'Behold, the tabernacle of God is with men, and he will dwell with them, and they shall be his people, and God himself shall be with them, and be their God' (v.3). The central significance of this vision and promise will, I hope, become clear in the examination of the iconography of mosaic and window.

Figure 1: East end of the presbytery, St Davids Cathedral, stained glass by John Hardman & Co. 1870, glass mosaic by Salviati & Co., 1871 (Photo: Martin Crampin)

The *motif* is not to be confused with the very familiar stylized 'gothic canopy' which so often appears over the heads of standing figures in nineteenth-century glass (and some twentieth, for that matter).[12] Although here it possesses the same flat two-dimensionality that one associates with many of the gothic canopies designed by Pugin towards the end of his life, based on those of the Decorated period he favoured, the subject matter here is not merely decorative. Implying as it does a vision of the heavenly Jerusalem it makes the point that all that is within the frame is *sub specie aeternitatis*, and should be read accordingly.

III

The mosaics lie at the heart of the scheme. Writing in the 1907 guide-book to the cathedral, the architect Philip Robson described the effect of the mosaics as 'by no means bad'.[13] He was damning with faint praise. Artistically they are not a success, a judgement tactfully conceded by Roger Stalley: 'A logical alternative to stained glass, but without artificial light rather dull; the detail struggles against the dense Romanesque ornament alongside'.[14] The existence of the Trinity Chapel as an enclosed space beyond the windows to the east from the early sixteenth century severely compromised these lancets as a means of illumination and made glazing problematic. The newly revived technique of glass mosaic in the nineteenth century provided a solution, but the confined space, as Stalley observed, meant that the execution of the design adopted was not totally successful. In particular, the small scale of the three panels below the principal subjects makes them difficult to interpret from any distance in anything other than the brightest light. The deep splay and rich ornamentation of the lancets themselves overwhelms the subject-matter, and places it in shadow.[15]

Some of the blame for this should be laid at the door of the cathedral's architect at the time, Sir George Gilbert Scott. In his 1862 Report to the Dean and Chapter, Scott had been dismissive of the question of glazing. 'I think I have now touched upon everything but the *very subordinate subject* [my italics] of decorations, such as stained glass, suitable decorations of the East end, etc.' he wrote.

I think that stained glass for the few and scanty windows of the choir should be a part of the work of restoration – possibly; that

'The Glow and the Glory'

for other windows may be left to the probability of individual benefactions.[16]

It was clearly not a subject that was high on his agenda, or one to which he was inclined to pay too much attention. It was not an attitude that would have endeared him to Whall or Piper – or to Pugin either.

As it happened, it was just such an individual benefaction that financed the mosaics and the stained-glass in the windows above. The Revd John Lucy, of the family of William Lucy, Bishop of St Davids from 1660–1677, presented both as a memorial to his co-lateral ancestor.[17] John Lucy was a wealthy and munificent patron. His family had been settled at Charlecote in Warwickshire since at least the thirteenth century. He was the second son of the Revd John Hammond Lucy, and had succeeded to one family living – Hampton Lucy – in 1815, at the age of twenty-five, and to another, Charlecote itself, eight years later. In 1822 he had begun the total rebuilding of Hampton Lucy church, using Thomas Rickman as his first architect, and inserting in 1837 an east window by Thomas Willement, who the family had already employed as architect for rebuilding at Charlecote Park. That window, depicting episodes from the life of St Peter, the church's patron, was described by an unnamed contemporary as 'the most magnificent window in stained glass that has been produced in modern times, in imitation of the ancient style'.[18] The choice of Willement, an established designer and maker of glass by this date, meant that no expense was spared by Lucy. (Only four years later Pugin stopped using him as his charges were too high.[19]) Twenty years on, Lucy, intent on completing the work on his church, employed Sir Gilbert Scott as architect. The chancel at Hampton Lucy is to his design.[20] Thus fifteen years before the work at St Davids, patron and architect were known to one another and had collaborated. By 1870 John Lucy was eighty years of age, but clearly his enthusiasm, pride in his ancestry, concern with posterity – and the contents of his pocket – were undiminished. It can be safely assumed that the old man knew exactly what he wanted, and how to set about achieving it. He also lived long enough to see the work completed. He died, as a canon of St Davids, in 1874.

Despite his earlier rather dismissive attitude, because of his key role in the cathedral restoration, and his previous acquaintance with the patron, Scott must have been involved in the work. The design for the glass and for the mosaics was entrusted to John Hardman Powell (1827–1895), the cousin of John Bernard Hardman who had succeeded to his father's Birmingham stained-glass, church metalwork and textile business in 1867. John Hardman Powell was the firm's chief designer, and the firm's work was used by many of the prominent ecclesiastical architects of the day, Scott among them. Although the subject matter of the glass and mosaics may well have been Lucy's choice, the suggestion of using Hardmans for their design almost certainly came from Scott.[21]

Hardmans undertook the cutting, painting and firing of their own glass, as well as designing it, but glass mosaic was another matter.[22] That is where Salviati and Company come into the picture.

It is necessary here to make a short excursion into the story of glass mosaic. Venice and glassmaking had through the centuries become almost synonymous, and from at least the end of the thirteenth century the industry had been localized on the island of Murano in the lagoon. The fall of the Republic in 1797 to the forces of Napoleon, and the transfer in 1814 of its territories to the Austro-Hungarian Empire had all but eclipsed the age-old tradition (the Habsburgs, naturally, overtly favoured the glassmakers of Bohemia) and by the mid-nineteenth century the industry was in a parlous state. However, the founding of the firm of *Fratelli Toso* on the island in 1854, followed by the arrival in 1859 of Antonio Salviati, reversed the decline. *Dottore* Salviati was not an artist; he was a lawyer and business entrepreneur from Vicenza, with an eye for the main chance.[23] His 'laboratory of mosaic art' had as its objective the production of glass tesserae and tiles to repair the Venetian mosaics, and to produce new ones. Salviati employed a number of notable craftsmen and the venture met with almost immediate success. Salviati was an enthusiastic marketer, promoting the work of his factory internationally. In 1862 he came to London, to the Exposition of that year, and his work was well received. He had the vision and the energy, he also had a saleable product, and the means for its mass production, but he lacked the requisite capital to fully exploit it. This he was to find in London, thanks largely to Sir William Drake, chairman of the Burlington Fine Arts Club, and Austen Henry Layard, archaeologist, diplomat, politician, art connoisseur and banker, who with others, agreed to invest in the project.[24] In 1866 the London-based Salviati and Company was founded, and in the summer of that year opened their first London showroom, at 431 Oxford Street. The manufacture of the glass tesserae may have been on an island in the Venetian lagoon but the financial base of the enterprise was London. Not surprisingly, some of the earliest and most

152

'The Glow and the Glory'

prestigious commissions came from this country; the reredos of the Last Supper behind the High Altar of Westminster Abbey in 1867, and the chapel apse mosaic at Gonville & Caius College, Cambridge in 1870.[25]

Here again Sir Gilbert Scott enters the picture. The reconstruction of the screen and installation of the reredos at Westminster was his work.[26] He had therefore used Salviati before the work was undertaken on the St Davids lancets in 1871. By this date the ecclesiastical art world in the United Kingdom was well aware of the potential and worth of the work of Salviati's factory, and neither architects nor potential patrons would have had to have journeyed further than Oxford Street to discuss their contract.[27]

As the centrepiece of John Hardman Powell's overall design, the subject matter of the three mosaics is of particular interest. The centre light contains a representation of the Crucifixion, with the conventional flanking figures of the Blessed Virgin Mary and St John the 'beloved disciple', and the anguished figure of Mary Magdalene at the foot of the cross. The features of all of the figures deserve close attention, from the mingled pain and compassion in the face of Christ, to the deep sorrow in the eyes and expressions of Mary, John and the Magdalene. From the wounds in Christ's hands and feet, streams of blood flow into three chalices.[28] Above the crucifix, two angels veil the sun and the moon (a reference to the 'darkness over all the earth' at the crucifixion (Lk. 23:44–5). The composition, based ultimately upon John 19:25–7, draws its inspiration from countless medieval examples. John Hardman Powell was, like all of his family, not only a fervent Catholic, but also the dutiful disciple of Pugin, who had been the firm's chief designer until 1852. Powell's work here is entirely in harmony with his master's principles. The work should be beautiful, edifying and appropriate, with the crucifixion central. Pugin had written in 1851 'you cannot have the crucifixion as a pendant to anything'.[29]

What is interesting about Hardman's design is his use of typology. The small panel beneath the crucifixion scene illustrates Numbers 21:9, the setting up by Moses of a brazen serpent on a pole in the wilderness.[30] Typology was well known to the Victorian artist. Ruskin had drawn attention to it in his *Modern Painters*, and Holman Hunt enthusiastically embraced it. As George Landow has pointed out, typological interpretations of the Bible narrative were widespread, generally accepted, and characteristic of contemporary hermeneutic and exegesis.[31]. The juxtaposition of the Crucifixion and the raising of the brazen serpent was not

Figure 2: Salviati & Co., The Brazen Serpent, 1871, designed by John Hardman Powell, presbytery (Photo: Martin Crampin)

only an obvious one; it had impeccable gospel credentials. Jesus himself in John 3:14–5 had prophesied 'As Moses lifted up the serpent in the wilderness, even so must the Son of Man be lifted up: that whosoever believeth in him should not perish, but have eternal life'.

Bishop Westcott in his magisterial commentary on John's gospel very clearly explored this typology.[32] The brazen serpent is lifted up on its pole as a conspicuous object in the sight of all of the people. As the afflicted and wounded look upon it, they are restored to temporal health; life is restored to them. As a 'type' of the crucifixion, it is obvious. Jesus is nailed to the cross at a place, where, as both Mark and Matthew indicate, there were those who 'passed by' (Mk. 15:29; Matt. 27:39) and looked upon Him (Jn 20:37, quoting Zech. 12:10). But, as Westcott pointed out, for those who 'look upon' the crucified Christ with the faith of the believer, the healing is not temporal but eternal (the promise of Jn 3:14), it is healing from the death of sin. As St Augustine said, the serpent was 'a present help for the hurt and a type of the future destruction of death by death in the Passion of Christ crucified'.[33]

The brazen serpent in the St Davids mosaic is flanked by two figures. That on the left, shown with the conventional 'horns' and rod (Num. 20:11) is that of Moses. That on the right in the priestly robes with

'The Glow and the Glory'

the breastplate and the Urim and the Thummim (Lev. 8:8) is presumably intended to represent Aaron. The figure is holding the budding rod, his attribute in art since at least the thirteenth century, and inspired by the account in Num. 17:1–8. This identification poses a problem for Aaron had died on Mount Hor, and his son Eleazar had been invested as his successor by Moses before the raising of the serpent.[34] Unless, therefore, we are to assume that Aaron's rod passed with the High Priestly office – and Num. 17:10 would seem to indicate that this was so – the presence of Aaron in this tableau is anomalous. However, the overall intention is clear; the 'type' of the crucifixion is flanked by the giver of the Law, himself seen as a 'type' of Christ, and by the High Priest, whose priesthood was seen as a 'type' of the superior High Priesthood of Christ – as explored in chapter 7 of the epistle to the Hebrews.[35]

It is this juxtaposition of the brazen serpent with the crucifixion, and the former being seen as the type of the latter, that is the link between the mosaic of the central lancet and those in the two lancets which flank it, containing the figures of Ecclesia and Synagoga.[36] This composition can be traced back at least to the tenth century, and incidentally from a period of rising tension between Christians and Jews. It derives in its present form from the image created in the writings of Albertus Magnus (c.1206–80) which in its turn owes much to Lam. 5:16–7. Albertus describes Synagoga as a blindfolded woman, who has lost her crown, and carries her head lowered. In the Lamentations, Jeremiah describes Jerusalem (and thus, in Christian understanding, by implication Synagogue, the church of the Old Covenant) as bewailing 'the crown is fallen from our head: woe unto us, that we have sinned! For this our heart is faint; for these things our eyes are dim.' It is the standard medieval representation of Synagoga that we have here, blindfolded, her crown hanging loosely from her hand, and with the broken lance, which is a 'type' of that which pierced the side of Christ on Calvary. John 19 (v.34). John asserts (v.37) that this was in fulfilment of 'another scripture' (Zech. 12:10): 'they shall look upon me whom they have pierced'. The blindfolded Synagogue cannot fulfil that prophecy. She is not a participant in the 'blood and water', traditionally interpreted as the grace flowing from the dominically constituted sacraments of Baptism and Eucharist. It is worth noting of this figure that she is shown wearing the breastplate of the High Priest, and that the broken lance she carries is floriate. Both are 'back-references' to the priesthood of the Old Covenant that had been superseded by that of Christ. The governing text here is

Hebrews chapter 9 verses 11–15, and especially verse 14: 'How much more shall the blood of Christ, who through the eternal Spirit offered himself without spot to God, purge your conscience from dead works to serve the living God?'

The superseding of the Old Covenant by the New and by the teachings of the Church, is symbolised by Ecclesia, the stately, crowned figure shown in the other flanking lancet holding a cross in her right hand and a chalice in her left.[37] Two things in particular call for comment here; first, although the figure of Ecclesia is placed in the left-hand lancet, as we view it, it is, in fact, in the place of honour, to the 'right hand' of the crucified Lord. Secondly, the female figure of Ecclesia is here robed in Eucharistic vestments, the alb and chasuble of the priest. The church is traditionally female; she is 'Holy Mother Church' and the author of the Epistle to the Ephesians (ch. 5), uses the simile of bride and church.[38]

IV

The subject-matter of the lancets above is not entirely clear at first sight. The windows are set high, and the imagery is detailed. Robson maintained that the windows represented the Last Supper, Gethsemane, the Transfiguration and the Nativity[39] (though not in that order, reading from left to right), but Stalley gives the subjects as the Nativity, the Resurrection, the Ascension and (possibly) the Supper at Emmaus.[40] Robson is right; Stalley is wrong three times out of four. Reading from left to right, the first subject is the Nativity, depicting the Virgin Mary, the Christ-child, and an attendant St Joseph, with his staff, a traditional grouping inspired by Luke chapter 2 (vv.1–7). This composition, in which the Blessed Virgin occupies pride of place, but which nonetheless, because of the focus of her gaze upon the Christ-child, is imbued with tenderness and humanity, emerged into western iconography during the thirteenth century. It seems to have two roots, namely, the development of Franciscan piety and spirituality[41] and the rapid and widespread popularity of the *Revelations* of the fourteenth century St Bridget of Sweden. Bridget believed that she had been vouchsafed a vision of the nativity by the Virgin herself, in which the birth occurred instantaneously and painlessly while Mary knelt at prayer.[42] St Davids has here a good example of the resulting image; the Christ-child, at ground level, a kneeling figure of the Blessed Virgin, and a standing, thoughtful figure of Joseph. What is captured is

Figure 3: John Hardman & Co., The Nativity, 1870, designed by John Hardman Powell, presbytery (Photo: Martin Crampin)

the moment of the miraculous birth in the Brigettine tradition. A word should be said of Joseph's staff. This is not an indication of his old age or frailty, but a reference to the story in the apocryphal *Protoevangelium of James*, in which Joseph is seen to be divinely chosen to be the spouse of the Virgin by the flowering of his staff. The inspiration of the story of Aaron's rod here is, of course, obvious.[43]

The next window, reading from left to right, is the Transfiguration of Jesus, recorded in all three synoptic gospels. With Jesus are shown Moses (again 'horned', from the Vulgate mistranslation of Exodus 34:29) holding the Book of the Law and his rod; Elijah, and the three apostles Peter, James and John. The composition, as with the Nativity lancet, is conventional and unremarkable.

The third window depicts the agony of Jesus in the Garden of Gethsemane. Again we have, in accordance with Matthew 26:37, Peter, James and John in the foreground (shown asleep, as recorded in v.40) and the praying figure of Jesus beyond. What is depicted here is the prayer of Jesus, in v.39, that 'the cup' of the forthcoming suffering should pass from Him, but only if it be His Father's will. Before Jesus, bending from Heaven, is an angel, holding that cup in the form of a chalice.

The fourth window shows the moment at the Last Supper when Jesus intimates to John, 'one of his disciples, whom Jesus loved' (Jn. 13:25) and who 'was leaning on Jesus' bosom' that Judas Iscariot was to be the instrument of his betrayal (vv.25–30). This is a very clever use of the restricted space by Hardman Powell. It would have been impossible to have shown the entire apostolic company gathered together. The bread and the cup on the table, and this moment of intimacy, are used to encapsulate the narrative.

Chronologically, reading from left to right, the sequence does not make sense. Gethsemane and the Last Supper would need to be juxtaposed. Theologically, the order is less important, in fact, arguably, makes rather more sense. In the first three lancets the Incarnate life of the Son of God is summarized. In the fourth, the Last Supper, and the institution of the Eucharist, the continuing work of the church, the continuing Incarnation, is revealed.[44]

V

Finally in this section the two small panels in the mosaic, those respectively beneath the figures of Ecclesia and Synagoga, require comment. Here there is a departure from the Biblical narrative and a move forward in time to the life of the cathedral's patron, St David. This is a reference to the continuing work of the Incarnate Lord, the work of the church. The panel beneath the figure of Ecclesia does not depict a specific incident in the life of the saint, but rather that which characterized the whole of his life, that of the community which he founded and over which he presided. The panel shows David giving sustenance to the poor, exemplified here by a woman and a young child, the saint himself dressed simply in a grey monastic habit.

Rhygyfarch's *Life of St David* stresses the saint's life of charity; David gave constant attention to the 'feeding [of] a multitude of orphans, wards, widows, needy, sick, feeble and pilgrims: so he began; so he continued; so he ended.'[45] The placing of this image under that of Ecclesia is quite deliberate. David and his community epitomize the corporate works of mercy enjoined upon the Christian church,[46] which derive from

Matt. 25:31–46, Jesus' account of the Last Judgment, when those who have fed the hungry, sheltered the homeless, clothed the naked, visited the sick and the imprisoned, enter into the inheritance of the Kingdom of God, and those who have failed in these obligations are condemned to everlasting punishment. 'Inasmuch as ye have done it unto one of the least of these my brethren, ye have done it unto me.' (v.40). The juxtaposition of the figure of Ecclesia with David and the works of mercy was intended to be both a message and a challenge to the church and to individual Christians.

The choice of a simple monastic habit for the clothing of the saint here serves to emphasize the point. 1871 is an early date for the depiction of David in this way; more common was the hieratic image of David sumptuously and anachronistically robed as a metropolitan archbishop, an image which lingered into the twentieth century. By that date the fashion was changing. Sir William Goscombe John's David in the Cardiff City Hall was put in place in 1917.[47] The emphasis is on the holy poverty and humility of the saint, rather than on the power, pride and pomp of the medieval prelate.

By contrast, the panel under the figure of Synagoga does depict a specific incident in the life of David, and one to which Rhygyfarch devotes several chapters, namely, the Synod of Llanddewi Brefi at which the saint decisively confounded the adherents to the Pelagian heresy.

In the mosaic, the placing of the image of his preaching of the orthodox Christian faith beneath the blind figure of Synagoga is quite deliberate. The years immediately preceding the insertion of this mosaic were a time of theological ferment in the western churches. 1864 had seen the publication by Pope Pius IX of the Syllabus of Errors, widely interpreted as an attack on liberal thinking both inside and outside of the Catholic Church. In the Established Church the theological liberalism of Rowland Williams (vice-principal of St David's College, Lampeter until 1862 under Dean Llewelyn Lewellin) and of Bishop Colenso of Natal had resulted in charges of heresy being brought against them. It is in the context of this climate that this depiction of the Synod of Llanddewi Brefi is to be understood. For the Catholic Hardman Powell and the Anglican John Lucy it was only when adherence to what they believed to be false teaching was rooted out that the church could be true to its calling.[48] Lucy's bequest may be a nineteenth century sermon in glass and mosaic, but it is more than that; it is a robust essay in contemporary Christian apologetic.[49]

John Morgan-Guy

VI

The other stained-glass in the cathedral all dates from the twentieth century, and although overall it may be subject to Piper's critique quoted earlier, some of the chosen subjects are entirely appropriate for their situation. Chronologically the cathedral had to wait for more than thirty years after the Lucy bequest before any more pictorial glass was inserted.

The chapel of St Nicholas in the north aisle of the retrochoir was restored at the turn of the nineteenth and twentieth centuries as a memorial to Dean David Howell, and the glazing of the east window, dating from 1904, marks the culmination of the work.[50] Nicholas, a fourth century bishop of Myra, was in the Middle Ages one of the most popular saints in Christendom. As the patron of seafarers, the dedication to him of a chapel here at St Davids, within sight and sound of the sea, was particularly appropriate.[51] The image of the saint in the window is a conventional one; he is shown robed as a bishop, holding the book of the gospels, and is identified by his emblem of three golden balls. This is a reference to the story in the ninth century Life of the saint that he saved three girls, daughters of an impoverished

Figure 4: James Powell & Sons, St Nicholas, 1904, Chapel of St Nicholas, east wall of the north aisle of the retrochoir (Photo: Martin Crampin)

'The Glow and the Glory'

nobleman, from a life of prostitution by throwing three bags of gold, to serve as a dowry for them, into their window under cover of darkness. The glass is the work of the firm of James Powell & Sons of the Whitefriars Glassworks in London. Established in 1844, the firm commissioned designs from distinguished artists such as Sir Edward Burne-Jones and Henry Holiday, often employing more than one artist in the preparation of a single window. Unfortunately, although this St Nicholas window features in the company's Order Book for 1904, in this instance no artist is recorded by name.[52]

Five years later, in 1909, 'a wayfarer' donated the window in the chapel of St Thomas à Becket depicting St David and St Asaph.[53] Both are shown in full medieval episcopal regalia – what Roger Stalley called 'outrageously detailed vestments'.[54] The style of the design is reminiscent of Charles Eamer Kempe, but is the work of the Lancaster firm of Shrigley and Hunt, which began the manufacture of stained glass in 1874. At the date of this window's design and installation, the firm's chief designer was the Swedish-born Carl Almquist (1848–1924), who had trained as an assistant to Henry Holiday.[55] It is likely that Almquist was responsible for the David and Asaph window, as he was the designer of two other windows donated by 'a Wayfarer', that of SS. George, Michael and Alban in St Mary Redcliffe, Bristol, and of SS. Richard and Nicholas in the cloister of Chichester Cathedral.[56] 'A Wayfarer' was a specific person, whom Birgitta Lovgren identified with 'the pseudonym of a rather prolific author whose books regularly turn up in English antiquarian bookshops';[57] in fact, the window was something of an advertising gimmick, as in this case the 'Wayfarer' was Arthur Hunt, a partner in the firm of Shrigley & Hunt, and it was obviously intended to awaken interest in the firm's work.[58] In this it was successful, as further commissions followed within the diocese.

It has to be said that neither the Powell of Whitefriars nor the Shrigley & Hunt windows show those firms at their best.[59] In particular, Almquist was in declining health by the early years of the twentieth century, and inclined to recycle earlier designs. Both his St Mary Redcliffe and Chichester cathedral 'Wayfarer' windows contained figures he had used elsewhere.[60]

The 1923 windows at the west end of the cathedral, by Kempe and Company, also reveal the declining power of that firm's designs by this time.[61] Charles Eamer Kempe opened his stained glass studio in 1866, after graduating from Oxford and studying under G. F. Bodley, one of the most distinguished of the 'Gothic Revival' architects. Kempe, like his master, was much influenced by the Oxford 'Tractarians', and, though he was never a thoroughgoing 'Anglo-Catholic', his richly robed, hieratic figures had a great appeal to clergy and laity sympathetic to that movement in English church life. 'The silvery, detached, spiritual image Kempe managed to convey was the perfect fulfilment of the Anglican churchman's dream for a mystical atmosphere in the uplifted church ritual of the late nineteenth century.'[62] However, after his death in 1907 and the removal from the scene of his personal 'fastidious supervision',[63] the work of the firm stagnated under his nephew, Walter Ernest Tower. By 1923 the designs were all-too-often rigid, old-fashioned and derivative, and the attempt to inject colour, as in the west windows at St Davids, did little to rescue them.

The Kempe glass was inserted into Scott's late-nineteenth-century fenestration, and it exemplifies several of the firm's characteristics, notably the richly ornate clothing of the figures, and the extremely elaborate canopy work which frames them.[64] The principal subject, in the three main lancets, is the Risen Christ, supported by St David and St George. The Christ figure is standing, holding the gonfalon, and with the wounds

Figure 5: C.E. Kempe & Co., The Risen Christ with St David and St George, and Archangels, 1923, west wall of the nave (Photo: Martin Crampin)

'The Glow and the Glory'

in his hand, feet and side visible. To his left (and our right) is the figure of St George, in full plate armour, with both his shield and banner bearing his emblem of the red cross. On the right hand of Christ (our left) is St David, with the dove of the Holy Spirit on his shoulder. The saint is robed as a medieval bishop, but, interestingly, not as a metropolitan archbishop. He carries a pastoral staff and not a metropolitical cross, and wears no pallium.

In the five smaller lancets above appear the figures of three archangels, with Michael at the centre, Gabriel to his right and Raphael to his left.[65] They are supported by two flanking angels, bearing musical instruments. Michael, like St George, is shown in full plate armour, with sword and banner, as befits the captain of the Heavenly Host, the celestial army that defends the Church. He is the angel who defeats the rebel angels and the dragon of evil (Rev. 12:7–9). Gabriel, the messenger of God and angel of the Annunciation (Lk. 1:26–38) bears his emblem of lilies, the symbol of purity,[66] and a scroll with the opening words of his salutation to Mary 'Ave Maria, gratia plena' (Lk. 1:28). The third archangel is Raphael, who figures prominently in the apocryphal book of Tobit, and who, because of his role there (Tob. 5) as guide and protector to Tobias, is assigned the responsibility of protecting travellers and pilgrims.[67]

The date of this ensemble is important in the uncovering of its meaning. 1923 was only three years after the disestablishment of the Church in Wales, the culmination of a protracted and often bitter campaign. Both the bishop of St Asaph and John Owen, the bishop of St Davids, had been doughty, determined – and sometimes politically devious – opponents of this severance of the Welsh dioceses from those of the Established Church of England, and although they were to be prominent in the forging of a sense of identity for the disestablished church, at the same time they still had, in common with most if not all Welsh Anglicans, a deep-rooted Establishment 'mind-set'.[68] The essential unity of the English and Welsh Anglican provinces, despite the coming into force in March 1920 of the Welsh Church Act, is here proclaimed by the figures of St David and St George. The presence of the archangels, protectors of the church,[69] in the lancets above, recalls the promise of Jesus to Peter that the gates of hell shall not prevail against that church, founded as it is upon the rock of the apostles and prophets (Matt. 16:18. cf. Eph. 2:19–22).

If it is possible to see in the 1909 and 1923 windows echoes of the disestablishment campaigns, then the 1924 Lady Chapel window, also by Kempe & Co., breathes a less polemical air. It would not be inappropriate to refer to this as 'the singing window'. The central figure in the five lights is a charming depiction of the Blessed Virgin Mary, holding the Christ-child in her arms. The child is lively, stretching out his left hand to grasp the clasp of His mother's cloak. Above are the opening words of the Magnificat, the song of Mary: 'My soul doth magnify the Lord' (Lk. 1:46). This central figure is flanked in the two lights on either side by figures of the four evangelists, Matthew, Mark, Luke and John, each – with the exception of Matthew – accompanied by their symbol, the lion, the bull and the eagle.[70] Above each of the evangelists is an angel musician, with associated texts.

The window is thus full of sound. In the medieval understanding, that which was depicted could be heard. Thus a representation of the hand of God was interpreted as the voice of God speaking – as, for example, at the baptism of Jesus (Mk. 1:11) or at the Transfiguration (Lk. 9:35). When a text is enrolled, as with the Biblical quotations in this window, they are to be heard by the viewer, as if they were being read or sung.[71] Similarly, when a musical instrument is portrayed, then it is heard. The English mystic Richard Rolle provides an illustration of this when he recalls an occasion when he was sitting in a chapel with carved angels in the roof above, and, as he quietly sang psalms, 'I beheld above me the noise as it were of readers, or rather singers. . .' To behold was also to hear.[72] In this Lady Chapel window, Mary sings her Magnificat, as the angels accompany her, as well as themselves singing (several of the Biblical quotations are taken from the psalms). The sound that goes out into all lands (cf. Rom. 10:18) is that of the gospel message of salvation, to which the writings of the four evangelists bear witness.[73]

It was to be more than thirty years before more stained glass was added to the cathedral windows, again at the west end. The two rose windows in the west walls of the north and south nave aisles were glazed in 1955–56 by William Morris Studios of Westminster. In the opinion of Roger Stalley, with their brilliant, intense colouring, this is 'the best glass in the cathedral', and it is a fair judgement.[74] The firm of William Morris is not to be confused with that of his great, Pre-Raphaelite namesake, but flourished in the middle years of the twentieth century, particularly when its chief designer was the artist Frederick W. Cole.[75]

The rose window in the south-west corner of the nave, above the font, explores the typology of baptism. At the apex, like a Norse god, stands the figure of Moses, his arms outstretched, as the waters of the Red Sea roll behind him. To Moses God had entrusted the release of His chosen people from bondage (Ex. 3:10) and at the Red Sea, Moses, in obedience to God's command, stretched out his hand over the waters, so that the Israelites could pass on dry ground (Ex. 14:16, 21–2). Medieval authors interpreted this passage of the Red Sea as a type of salvation wrought through baptism, and the Israelites' passing into the Promised Land from their slavery in Egypt as freedom from the bondage of sin, and this is the understanding explored here. The passage of the chosen people (Ex. 14:22), represented here by a father and two sons, and the pursuing army of pharaoh (Ex. 14:26–8), about to be overwhelmed by the returning waters, are also shown.

At the bottom of the window, the scene changes to the story of the Flood and the Ark (Gen. 7 and 8). The Ark was interpreted as a type of the Christian church, following 1 Pet. 3:20–1. Just as Noah had been obedient to the command of God in the building of the Ark, thus providing a refuge for his family and the animals, so the church was seen

Figure 6: William Morris & Co. (Westminster), The Israelites Crossing the Red Sea and the Ark of the Church, 1956, designed by Frederick Cole, baptistry window, west end of the south aisle (Photo: Martin Crampin)

as a redemptive community called into being by Christ. The deluge (Gen. 7:12) which overwhelmed the earth, but upon the floodwaters of which the Ark floated (Gen. 7:18) was seen as the type of Col. 2:12; through baptism the Christian is buried with Christ, and raised to new life. The typology is made clear in the window by the image of the west front of the cathedral behind the Ark, and also by the baptismal shell in the foreground.

The message of the window is further reinforced by the presence of four symbols, the fish, the anchor, the cross and the flaming heart. The fish has, from the days of the early church, been associated with the sacrament of baptism through its evocation of the name of Jesus. (The Greek *ichthys*, fish, was read as an acrostic of *Iesus Christos Theou Yios Soster* – Jesus Christ, Son of God, Saviour.) Here the fish encircles the cross, the circular form standing for eternal life. The anchor, from Hebrews 6:19, is the symbol of hope in the resurrection, which hope is brought to birth through baptism. The cross, symbol of Christ and of the church, with which all candidates for baptism are signed, needs no explanation. The flaming heart is the symbol of faith, and of the consecration and dedication of the believer to the service of Christ, which is the ordination of baptism. So, symbolically and typologically, the theology and Christian understanding of baptism is explored in this window. And at the centre is the descending dove of the Holy Spirit, which rested upon Christ at His baptism (Mk. 1:10) and through whom God's gifts of grace are bestowed at the waters of the font.

The other rose window has as its theme the vision of St John. The imagery is dominated by the Four Living Creatures (Rev. 4:6–8), which from the fifth century onwards came to symbolize the evangelists. The seven golden candlesticks (Rev. 1:20), symbols of the seven churches of Asia; the four winds (Rev. 7:1) which blow around the four corners of the world; the great seven-headed dragon (Rev. 12:3) cast down by Michael and his angels; and the Holy City (Rev. 21:10) wherein is found the glory of God, completes the imagery, all circling around the figure of the Lamb (Rev. 7:17). The two windows have to be taken together, as the Greek letters Alpha and Omega, the beginning and the end, which feature in the Apocalypse window, indicate. In the former is the proclamation of the gospel message of new birth and new life in Christ; in the latter the promise that 'the Lamb which is in the midst of the throne shall feed them, and shall lead them unto living fountains of waters; and God shall wipe away all tears from their eyes'.

The site chosen for the most recent window (1958) was again the chapel of St Thomas Becket, where now the east window was glazed in memory of the Revd Ernest Evans, a benefactor of the cathedral. The subject, appropriately, was the martyred archbishop himself, and pride of place is given in the centre light to his standing figure.[76] Below left is shown his enthronement as archbishop of Canterbury in 1162, and below right riding on horseback, bestowing a blessing. Beneath the standing figure in the centre light is the aftermath of the martyrdom, the assassinated Thomas lying surrounded by the three knights who killed him in his cathedral church in 1170, their drawn swords pointing towards his body. Becket was swiftly canonized, and for four hundred years his shrine at Canterbury became (like that of St David in this cathedral) a focal point for pilgrimage and devotion.

Figure 7: Carl Edwards, Thomas Becket Enthroned, 1958, east wall of the Chapel of St Thomas Becket (Photo: Martin Crampin)

The window was designed by Carl Edwards (d. 1985), a prolific artist who received a number of important commissions in England, including work for Liverpool Anglican cathedral, the Temple church in London and the Palace of Westminster, but other than this window undertook little in Wales.[77] In the recollection of his daughter Caroline Benyon, who took over his studio, Edwards was 'a precise man and he expected his instructions to be carried out to the letter' and it was 'these often infuriating qualities that enabled his half-inch to the foot sketch to be photographically blown up to full size and become the basis of the cartoon which he inked in. It made the painting easy though strenuous, with each line having to be traced exactly, not interpretively.'[78] Edwards had trained under James Hogan, whose work is better represented in Wales, as he was one of the designers commissioned by Powells of Whitefriars.[79] However, for all Edwards's meticulous attention to detail – or, perhaps, because of it – the drawing of the figures in the Becket window is 'stiff', and, although the scenes from the saint's life and martyrdom require a sense of movement, they appear curiously frozen.

Compared with many churches and cathedrals, St Davids has little stained glass, but what there is deserves attention. The chosen themes explore complex Biblical and theological doctrines, as well as in some cases recalling, perhaps only by implication, episodes in church history which impinged upon the cathedral's life. The windows require more than the visitor's passing glance.

Notes

[1] J. Piper, *Stained Glass: Art or Anti-Art* (London, 1968), p. 14.

[2] Piper, *Stained Glass*, p. 37.

[3] Piper, *Stained Glass*, p. 39. In the Kempe and Shrigley & Hunt windows, discussed below, he would have typical examples of that which he was criticising.

[4] Piper, *Stained Glass*, p. 58.

[5] Piper, *Stained Glass*, p. 37.

[6] C. Whall, *Stained Glass Work: A Text-Book for Students and Workers in Glass* (London, 1905), p. 155.

[7] Whall, *Stained Glass Work*, p. 199.

[8] Piper, *Stained Glass*, p. 14.

[9] He also knew his Gerard Manley Hopkins. 'The Glow and the Glory' comes originally from Hopkins's 1875 poem 'The Wreck of the Deutschland', W. H. Gardner and N. H. MacKenzie (eds), *The Poems of Gerard Manley Hopkins* (Oxford, 4th rev. edn 1970), pp. 51–63, stanza 5. Whall and Piper shared the vision Hopkins expresses here, a vision summarized by J. Pick, *Gerard Manley Hopkins: Priest and Poet* (Oxford, 3rd imp. 1946) p. 44.

'The Glow and the Glory'

[10] Wyn Evans and Roger Worsley, *St Davids Cathedral 1181–1981* (St Davids, 1981), p. 89.

[11] The inscription on the brass plaque beneath the central lancet makes it quite clear that the glass and mosaics form a unified scheme.

[12] There are elaborate examples of such canopies over the figures of St David and St George in the lancet windows of the west wall of the nave of the cathedral, glazed by Kempe and Co., in 1924, See below.

[13] Philip A. Robson, *The Cathedral Church of St David's. A Short History and Description of the Fabric and Episcopal Buildings* (London, 1907), p. 41.

[14] Roger Stalley, 'The Cathedral', in T. Lloyd, J. Orbach and R. Scourfield, *Pembrokeshire*, The Buildings of Wales (New Haven CT and London, 2004), pp. 386–414 at p. 410.

[15] Not everyone would concur with this judgment; Marjory Wight, in the *Pilgrim's Guide to St David's and its Cathedral* (Gloucester, nd. but *c.*1930) p. 32, says 'These shimmering mosaics harmonise admirably with the ancient stonework'.

[16] George Gilbert Scott, *Report made by Order of The Dean and Chapter on the State of the Fabric of St David's Cathedral* (London, 1862), p. 32.

[17] Bishop Lucy was responsible for repairs to the Collegiate Church in Brecon, and his fine, if intimidatingly grim-faced, portrait bust can still be seen in the ante-chapel at what is now Christ College, along with lifesize alabaster figures of his son, the Revd Richard (d. 1690) and daughter-in-law, Florence Games (d. 1706).

[18] Quoted in Nikolaus Pevsner & Alexandra Wedgwood, *Warwickshire*, The Buildings of England (London, repr. 1974), p. 305.

[19] Stanley A. Shepherd. 'Stained Glass', in Paul Atterbury & Clive Wainwright (eds), *Pugin: a Gothic Passion* (London, 1994), pp. 194–206, at p. 197.

[20] This meant that Willement's east window had to be re-housed. The glass was 're-arranged' by Scott.

[21] For a useful introduction to the history of Hardmans, and the firm's close association with A. W. N. Pugin, see Brian Doolan, *The Pugins and the Hardmans* (Birmingham, 2004).

[22] Doolan, *The Pugins and the Hardmans*, p. 22.

[23] A good example of Salviati's flair for publicity is the memorial mosaic to President Abraham Lincoln, accepted as a gift by the United States House of Representatives in July 1866. Salviati may well have been an admirer of the assassinated president, but the portrait was just as much a well-judged promotional exercise.

[24] J. Mordaunt Crook, *William Burges and the High Victorian Dream* (London, 1981) p. 80 and n. 11; *Oxford Dictionary of National Biography*, 32, pp. 915–19. William Burges, who was to be the 3rd Marquess of Bute's favoured architect, was an early supporter of Salviati's work (Crook, p. 216) and Layard had south Walian connections. In 1869 he married Mary Enid Evelyn, daughter of Sir John and Lady Charlotte Guest – having been earlier, it is rumoured, romantically associated with Lady Charlotte herself. (He was 26 years older than his new wife.)

[25] The apse was the work of Alfred Waterhouse (1830–1905), who had been undertaking work at the college since 1868. In a typically forthright verdict, Pevsner called it 'self-possessed. . . insensitive. . . blatant' and said of Waterhouse that his designs showed the 'High Victorian way, utterly unconscious of the character into which it should fit – individualism and no cooperation'. Nikolaus Pevsner, *Cambridgeshire* (Buildings of England: London, repr. 1977), pp. 37 and 81. Contemporary taste differed; Waterhouse's work at the college was judged an outstanding success, as Pevsner had to admit.

[26] Christopher Wilson et al., *Westminster Abbey* (The New Bell's Cathedral Guides: London, 1986), p. 177. The cartoon for the reredos was prepared by Clayton & Bell.

169

27 Other firms were quick to realize the potential, especially James Powell of Whitefriars, and Clayton & Bell. The former firm was responsible for the reredos in St Peter, Glasbury, Breconshire and the latter for the very fine, but almost unknown, Christ in Majesty in the Bute Mausoleum in St Margaret's, Roath, Cardiff. The 1888 Christ in Majesty over the chancel arch in St Mary's, Llanfair Kilgeddin, is again almost certainly the work of Powells of Whitefriars, though part of Heywood Sumner's overall design.

28 The confined space of the lancet means that the angel figures, usually shown holding the chalices, are here omitted. Artistically, this is rather unfortunate, as the chalices beneath the arms of the cross are free-floating, and at the base, the fingers of the right hand of Mary Magdalene are interposed between the viewer and the stream of blood flowing from the feet of Christ.

29 Quoted by Shepherd, 'Stained Glass', p. 206.

30 Stalley, 'The Cathedral', p. 410 mistakenly identifies this subject as the worship of the golden calf, from Ex. 32, which completely destroys its typological significance.

31 See George P. Landow, *William Holman Hunt and Typological Symbolism* (New Haven CT, 1979), especially pp. 7–17.

32 B. F. Westcott, *The Gospel according to St John*, 2 Vols. (London 1908), vol. I, pp. 116–17.

33 Augustine, *De Civitate Dei*, ix, chap. 8.

34 Num. 20:23–9. Robson, *The Cathedral Church*, p. 40.

35 It is worth noting that the budding rod of Aaron was itself seen as a 'type' of the cross of Calvary.

36 Perhaps the best medieval English examples of these figures are to be found at Rochester Cathedral, where they flank the door to the Chapter House.

37 The figure has a somewhat grim expression – an expression, rather unfortunately, reproduced on the face of Mary on the Mothers' Union banner in the Lady Chapel. Mary here is clearly modelled on Ecclesia. By contrast, the Christ-child on the banner has, one is relieved to note, a particularly joyful air.

38 See also 2 Cor. 11:2.

39 Robson, *The Cathedral Church*, p. 40.

40 Stalley, 'The Cathedral', p. 410.

41 This may – or may not – be associated with St Francis's celebrated 'living crib' of 1223 in the cave at Gubbio.

42 Henrik Cornell, *The Iconography of the Nativity of Christ* (Uppsala, 1924), p. 12.

43 David R. Cartlidge and J. Keith Elliott, *Art and the Christian Apocrypha* (London, 2001), pp. 24–5.

44 At the foot of each lancet, all but invisible to the naked eye, even from the quire, are the emblems associated with the four Evangelists, Man, Lion, Ox, Eagle. The order is that of the gospels in the New Testament, Matthew, Mark, Luke, John.

45 R. Sharpe and J. R. Davies, 'Rhygyfarch's Life of St David', in J. W. Evans and J. M. Wooding (eds), *St David of Wales. Cult, Church and Nation* (Woodbridge, 2007) p. 129.

46 *Catechism of the Catholic Church*, section 2447.

47 The statue is the dominant figure in a group of 'Welsh' heroes, executed by a number of prominent sculptors, and paid for by Lord Rhondda. It includes Hywel Dda, Dafydd ap Gwilym, Giraldus Cambrensis, Llewellyn the Last, Owain Glyndwr, Henry VII, Bishop William Morgan, William Williams Pantycelyn, Sir Thomas Picton (removed 2022) and, rather curiously, Boadicea.

48 For a succinct account of the background and content of the Syllabus of Errors, see E. E. Y. Hales, *Pio Nono* (London, 1954), pp. 255–62, and for a recent overview of the heresy of

'The Glow and the Glory'

Williams and Colenso, see Gerald Parsons, 'From Heresy to Acceptance? Rowland Williams and John William Colenso in Perspective', *Welsh Journal of Religious History*, 1 (2006), pp. 59–87.

49 It is necessary to bear in mind the personalities involved. Dean Llewelyn Lewellin and John Lucy were what is sometimes called old-fashioned 'High and Dry' churchmen, not afraid to embrace at least some of the principles of the Oxford or Tractarian Movement. The theological liberalism of Rowland Williams or Bishop Colenso would have been repugnant to them. So would the theological standpoint of the reigning and unpopular Bishop of St Davids when the windows and mosaic were put in place, Connop Thirlwall. It is possible to see in the choice of David's triumph over heresy at the Synod of Llanddewi Brefi a covert criticism of the liberal views of this successor of David, whose theology would have appeared to his Dean and to Lucy as at least heterodox.

50 The glass, however, is not part of that memorial. It was given in memory of Mary Elizabeth, the daughter of Canon William Beach Thomas, and is thus, like the Lucy bequest, an example of the private benefaction that Scott had thought likely. The relics of St Nicholas were translated to Bari in 1087. His shrine there became a recognized 'stopover' for pilgrims to the Holy Land. It is likely that his chapel in St Davids served as a similar focus of devotion, pilgrims praying there *en route*, as it were, to the shrine of Dewi Sant.

51 Many of the miracles ascribed to Nicholas took place at sea, hence the connection of the saint with sailors and seafarers.

52 Victoria & Albert Museum Archive of Art and Design; Denis Hadley (comp.), *James Powell and Sons. List of Figurative Windows and Opus Sectile 1847–1973* (2 parts, October 2000, rev. November 2001). In the same year as this St Nicholas window, the firm produced windows for St David's, Brawdy. There the artist is recorded as 'Hardgrave'. This was Charles Hardgrave, who worked for Powells as a freelance designer from 1874 and was a protégé of Henry Holiday.

53 Asaph is the somewhat shadowy sixth-century figure who is the patron of the north Walian cathedral and diocese that bears his name.

54 Stalley, 'The Cathedral', p. 412.

55 Birgitta Rengmyr Lovgren, 'Carl Almquist (1848–1924), His Life and Work', *Journal of Stained Glass*, 21 (1997), pp. 11–40.

56 Lovgren, 'Carl Almquist', Plates IV and V, pp. 29 and 28.

57 Lovgren, 'Carl Almquist', p. 30.

58 *Pembroke County Guardian and Cardigan Reporter*, 17 Sep. 1909. I would like to thank Dr Martin Crampin for this identification.

59 Perhaps the best of Almquist's glass in Wales is in Betws Bledrws Church, near Lampeter, which dates from the late 1880s when he was at the height of his powers.

60 At Lancaster Priory and Ham (Richmond) respectively.

61 The date is given in Philip N. H. Collins (ed.), *The Corpus of Kempe Stained Glass in the United Kingdom and Ireland* (The Kempe Trust, 2000) p. 332.

62 Margaret Stavridi, *Master of Glass: Charles Eamer Kempe 1837–1907 and the Work of his Firm in Stained Glass and Church Decoration* (Hatfield, 1988) p. 50.

63 Stavridi, *Master of Glass*, p. 29.

64 Stavridi, *Master of Glass*, p. 98.

65 For a useful introduction, see Clara Erskine Clement, *Angels in Art* (London, 1899).

66 Because of its symbolic meaning and association in art with the Annunciation, the lily became the particular emblem of the Virgin Mary.

67 Hence his attributes here of the staff (with a banner bearing his name) and a sword.

68 That the anti-disestablishment campaign in the early years of the twentieth century was so closely identified with the bishops of St Asaph and St Davids may explain why the 1909 'wayfarer' window in the Becket Chapel features these two diocesan patron saints.

69 And of all who journey to the shrine of St David on pilgrimage – thus the presence of St Raphael.

70 The symbols, from Rev. 4:1–11 and deriving ultimately from Ez. 1:1–28, are those already discussed for the Hardman glass in the presbytery. The symbol for Matthew, being a man, is omitted here probably for artistic reasons – a manikin at the evangelist's feet would have scarcely been appropriate.

71 Our modern practice of silent reading was not that adopted by our medieval forebears.

72 Quoted by Frances M. M. Comper, *The Life of Richard Rolle, together with an Edition of his English Lyrics* (London & Toronto, 1928), p. 92.

73 The window was put in place in memory of Evan Phillips, Dean 1895–97, and of his father, who had been the first vicar of Aberystwyth.

74 Stalley, 'The Cathedral', p. 414.

75 Many of Coles's designs and papers, as well as portraits and landscapes, for the years 1938–98 are kept at the Victoria & Albert Museum Archive of Art and Design.

76 Rather strangely, he is shown robed as a bishop and not an archbishop. He holds a pastoral staff and not his metropolitical cross, and is not wearing the pallium. Over his head two angels hold the crown symbolizing his martyrdom. Otherwise the figure is very much a 'stock' episcopal image.

77 There are four small windows, for example, at Llyswen in Breconshire.

78 Caroline Benyon in 'Stained Glass 1921–1996: A 75th BSMGP Anniversary Retrospective', *Journal of Stained Glass*, 20 (1996), pp. 68–86, at pp. 69–70.

79 For Hogan, see *Journal of Stained Glass*, 8 (1941) pp. 109–25, and his obituary in *Journal of Stained Glass*, 10 (1948), p. 50.

INDEX

A
Aberystwyth 69
Abraham, Bishop 7
Albert, Prince 135
Albertus Magnus 155
Alexander III, Pope 89
Allen, Dean James 140–1, 143–4
Amroth 102
Angle 102
Anselm le Gras, Bishop 63
Appleby, Revd Philemon 121
Asser 4–5, 7–8
Augustine, St 10, 32, 154
Aurelian, Paul 3

B
Baldwin, Archbishop 19
Bangor Cathedral 5, 100, 102, 136
Barlow, Bishop William 91–2
Barry, Sir Charles 131
Bath stone 64–8
Bek, Bishop 115
Bernard, Bishop 8–9, 37
Beverley Minster 136
Bitton, St Mary (Glos.) 35
Blore, Edward 131
Book of Llandaf 7
Brakspear, Sir Harold 34
Brecon Priory 103, 136
Bristol 33, 35–7, 46, 62, 64, 67, 69, 161
Brycheiniog, Gwynfardd 39
Burgess, Thomas Bishop 95, 98, 114
Butterfield, William 101, 137

C
Caerbwdi sandstone 45–51, 53–5, 65, 85, 137, 142
Caerfai Bay 45–7, 53, 55
Caernarvon 75
Calixtus II, Pope 6, 8
Canterbury 2, 4, 19, 30, 32–3, 37–9, 75, 88, 136, 167
Caradoc, St 89–90
Cardiff 159
Cardigan Priory 39
Carmarthen 6, 62, 91, 96, 121
Carpenter, R. C. 131

Carreg Frân 51
Carreg yr Esgob 51
Celtic Church 3, 12
Charlecote Park (Warks.) 151
Chichester 92, 107, 131, 136, 161
Clear, James 136–7, 141
Clynnog Fawr 9
Cogitosus 10, 12
Cuthbert, St 7, 71

D
Darlington 136–7
David, St 1, 3–4, 6–8, 13, 30, 71–92, 158, 161–3, 167
Davies, Revd Nathaniel 111–25
Davies, Archdeacon Richard 117–18
Dinefwr 39
Dundry stone 30, 37, 46, 62–9
Durham Cathedral 24, 32–3, 39, 131, 136

E
Ecclesiastical Commission 103, 105, 115, 119–20, 124
Edward I, King 74, 115
Eleanor, Queen 75
Ely Cathedral 103, 106, 136
Etheldreda, St 71
Evans, Revd Ernest 167
Ewenny Priory 34

F
Ferrey, Benjamin 131
Ffos y Mynach 12

G
Gerald of Wales 2, 5–8, 13, 19, 54, 74, 89
Gervase 38
Gildas 4
Glastonbury Abbey 25, 30, 33, 35–9
Gloucester Cathedral 24, 33–5, 103, 136
Glyn Rhosyn 48, 50–1
Gower, Bishop 24, 30, 53, 137
Gruffydd ap Cynan 6, 74
Gryg, Rhys 62

H
Hafodunos (Denbigh.) 134
Harries, Revd George 104–5

Index

Haverfordwest 69, 118, 138
Henfynyw 6–7
Henry II, King 8, 74
Henry of Blois 33–4
Hereford Cathedral 33, 96, 136–7
Herefordshire School 33
Hiot, Archdeacon John 63
Howell, Dean David 144, 160
Hugh of Lincoln, St 88
Hull 136

I
Iorwerth, Bishop 63
Ireland 5–6, 8, 10–12, 33, 52, 64, 74

J
James Powell & Sons 140, 151–4, 157–61, 168
Jedburgh Abbey 30
Jerusalem, Church of the Holy Sepulchre 88
John de Gamages, prior 74
John Hardman & Co. 138, 140, 148–9, 151, 157
John of Anagni 19
Jones, Bishop W. Basil 125, 141–4

K
Kelham Hall (Notts.) 134
Kempe & Co. 161–3
Keynsham Abbey 33, 35–6

L
Lampeter, St David's College 104–5, 107, 118, 159
Leeds 135
Lewellin, Dean Llewelyn 100, 102, 104–5, 107, 111–25
Lincoln Cathedral 107
Lindisfarne Priory 24
Liverpool Cathedral (Anglican) 168
Llancarfan 5
Llandaff Cathedral 9–10, 34, 62–3, 69, 95, 100, 106, 131
Llanddewi Brefi 4, 159
Llandovery 39
Llanelian 9
Llangennith 69
Llanilltud Fawr 5
Llanllŷr 39
Llannarth 69
Llanrhian 69
Llanthony Priory 24–6

Llanwnnen 113–16, 121
Llanychaearn 69
Lock, Adam 37
Lucy, Revd John 151, 159–60
Lucy, Bishop William 151

M
Malmesbury Abbey 24, 34
Mary I, Queen 87
Mathry 119
Morgan, Bishop 62
Morris, William 136
Much Wenlock 39

N
Nash, John 95–8, 141–2
Newport 69
Ninian, St 11
Nolton Haven 52
Norwich Cathedral 107, 131
Notes on the Cathedral Church of St Davids (1853) 111–12

O
Oakham (Rutland) 39
Oengus 5
Owen, Bishop John 163
Oxford 30, 111, 117–18, 125, 131, 136, 161
Oystermouth 69

P
Payne, Canon H. T. 98–9, 114, 120
Penbryn 69
Pen-rhiw quarry 48, 50
Penson, Richard Kyrke 102
Peter de Leia, Bishop 19–20, 39, 77
Piper, John 147–8, 151, 160
Porth Clais 47, 51–3
Porth Lisgi 50–1
Porth Lleuog 53
Porth Melgan 53
Preston 135
Prichard, John 106, 131
Pugin, Augustus W. N. 131–2, 137, 142, 148, 150–1, 153
Purbeck marble 45–6, 61–2

R
railways 118
Reading Abbey 30
Rhayader 39
Rhygyfarch ap Sulien 2–7, 11, 13, 74, 158–9

Index

Rhys ap Tewdwr 74
Rhys of Deheubarth, Lord 20, 39–40, 62, 158–9
Richard de Wych, St 92
Richardson, Revd Richard 98–9
Richardson, Revd William 105–6, 122, 124
Roger of Pont l'Eveque, Archbishop 33–4
Roger of Salisbury, Bishop 32, 34
Romsey Abbey 30

S
St Albans Cathedral 32, 136
St Andrews Cathedral Priory 38–9
St Asaph Cathedral 100, 102, 136
St Davids
  Bishop's Palace 48, 51, 63
  County School 118
  Cross Square 65
  Porth y Tŵr 45, 48–52, 55, 145
  St Mary's College 45, 48, 50–1, 53, 55
St Davids Cathedral
  Bishop Vaughan's Holy Trinity chapel 64–7, 96, 141, 144
  chapel of St Edward the Confessor 55, 144
  chapel of St Thomas Becket 9, 32, 49, 99, 140–1, 161, 167
  chapter school 111–25
  construction materials 45–69
  crossing, description of 20–1
  Lady chapel 20, 49–50, 103, 144–5, 163–4
  nave, description of 21–5
  predecessor churches 1–13
  presbytery, description of 25–31
  rebuilding (post-1182) 19–40
  restoration of Sir George Gilbert Scott 23, 26, 77, 82, 84–6, 97, 102–7, 125, 131–45, 148–50, 162
  Shrine of St David 71–92
  situation 5, 45
  stained glass 147–68
  structural collapses 5, 20, 78, 95, 138
  transepts, description of 31
St Dogmael's Abbey 69
St Paul's Cathedral 108
St Petrox 102
Salisbury Cathedral 88, 136–7
Salviati & Co., London 140, 149, 152–4
Salvin, Anthony 131
Sarum Cathedral 32–4, 38, 88
Silian 113, 115–16, 121

Slebech 39
Smirke, Sydney 131
Society for the Protection of Ancient Buildings 143
Staffordshire 53, 131–4, 138
Strata Florida Abbey 39–40, 69
Sulien, Bishop 7
Swithun, St 9, 71, 88

T
Talley 39
Tewkesbury Abbey 30, 35, 136
theological colleges 107
Thirlwall, Bishop Connop 102–4, 114–15, 118–19, 123, 141
Thomas, Revd W. H. 105
Trollope, Anthony 111–12, 124
Tudor, Edmund (First Earl of Richmond) 62

U
Urban, Bishop 7, 9, 10

V
Vallis Rosina 5, 7
Vetus Rubus 5–7
Victoria, Queen 135, 142

W
Walton West 102
Wells Cathedral 35–40, 131
Welsh annals 1–4, 19, 74
Welsh Council 92
West Country School 34, 36–7
Westminster Abbey 136, 140, 142, 153
Whall, Christoper 147–8, 151
Whitchurch Canonicorum 88
Whitesands 7, 10
Whitland Abbey 39, 69
Wigmore Abbey 35
William I, King 13, 74
Williams, Sir Erasmus 104–6, 140
Williams, Revd James Propert 118, 122
Williams, Revd Rowland 104, 159
Willis, Browne 75–6, 81, 86
Winchester 8–9, 32–3, 38, 136
Windsor 135
Wood, John 95
Worcester Cathedral 34–5, 136
Wotton, William 75–6, 86, 90

Y
York Minster 33–4, 131

ISBN 978-1-83772-087-3
eISBN 978-1-83772-088-0
ISSN (Print) 2057-4517
ISSN (Online) 2057-4525
The Journal of Religious History, Literature and Culture
© University of Wales Press, 2023
Articles and reviews © The Contributors, 2023

Printed by CPI Group (UK) Ltd

Contributors to *The Journal of Religious History, Literature and Culture* should refer enquiries to the journal page at *www.uwp.co.uk* or e-mail press@press.wales.ac.uk requesting notes for contributors.

Advertising enquiries should be sent to the Sales and Marketing Department at the University of Wales Press, at the address below.

Subscriptions: *The Journal of Religious History, Literature and Culture* is published twice a year in June and November. The annual subscription for institutions is £95 (print only), £85 (online only) or £140 (combined); and for individuals is £25 (print or online only) or £40 (combined). Subscription orders should be sent to University of Wales Press, University Registry, King Edward VII Avenue, Cardiff CF10 3NS. E-mail: press@press.wales.ac.uk.

Open Access: The University of Wales Press (UWP) is fully committed to the principle of Open Access for those authors requiring it, whether by funder mandate, REF or otherwise. It is incumbent on contributors to state clearly if they have an Open Access requirement when submitting an article.

UWP's policy is to require an embargo period of eighteen months for Green Open Access, to begin on the last day in the month of publication of the print version. We also welcome submissions for Gold Open Access: if required, please contact the Commissioning Department at UWP to discuss an Article Processing Charge (APC) for your article.

The version of record for deposit should be the author's accepted and final peer-reviewed text, for non-commercial purposes.

The inclusion of third-party material in the deposited article will be at the author/institution's own risk. Authors should continue to ensure clearance of rights for third-party material for print and e-publication in the usual way for the purposes of the version published by UWP and for Open Access, if your article is Open Access.

UWP will continue to accept and publish articles by authors without requirements for REF under pre-existing arrangements.

For more information on our current Open Access policy, please visit our website: *www.uwp.co.uk/open-access*.